DATE DUE

DEMCO 38-296

GREAT WRITERS OF THE ENGLISH LANGUAGE

Index

GREAT WRITERS OF THE ENGLISH LANGUAGE

Index

General Index
Index of Writers
Index of Literature
Glossary

MARSHALL CAVENDISH · NEW YORK · TORONTO · LONDON · SYDNEY

STAFF CREDITS

Executive Editor
Reg Wright

Series Editor
Sue Lyon

Editors
Jude Welton
Sylvia Goulding

Deputy Editors
Alice Peebles
Theresa Donaghey

Features Editors
Geraldine McCaughrean
Emma Foa
Ian Chilvers

Art Editors
Kate Sprawson
Jonathan Alden
Helen James

Designers
Simon Wilder
Frank Landamore

Senior Picture Researchers
Julia Hanson
Vanessa Fletcher
Georgina Barker

Picture Clerk
Vanessa Cawley

Production Controllers
Judy Binning
Tom Helsby

Editorial Secretaries
Fiona Bowser
Sylvia Osborne

Managing Editor
Alan Ross

Editorial Consultant
Maggi McCormick

Publishing Manager
Robert Paulley

Reference Edition Published 1989
Published by Marshall Cavendish Corporation
147 West Merrick Road
Freeport, Long Island
N.Y. 11520

Typeset by Litho Link Ltd., Welshpool
Printed and Bound in Italy by
L.E.G.O. S.p.a. Vicenza

LIBRARY OF CONGRESS
Library of Congress Cataloging-in-Publication Data
Great Writers of the English Language
   p. cm.
   Includes index vol.
   ISBN 1-85435-000-5 (set): $399.95
   1. English literature — History and criticism. 2. English
literature — Stories, plots, etc. 3. American literature — History
and criticism. 4. American literature — Stories, plots, etc.
5. Authors. English — Biography. 6. Authors. American — Biography.
I. Marshall Cavendish Corporation.
PR85.G66 1989
820'.9 – dc19   88-21077
                                                                              CIP

ISBN 1–85435–000–5 (set)
ISBN 1–85435–014–5 (vol)

CONTENTS

How To Use The Index 6

Volume List of Writers 7

Alphabetical List of Writers 8

Alphabetical List of Books 9

General Index 11

Index of Writers 51

Index of Literature 77

Glossary 92

How To Use The Index

The following pages are a complete index to volumes 1 to 13 of *Great Writers of the English Language*. The index is divided into three alphabetical sections: a General Index, an Index of Writers, and an Index of Literature.

THE GENERAL INDEX
This index includes entries on all topics – people, countries, technical terms, and historical events, as well, of course, as writers and literature – that appear in *Great Writers of the English Language*. Where possible, people are indexed under surnames; where this is inappropriate (for example, Victoria, Queen of England), the person can be found under his or her most familiar name. Famous names in all fields of art are listed in this index, but for writers, turn immediately to the Index of Writers.

THE INDEX OF WRITERS
In this section all writers appearing in the thirteen volumes are listed. Writers can be found under their surnames – for example: Shakespeare, William; Hemingway, Ernest – but where this does not apply – for example: Dante Alighieri – writers are listed under their best-known names. The entry on each of the fifty-seven featured writers is followed by detailed subentries on their lives and works; the works themselves are listed alphabetically at the end of the subentries.

If, however, you wish simply to locate a writer within a volume or a book featured in the Reader's Guide chapters, there are volume and alphabetical lists on pages 7-9.

THE INDEX OF LITERATURE
This index lists novels, plays, poems and other writing; other works of art can be found in the General Index. Each work of literature is, where applicable, followed by the writer's name in parentheses.

USING THE INDEX
The number immediately following an entry is the number of the relevant volume. This is followed by a colon and then the page numbers on which the entry appears. If an entry can be found in other volumes, these volume and page numbers are printed in numerical order and are separated by a semi-colon. Page numbers which refer to illustrations are printed in italic type in all three indexes, as are titles of all works of art. The names of the fifty-seven writers who are featured in *Great Writers of the English Language* are printed in bold type, both in the General Index and in the Index of Writers.

GLOSSARY
In this section, there are over one hundred definitions of specialist words used in English literature, including explanations of literary movements or schools and technical terms used by critics.

Volume List of Writers

1 Early English Writers
William Shakespeare
John Bunyan
Samuel Pepys
Henry Fielding

2 Nineteenth-Century British Writers
William Thackeray
Anthony Trollope
Oscar Wilde
Samuel Butler

3 Two English Masters
Charles Dickens
Thomas Hardy

4 British Women Novelists
Charlotte Brontë
Emily Brontë
Elizabeth Gaskell
George Eliot

5 Early Modern Novelists
Henry James
H. G. Wells
W. Somerset Maugham
John Galsworthy

6 Modern Novelists
D. H. Lawrence
Robert Graves
H. E. Bates
Graham Greene

7 American Classics
Mark Twain
F. Scott Fitzgerald
John Steinbeck
Ernest Hemingway

8 Women Writers
Jane Austen
Louisa M. Alcott
Katherine Mansfield
Virginia Woolf

9 Exotic Journeys
Charles Darwin
Herman Melville
Joseph Conrad
E. M. Forster

10 Satirists and Humorists
Jonathan Swift
Lewis Carroll
Evelyn Waugh
Aldous Huxley

11 Adventure Writers
Daniel Defoe
Sir Walter Scott
Robert Louis Stevenson
Rudyard Kipling

12 Writers of Mystery and Suspense
Mary Shelley
Edgar Allen Poe
Wilkie Collins
Sir Arthur Conan Doyle

13 Great Poets
Geoffrey Chaucer
William Shakespeare
Lord Byron
Samuel Taylor Coleridge
John Keats
Percy Bysshe Shelley
William Wordsworth
Rupert Brooke
Wilfred Owen
Isaac Rosenberg
Siegfried Sassoon

Alphabetical List of Writers

Writer	Volume
Alcott, Louisa M.	8
Austen, Jane	8
Bates, H. E.	6
Brontë, Charlotte	4
Brontë, Emily	4
Brooke, Rupert	13
Bunyan, John	1
Butler, Samuel	2
Byron, Lord	13
Carroll, Lewis	10
Chaucer, Geoffrey	13
Coleridge, Samuel Taylor	13
Collins, Wilkie	12
Conrad, Joseph	9
Darwin, Charles	9
Defoe, Daniel	11
Dickens, Charles	3
Doyle, Sir Arthur Conan	12
Eliot, George	4
Fielding, Henry	1
Fitzgerald, F. Scott	7
Forster, E. M.	9
Galsworthy, John	5
Gaskell, Elizabeth	4
Graves, Robert	6
Greene, Graham	6
Hardy, Thomas	3
Hemingway, Ernest	7
Huxley, Aldous	10

Writer	Volume
James, Henry	5
Keats, John	13
Kipling, Rudyard	11
Lawrence, D. H.	6
Mansfield, Katherine	8
Maugham, W. Somerset	5
Melville, Herman	9
Owen, Wilfred	13
Pepys, Samuel	1
Poe, Edgar Allen	12
Rosenberg, Isaac	13
Sassoon, Siegfred	13
Scott, Sir Walter	11
Shakespeare, William	1, 13
Shelley, Mary	12
Shelley, Percy Bysshe	13
Steinbeck, John	7
Stevenson, Robert Louis	11
Swift, Jonathan	10
Thackeray, William	2
Trollope, Anthony	2
Twain, Mark	7
Waugh, Evelyn	10
Wells, H. G.	5
Wilde, Oscar	2
Woolf, Virginia	8
Wordsworth, William	13

Alphabetical List of Books

Title	Volume
Adventures of Huckleberry Finn, The	7
Adventures of Sherlock Holmes, The	12
Alice in Wonderland	10
Barchester Towers	2
Bliss	8
Brave New World	10
Canterbury Tales, The	13
Comedians, The	6
Cranford	4
Diary (Pepys)	1
Fall of the House of Usher, The	12
Far from the Madding Crowd	3
For Whom the Bell Tolls	7
Forsyte Saga, The	5
Grapes of Wrath, The	7
Great Expectations	3
Great Gatsby, The	7
Gulliver's Travels	10
Hamlet	1
I, Claudius	6
Ivanhoe	11
Jane Eyre	4
Kim	11
King Lear	1
Little Women	8
Lord Jim	9
Love for Lydia	6
Midsummer Night's Dream, A	13
Mill on the Floss, The	4
Moby-Dick	9
Of Human Bondage	5
Passage to India, A	9
Picture of Dorian Gray, The	2
Pilgrim's Progress	1
Portrait of a Lady, The	5
Pride and Prejudice	8
Robinson Crusoe	11
Romeo and Juliet	1
Tale of Two Cities, A	3
Taming of the Shrew, The	13
Tess of the d'Urbervilles	3
To the Lighthouse	8
Tom Jones	1
Treasure Island	11
Twelfth Night	13
Vanity Fair	2
Vile Bodies	10
Virgin and the Gipsy, The	6
Voyage of the Beagle, The	9
War of the Worlds, The	5
Way of All Flesh, The	2
Woman in White, The	12
Wuthering Heights	4

GENERAL INDEX

Note Page numbers in italic type refer to illustrations.

A

A Rebours (Huysmans) 2:*61, 72*
Abbey, Ned 5:27
Abbotsford 11:*32*, 33, 35, 42, *42*, 50
Abolition movement 8:*33*, 48, 50, 51
Absent-Minded Beggar, The (Kipling) 11:*96*
Absolution (Fitzgerald) 7:46
Ackerley, J. R. 9:82, *82*
Across the Bay (Bates) 6:71, *71*
Across the River and into the Trees (Hemingway) 7:92, *92*, 95, *95*
Acton, Harold 10:56, 57, 59, *66*
Acton, William 2:96, 97
Acushnet 9:30, *32*, 49
Adam Bede (Eliot) 4:*78, 81*, 82, 83, 90, *90*, 91, *91*, 93, *93*
'Adams, Nick' of *In Our Time* 7:93
Addison, Joseph 10:9, 23
Adl, Mohammed el 9:*81*, 82
Adonais (Shelley) 13:61, 63, *70*
Adventures of One Hans Pfall (Poe) 12:51
Adventures of Sherlock Holmes, The (Conan Doyle) 12:84–89, *84-89*
Adventures of Brigadier Gerard, The (Conan Doyle) 12:92
Adventures of Tom Sawyer, The (Twain) 7:9, 11, 18, 19, 20, 21, *21*
Adventures of Huckleberry Finn, The (Twain) 1:64; 7:9, 11, 12-17,

12-17, 18, *18*, 19, 20, 21, 24; 11:86
Advertisement and Preface (Wordsworth) 13:76
Aeneid (Virgil) 6:50
Aestheticism 2:72-76, *72-76*
After a Journey (Hardy) 3:87
After Dark (Collins) 12:70
After Many a Summer (Huxley) 10:92, 93, 94, *94-95*, 95
Aftermath (Sassoon) 13:*92*
Afternoon of an Author (Fitzgerald) 7:44
Afterwards (Hardy) 3:87
'Aged Parent' of *Great Expectations* 3:37, *37*
Agnes Grey (A. Brontë) 4:10, 24, 28, 32, 44, 47, *47*
agriculture
   19th century England 3:92-96, *92-96*
   20th century England, mechanization 6:72-76, *72-76*
'Ahab, Captain' of *Moby-Dick* 9:36, 37, 38, 39, 40, *40*, 41
Ahmed Khan, Sir Syed 9:81
Ahuitzotl 6:28
Al Aaraaf, Tamerlane and Minor poems (Poe) 12:32
Albert, Prince 10:*33*; 11:52, *52*
Alchemist, The (Jonson) 13:52, *52*
Alcott, Abigail May (Abba) 8:30, *30*, 31, 32, 34
Alcott, Amos Bronson 8:30, 31, *31, 33*, 34, 35, 43, *44*, 45
Alcott, Anna 8:30, 31, 32, 34, 35, *35*, 42
Alcott, Elizabeth 8:30, 31, 32, 38
Alcott, Louisa May see *Index of Writers*
Alcott, May 8:30, 35, *35*
Aldiss, Brian see *Index of Writers*

Alexander, F. M. 10:82
'Algernon' of *The Importance of Being Earnest* 2:71
'Alice' of *Alice in Wonderland* 10:36, *36*, 37, *37*, 38, *38*, 39, *39*, 40, *40*, 41, 43, *45*
Alice in Wonderland (Carroll) 10:30, *30-31*, 32, 33, *33*, 34, 36-41, *36-41*, 43, *43*, 44, *44*, 45, *45*, 46, 48, 49, 52, 82
Alice's Adventures in Wonderland see *Alice in Wonderland*
All-India Muslim League 9:99
All Quiet on the Western Front (Remarque) 6:43
All the Sad Young Men (Fitzgerald) 7:43, 45, 46, *46*
All the Year Round 3:13, 17, 42
Allan, Frances 12:30, 31, *31,* 32
Allan, John 12:30, 31, *31,* 32, 33
Allen, Percy 13:31
Allen, Ralph 1:*86*, 87, *87*
Alleyn, Edward 1:30
'Allworthy, Squire' of *Tom Jones* 1:87, 88, *88*, 89, 90, 91, 92, *92*
Almayer's Folly (Conrad) 9:56, 57, *57*, 69
Aloe, The (Mansfield) 8:67
Alone (Poe) 12:43
Along the Road (Huxley) 10:90
Alps and Sanctuaries (Butler) 2:92
Amateur Emigrant, The (Stevenson) 11:57, 66, *66*
Amazing Stories 5:*42*, 52
Ambassadors, The (James) 5:10, 20, 21, *21*, 24
Amelia (Fielding) 1:85, 87, 97, 99, *99*
American, The (James) 5:7, 8
Ames, Ezra 9:*30*
Amis, Kingsley see *Index of Writers*
Amos Barton (Eliot) 4:*81*
Amritsar Massacre 9:100

Alice finds herself bemused by the rules of croquet in Wonderland. The balls are live hedgehogs, the mallets live flamingos and the soldiers bend over to provide the arches. A game with animate equipment, decides Alice, is a very difficult game indeed.

Andersen, Hendrik 5:9
Anderson, Mary 2:56; 5:27
Anderson, Robert 8:52
Anderson, Sherwood 7:80
'Andres' of *For Whom the Bell Tolls* 7:85, 87
Andrew, Sarah 1:83-84
Androcles and the Lion (Shaw) 5:*99*
Ann Veronica (Wells) 5:33, 43, 45, 47, *47*
Anne, Queen of England 1:100; 10:14, 15, 18; 11:11, *11*; 13:*9*
'Annette' of *The Forsyte Saga* 5:86, *86*, 88, *89*
Anon (Woolf) 8:83
'Anselmo' of *For Whom the Bell Tolls* 7:84, 87, 88, *89*
Anthem for Doomed Youth (Owen) 13:83
'Anthony, Captain Roderick' of *Chance* 9:71
Anti-Corn-Law League 4:76
Antic Hay (Huxley) 10:90
Anticipations (Wells) 5:42
Antigua, Penny, Puce (Graves) 6:44, 45, 46, *46*
Antonina (Collins) 12:55, 56
Antony and Cleopatra (Shakespeare) 1:22, 27, *27*
Ape and Essence (Huxley) 10:93
Apologia pro Poemate Meo (Owen) 13:91
'Apostles, The' 9:78
Arabian Nights, The 4:*43*
'Arabin, Dr Francis' of *Barchester Towers* 2:37, 38, 39, *39*, 40
Arbuthnot, John 10:11, 21
Arcadia (Sidney) 1:23
Archer, Frederick Scott 10:49
'Archer, Isabel' of *The Portrait of a Lady* 5:9, 12, *12*, 13, *13*, 14, *14*, 1̣5, *15*, 16, 17, *17*
Archer, William 5:97; 11:66
Archer, Laura 10:83
Armadale (Collins) 12:69, 70, 71, *71*
Armfield, Maxwell 2:*76*
Armin, Robert 1:22
Armstrong, Louis 7:*50*, 51
Arne, Thomas 1:83
Arnim, Countess von *see Index of Writers*
Arnold, Edward 3:72
Arnold, Matthew *see Index of Writers*
Arnold, Thomas 10:30, 78
Arrow of Gold, The (Conrad) 9:57, *68*
Art of Seeing, The (Huxley) 10:82
As You Like It (Shakespeare) 1:22; 13:39, *39*
Ashenden (Maugham) 5:69, 70, *70*, *75*, 76
Ashmole, Elias 1:38
Aspects of the Novel (Forster) 9:93

In this illustration by Lewis Carroll, *an unsuspecting Alice gazes at a door which, when opened, reveals the bizarre residents within – the Duchess, the pig baby and the grinning Cheshire cat.*

'Aspen, Lydia' of *Love for Lydia* 6:60, *60-61*, 61, 62, *62-63*, 63, 64, *64*, 65, *65*
'Aspen, Miss Bertie and Miss Juliana' of *Love for Lydia* 6:60, 64, *65*
Aspern Papers, The (James) 5:19, 21, 23, *23*
Asquith, Herbert 5:11; 8:72
At Tea (Hardy) 3:88
At the Back of the North Wind (MacDonald) 10:34, *34*
At the Bay (Mansfield) 8:66
At Wynyard's Gap (Hardy) 3:87
'Athelstane of Coningsburgh' of *Ivanhoe* 11:36, 37, 40, 41
'Athenodorus' of *I, Claudius* 6:37
'Augustus' of *I, Claudius* 6:36, *36*, 37, 38, 39, 40, 41, *41*, 49, 52
Atlee, Clement 5:35
Attack (Sassoon) 13:*91*
Attwood, Thomas 4:74-75
Aubrey, John 1:12
Audubon, Jean Jacques 9:25; 12:*49*, 50

August 1914 (Rosenberg) 13:85
Austen, Anna 8:9, *20*
Austen, Cassandra (mother of Jane Austen) 8:6, *6*, 7, 9, *9*, 10, *10*, 11
Austen, Cassandra (sister of Jane Austen) 8:6, *6*, 7, 8, 9, 10, 11, *11*, 20, 21
Austen, Charles 8:6
Austen, Edward 8:6, *6*, 7, 8, 9, *9*, 10, *10*
Austen, Francis (Frank) 8:6, 9
Austen, George (brother of Jane Austen) 8:6
Austen, George (father of Jane Austen) 8:6, 7, *7*
Austen, Henry 8:6, 7, 9
Austen, James 8:6, 7
Austen, Jane *see Index of Writers*
Author's Farce, The (Fielding) 1:84
Authoress of the Odyssey, The (Butler) 2:91, *91*, 95, *95*
Autobiography (Twain) 7:6, *6*, 11
Autobiography (Trollope) 2:34, 44, 49

'*Avenue, Middelharnis, The*'
    (Hobbema) 3:*70-71*
Avery, John 'Long Ben' 11:24, 27
Aykroyd, Tabitha 4:31
'Aziz' of *A Passage to India* 9:*81*, 84,
    84, 85, *85*, 86, 87, *87*, 88, *89*
Aztec Indians 6:24, *24*, 26, *26*, 27,
    28, *28*

B

Baa, Baa, Black Sheep (Kipling)
    11:79
Babbage, Charles 4:80
Bacon, Delia 13:31
Bacon, Francis *see Index of Writers*
Bacon is Shakespeare (Durning-
    Lawrence) 13:31
Baden-Powell, Sir Robert *see Index
    of Writers*
Bagehot, Walter *see Index of Writers*
Baker, Ida Constance 8:55, 56, *56*,
    57, *58*, 59
'Baker, Jordan' of *The Great Gatsby*
    7:36, *37*, *38*, 40, 41
Baldwin, Stanley 11:80
Balestier, Beatty 11:81
Ball, John 13:28
Ballad of Reading Gaol, The (Wilde)
    2:59, 69, 71, *71*
Ballantyne, James 11:34
'Banford' of *The Fox* 6:14, 15, *15*,
    16, *17*
'Bankes, William' of *To the
    Lighthouse* 8:85, 86, 88
Barchester Chronicle (Trollope) 2:33,
    35, 43, 45
Barchester Towers (Trollope) 2:33,
    36-41, *36-41*, 42, 43, 44, 45
Barger, Florence 9:82, *82*
'Barkis' of *David Copperfield* 3:26, 43
Barnard, A. M. *see* Alcott, Louisa
    May
Barrack-Room Ballads (Kipling)
    11:80, 91, 93, 94, *94*
Barrie, J. M. *see Index of Writers*
'Barry, Redmond' of *The Luck of
    Barry Lyndon* 2:22, *22*
'Barsad, John' of *A Tale of Two
    Cities* 3:20
Bartholomew Fair (Jonson) 13:*52*
Bartleby (Melville) 9:43
'Bartlett, Miss' of *A Room with a
    View* 9:95
'Barton, John' of *Mary Barton* 4:69,
    74
Basil (Collins) 12:56
'Baskerville, Sir Henry' of *The
    Hound of the Baskervilles* 12:94

'Bast, Leonard' of *Howards End* 9:94
Bastille, storming of 3:32, *33*
Bastow, Henry 3:*53*
Bates, David 10:38
Bates, Henry 9:25
Bates, Herbert Ernest *see Index of
    Writers*
Bates, Lucy 6:54, *55*
Bates, Marjorie ('Madge') Cox 6:55,
    56, 57, 58, *58*, 59
Bath 8:8, 23, 24, *25*, 26, 27, 27
Battle of Dorking, The (Chesney)
    5:*39*
Battle of Life, The (Dickens) 3:27
Battle of the Books, The (Swift) 10:22,
    22
Baudelaire, Charles *see Index of
    Writers*
Bavarian Gentians (Lawrence) 6:19
Baxter, Charles 11:72
Baxter, William 12:7
Beadnell, Maria 3:9, *9*
Beagle (HMS) 9:7, 8, *9*, *11*, 12, *13*,
    14-15, *14-15*, *16*, 18, 22, 27
Beard, Frank 12:59
Beardsley, Aubrey 2:70, 73, *73*, 74,
    75, 76
Beaton, Cecil 10:*90*
'Beatrix' of *The History of Henry
    Esmond Esquire* 2:21, 23
Beauchamp, Annie (Mrs) 8:54, *54*,
    56, 57
Beauchamp, Charlotte 8:55

Beauchamp, Harold 8:54, *54*, 55
Beauchamp, Kathleen Mansfield *see*
    Mansfield, Katherine
Beauchamp, Leslie 8:58
Beauchamp, Vera 8:55
Beaumont, Francis *see Index of Writers*
Beaumont, Sir George 13:55
Beautiful and Damned, The
    (Fitzgerald) 7:33, 43, 45, *45*
Beaverbrook, Lord 5:58
Beckford, William *see Index of
    Writers*
Bedford, Francis 10:50
Beeny Cliff (Hardy) 3:87, 89, 91
Beerbohm, Max 2:72; 5:*11*, *32*
Beggar's Opera (Gay) 1:84; 10:11, *11*
Behn, Aphra 1:52-53, *53*
Belgium, Congo and 9:72-76
Bell, Clive *see Index of Writers*
'Bell, Currer, Ellis and Acton' 4:10,
    11, 35, 46
Bell, George 11:75
Bell, Joseph 12:78, 80, *80*, 90
Bell, Vanessa Stephen 8:76, 78, 79,
    79, *81*, 82, *82*, 83, *92*, 96, 97, *97*,
    98, 99, 100, *100*
Belle Dame Sans Merci, La (Keats) 13:63
Belloc, Hilaire *see Index of Writers*
Belsches, Williamina 11:31, 46
Bendall, Edith 8:55
'Bennet, Elizabeth' of *Pride and
    Prejudice* 8:12, *12*, 13, *13*, 14, *14*,
    15, *15*, 16, *16*, 17, 20, 21, 22

*In 1831, Charles
Darwin joined the
crew of the British
Royal Navy survey
ship, HMS Beagle.
His five years aboard
as naturalist were to
provide the
observations on
which The Origin
of Species was
based.*

'Bennet, Jane' of *Pride and Prejudice* 8:12, *12,* 13, *15,* 16, *17*
'Bennet, Lydia' of *Pride and Prejudice* 8:*13,* 15, 16, *17, 19*
'Bennet, Mr' of *Pride and Prejudice* 8:12, 14, 15, 16
'Bennet, Mrs' of *Pride and Prejudice* 8:10, 12, *12,* 13, 14, *15,* 16, *16*
Bennett, Arnold *see Index of Writers*
Bennett, Harry 10:100
'Bennett, Mr' of *Kim* 11:85, 88, *88*
Benson, A. C. *see Index of Writers*
Bentham, Jeremy *see Index of Writers*
Bentley, Richard 9:43
Berkeley, Countess 10:18
Berkeley, Lord 10:18
Berlin, Irving 7:51
Bernhardt, Sarah 2:*68*
'Bertha' of *Bliss* 8:62, *62,* 63, 64, *65*
Besant, Annie 4:100
Bethlehem or Bethlem Hospital ('Bedlam') 12:72, *73,* 76
Betjeman, John *see Index of Writers*
Betterton, Mary 1:52
Between the Acts (Woolf) 8:92, 93, 95, *95*
Beyond the Pale (Kipling) 11:93
Bhownagree, Sir M. M. 9:98
Bickerstaff Papers (Swift) 10:19
Big Two-Hearted River (Hemingway) 7:93
Bigg-Wither, Harris 8:9
'Bildad' of *Moby-Dick* 9:36, 39, 40
Billy Budd (Melville) 9:35, 44, 45, 46, 83, *92*
'Bingley' of *Pride and Prejudice* 8:12, 13, 14, *15,* 16, 17

Binyon, Laurence *see Index of Writers*
Biographia Literaria (Coleridge) 13:57, 76
Bishop, John Peale 7:31
Bishop's Apron, The (Maugham) 5:56
Bixby, Horace 7:7
Black Cat, The (Poe) 12:45, 46, 47, *47*
Black Death (Plague) 1:11, 12, 28, *30, 36,* 38, 39, 40, 42, 45, 47; 13:6, 7, 8, *8,* 25, *26, 32,* 43
'Black Dog' of *Treasure Island* 11:60, *60,* 64
'Black Knight, The' of *Ivanhoe* 11:36, 37, *38-39,* 49
Black Mischief (Waugh) 10:57, 66, 69
'Blackbeard' *see* Teach, Edward
Blackwood, John 4:82, 83
Blackwood's Magazine 9:61, 67
Blake, William *see Index of Writers*
Bleak House (Dickens) 3:15, *15,* 26, 40-41, 43, 44, *44,* 50; 12:67, 97
Blighters (Sassoon) 13:90
'Blind Pew' of *Treasure Island* 11:60–61, *61,* 64
Bliss (Mansfield) 8:60, 62-63, *62,* 64, 65, *65,* 70
Blomfield, Arthur 3:53
Bloomsbury group *see Index of Writers*
Blossoming World, The (Bates) 6:59
'Blount, Nina' of *Vile Bodies* 10:60, 63, 64, *64, 76*
Blue Carbuncle, The (Conan Doyle) 12:86–87, 88, 89, *89*
Boccaccio, Giovanni *see Index of Writers*

Boer War 11:82, *90, 96-97,* 99, 100, *100*
'Bois-Guilbert, Sir Brian de' of *Ivanhoe* 11:37, *37,* 38, *38,* 40, *40,* 41, 48
'Bold, Eleanor' of *Barchester Towers* 2:37, 38, *38,* 39, 40, *41,* 45, *45*
'Boldwood, William' of *Far from the Madding Crowd* 3:64, 65, *65,* 67, 68, *68,* 69, 72
Bolshevik Revolution 7:74
'Bolton, Harry' of *Redburn* 9:47
Bombs Away (Steinbeck) 7:57
Bonaparte, Joseph 2:26
Bone, Muirhead 13:99
'Bones, Captain Billy' of *Treasure Island* 11:60, *60,* 61, 63, 64
Bonnard, Pierre 8:98
Bonney, Anne 11:27, 28, *28*
Bonus Expeditionary Force 7:73, *73,* 74
Book of Nonsense (Lear) 10:38, *38*
Book of Snobs, The (Thackeray) 2:18
Book of the Duchess, The (Chaucer) 13:7, 20
bootlegging/bootleggers 7:37, 38, *38,* 49, 50, 51
Boots (Kipling) 11:100
Bosanquet, Theodora 5:20, *20*
Bose, Subhas Chandra 9:99
'Bosinney, Philip' of *The Forsyte Saga* 5:80, 84, *84,* 85, *85,* 87, 88, *88,* 89, 90
Bostonians, The (James) 5:8, 20, 21, 23, *23*
Boswell, James *see Index of Writers*
Boukman, High Priest 6:97, 98
Bourdin, Martial 9:68
Bow, Clara 7:52
Bowden, George 8:55, 56
Boy in the Bush, The (Skinner/ Lawrence) 6:10, 18, *19*
Boyle, Robert *see Index of Writers*
Boyne, Battle of the 10:24, *24-25,* 25
Brachygraphy (Gurney) 3:8
Bradlaugh, Charles 4:100
Branwell, Elizabeth ('Aunt') 4:6, *6,* 7, 8, 9, *9,* 30, 32, 33, 34, 38
'Brattle, Carry' of *The Vicar of Bullhampton* 2:46-47, *47*
Brave New World (Huxley) 5:52; 10:81, 83, 84-89, *84-89,* 90-91, 92, 93, 94
Brave New World Revisited (Huxley) 10:83, 93
Brawne, Fanny 13:63, *63*
Bray, Cara 4:79, *79,* 80, *80, 81,* 90
Bray, Charles 4:79, *79,* 80, *80, 81,* 82, 90
Breath of Fresh Air, A (Bates) 6:59
Brecht, Bertolt *see Index of Writers*
Brett, Dorothy 6:*10,* 11, *11;* 8:58
'Bretton, John' of *Villette* 4:22

Mr Darcy begins to discover the attractions of Elizabeth Bennet in Jane Austen's Pride and Prejudice. *Recalling his earlier slight and display of pride, Elizabeth responds with humour and indifference.*

'Bridehead, Sue' of *Jude the Obscure* 3:55, 61, 72, 75

Brideshead Revisited (Waugh) 10:58, *58*, 67, 69, 70, *70*

'Brierly' of *Lord Jim* 9:63, 64

Brighton Rock (Greene) 6:80, 90, 93, *93*

'Briscoe, Lily' of *To the Lighthouse* 8:85, *85*, 86, 87, *87*, 88, *88*

Bristol, Horace 7:59, *76*

British Association 9:*11*

Britten, Benjamin 9:46, 83, *92*

'Brocklehurst, Mr' of *Jane Eyre* 4:7, 12, 14, 16, *16*, 20

Broken-Link Handicap, The (Kipling) 11:93

Brontë, Anne *see Index of Writers*

Brontë, Charlotte *see Index of Writers*

Brontë, Elizabeth 4:7, 30

Brontë, Emily *see Index of Writers*

Brontë, Maria (mother of Brontës) 4:6, *6*, 30, *33*

Brontë, Maria (sister of Brontës) 4:7, 30

Brontë, Patrick Branwell 4:6, 7, 9, *9*, *10*, 11, 18, *18*, 24, 27, 30, *30*, 31, 32, 33, *33*, 34, *34*, 35, 43, 45, 46, 50, 51, 58, 59, *59*, 69

'Brooke, Dorothea' of *Middlemarch* (Eliot) 4:90, 91, *91*, 94, *94*

'Brooke, John' of *Little Women* 8:40, 41, 46

Brooke, Rupert Chawner *see Index of Writers*

Brookfield, Jane 2:10, *10*

Brookfield, William 2:10

Brother and Sister, The (M. Shelley) 12:22

'Brown' of *The Comedians* 6:84, *84*, 85, *85*, 86, *86*, 87, *87*, 88, *88*, 89

'Brown, Captain' of *Cranford* 4:60, *61*, 63, 64

Brown, John 8:51, *51*

Brown, John 13:70

Brown, Martha 3:53, 60

Browne, Hablot Knight ('Phiz') 3:*41*

Browning, Elizabeth Barrett *see Index of Writers*

Browning, Robert *see Index of Writers*

Brummell, George Bryan (Beau Brummell) 8:*28*

Brunel, Isambard 12:48

'Brunoni, Signor' of *Cranford* 4:61, *63*, 64, *65*

'Buchanan, Daisy' of *The Great Gatsby* 7:36, *36*, 37, *37*, 38, 39, *39*, 40, *40*, 41, 48

'Buchanan, Tom' of *The Great Gatsby* 7:36, 37, 38, *38*, 39, 40, *40*, 48

Buckhurst, Lord 1:54

Buckingham, Duchess of 1:101

Buckingham, Duke of 1:*53*, 54

Buckingham, Robert Morgan 9:82

Buckingham, May Hockey 9:82, 83

Buckingham, Bob 9:82, *82*, 83

Buckland, Frank 9:24

Budd, George 12:79, *79*, 92

Buddhism 11:86, *86*

Buellens, Abbe 5:74

bullfighting 7:*80*, 81, *81*, *85*, 91

Bulwer-Lytton, Edward *see Index of Writers*

'Bumble, Mr' of *Oliver Twist* 3:26

Bunney, John 10:*50*

Bunyan, Elizabeth 1:*61*, 62, 63

Bunyan, John *see Index of Writers*

Bunyan, Joseph 1:62

Bunyan, Margaret 1:58, *58*, 60

Bunyan, Mary or Margaret Bentley (mother of John) 1:58, *58*, 60

Bunyan, Mary (first wife of John) 1:60, 61, *61*, 62

Bunyan, Mary (daughter of John) 1:61, *61*, 62

Bunyan, Thomas (father of John) 1:58, *58*

Bunyan, Thomas (son of John) 1:62

Bunyan, William 1:58, *58*

Burbage, James 1:28, 29

Burbage, Richard 1:12, 28, 29, 30, *30*; 13:31

Burdett-Coutts, Angela 3:*41*, 47

Burgess, Anthony *see Index of Writers*

Burgess, Guy 6:81

Burne-Jones, Philip 11:*90-91*

Burne-Jones, Sir Edward 4:83; 5:27; 11:*52*, 80, *80*

'Burnell family' of *Prelude* 8:60, *60*, 61, *61*, 62, 64, *64*

Burning Wheel, The (Huxley) 10:79, *91*

'Burns, Helen' of *Jane Eyre* 4:7, 16, *16, 17*

Burns, Robert *see Index of Writers*

Burr, Charles 12:35

Burroughs, Edgar Rice *see Index of Writers*

Burrows, Louie 6:8

Butler, Josephine 2:100

Butler, Samuel *see Index of Writers*

Butler, Thomas 2:78, *78*, 79, 80, 81, 82, 87, 90

Button, Jemmy 9:*13*, 14

Byron, Annabella Milbanke 13:59

Byron, George Gordon, Lord *see Index of Writers*

Byron, H. J. *see Index of Writers*

Rupert Brooke greeted World War I as a welcome test of his manhood, but before he could reach the fighting, he died of acute blood poisoning.

C

Cadell, Robert 11:*32,* 35
Cadenus and Vanessa (Swift) 10:10
Cakes and Ale (Maugham) 5:59, *67,*
68, 69, 71, *71*
'Caligula' of *I, Claudius* 6:36, 38, *38,*
39, 39, 40, *40,* 41, 50, 51-52
'Calpurnia' of *I, Claudius* 6:38, *38,*
40, *40*
Camden, William 1:11
Camel's Back, The (Fitzgerald) 7:42,
46, *46*
Cameron, Cecil 5:73
Cameron, Julia Margaret 10:*35,*
48-49, 49, 52
'Campbell, Alan' of *The Picture of*
Dorian Gray 2:64
Campbell, Colin 11:69
Campbell, Mrs Patrick 5:*100*
Can You Forgive Her? (Trollope)
2:43, 46
Cannan, Gilbert 6:20
Cannery Row (Steinbeck) 7:66, 67,
69, 70, *70*
cannibalism 9:31, *32,* 33, 45, *49,* 50
Canning, George 12:18
Canterbury Tales, The (Chaucer)
13:6, 10, 11, 12-19, *12-19,* 20,
22, *22,* 23, 27
Canterville Ghost, The (Wilde) 2:66,
69, *69*
Cantos (Pound) 5:28
Capa, Robert 7:58
Cape (Jonathan) 6:55, 58, 59, 66
Capone, Al 7:*48,* 50
Captain Singleton (Defoe) 11:21, *21,* 24
Captain's Doll, The (Lawrence) 6:20
Captive of Seville, The (Alcott) 8:32
'Carbury, Sir Felix' of *The Way We*
Live Now 2:46
Carco, Francis 8:58, 68
Cardenio (Shakespeare/Fletcher) 1:22
Cardwell, Edward, Viscount 11:96,
97, 98, *98*
'Carey, Philip' of *Of Human Bondage*
5:55, 58, 60, *60-61,* 62, *62,* 63,
63, 64, *65,* 68
Carlos, Don, King of Spain 9:57
Carlyle, Thomas *see Index of Writers*
Carmichael-Smyth, Henry 2:6
Caroline, Queen of England 11:46
Caroline of Anspach 1:*96*
Carolling (Robinson) 10:*50-51*
Carpenter, Edward 8:76; 9:82, 92,
95
Carr, Sybil 5:79
'Carraway, Nick' of *The Great*
Gatsby 7:36, *38,* 39, 40, *41*
Carroll, Lewis (Charles Lutwidge
Dodgson) *see Index of Writers*

After Alice falls into a large pool of salt water (which, she soon realises, is the result of her weeping when she was nine feet high), she is soon joined by fellow victims of the flood – a duck, a dodo, an eaglet, a lory, 'and several other curious creatures'.

'Carson, Henry' of *Mary Barton* 4:69
Carson, Sir Edward 2:58
Carter, Theophilus 10:33
'Carton, Sydney' of *A Tale of Two*
Cities 3:18, *19,* 20, *20,* 21, 22,
23, *23*
'Casaubon, Reverend' of
Middlemarch 4:90, 94, *94*
Casement, Roger 9:75-76, *75;*
12:83, *83*
Castle of Otranto, The (Walpole)
12:25, *25*
Castlemaine, Lady 1:44, *44*
Castlereagh, Robert Stewart,
Viscount 13:69
Castro, Fidel 6:*82,* 83, *91;* 7:83, *83*
'Casy' of *The Grapes of Wrath* 7:60,
62, 63, 64, *64,* 65, 66, 68
'Caterpillar' of *Alice in Wonderland*
10:36, 38, 41, *41*
'Catherick, Ann (Woman in White)'
of *The Woman in White* 12:60,
61, 62, *62,* 64, 68, 72
Catherine of Braganza 1:*39,* 44
'Cathy (Earnshaw/Linton)' of
Wuthering Heights 4:36, *36,* 37,
37, 38, *38,* 39, *39,* 40, *40,* 41, 43,
48
Catriona (Stevenson) 11:69
Cavell, Edith 5:73, *73*
Caxton, William 1:51; 13:22
Cecioni, Adriano 12:57
'Cedric of Rotherwood' of *Ivanhoe*
11:36, 37, 39, 40, 41, *41*
Celebrated Jumping Frog of Calaveras
County and Other Sketches, The
(Twain) 7:18, 21
Celestial Omnibus, The (Forster)
9:93, 94

Cenci, The (Shelley) 13:61
Cervantes, Miguel de *see Index of*
Writers
Cezanne, Paul 8:98, *98-99,* 99
'Chadband, Mr' of *Bleak House*
3:26, 41
'Challenger, Professor' of *The Lost*
World 12:91, 92, 95
Chalmers, George 13:33
Chambers, Edmund 6:7
Chambers, Jessie 6:7, *7,* 8
Chambers, Sarah Anne 6:7
Chance (Conrad) 9:59, 68, 69, 71
Chandler, Raymond *see Index of Writers*
Change, The (Hardy) 3:88
Chaplin, Charles 7:52; 10:*82,* 87, *99,*
100
Chapman, George 13:32, 52, 62
Chapman, John 4:80, 81, 82
Chapman and Hall 3:50, 70; 4:67
Charke, Charlotte 1:97
Charles Edward Stuart (Bonnie
Prince Charlie) 11:44, *44,* 45,
46, 69
Charles I, King of England 1:34, *35,*
36, 40, 41, 52, 76, *76,* 77, *77,* 78,
78, 79, *79,* 80, *80;* 11:21, *26*
Charles II, King of England 1:36,
36, 37, *37,* 38, 39, 40, *40,* 41,
42-43, *42, 43,* 44, *44,* 45, 50, 52,
53, *53,* 54, 55, *55,* 62, 76; 8:24;
11:*8, 26,* 47
Charlotte's Row (Bates) 6:69, *69*
Chartism 4:51, 67, 72-76, *72-76*
Chase, Jack 9:46, 47
Chase, Owen 9:34
Chaucer, Agnes Copton 13:6
Chaucer, Geoffrey *see Index of*
Writers

Poised over the abyss, *Conan Doyle's singular hero of crime stories, Sherlock Holmes, grapples with arch-villain Professor Moriarty at the Reichenbach Falls in Switzerland. The outcome of this encounter was a watery grave for Holmes – much to the outrage of his public following. With the incentive of a large financial inducement, Holmes was to reappear ten years later, wet but still alive, with his uncanny crime-solving abilities intact.*

Mansell Collection

Chaucer, John 13:6, *6, 7*
Chaucer, Philippa Roet 13:7, *7*
Chaucer, Robert Malin le 13:6
Chaumpaigne, Cecily 13:9
Cheap in August (Greene) 6:95, *95*
Checkhov, Anton *see Index of Writers*
'Cheshire Cat' of *Alice in Wonderland* 10:37, 38, 41, *41*, 43
Chesney, Sir George *see Index of Writers*
Chesterton, G. K. *see Index of Writers*
'Chicoy, Juan' of *The Wayward Bus* 7:67, 71

Child's Garden of Verses, A (Stevenson) 11:*54*, 58, 69, *70-71*, 71
Child's History of England, A (Dickens) 3:14; 12:67
Child-Who-Was-Tired, The- (Mansfield) 8:66-67
Childe Harold's Pilgrimage (Byron) 13:58, *68*, 76
Chimes, The (Dickens) 3:16, 24, 26, 27, 50
Chivalry, Age of 11:48-52, *48-52*
Christabel (Coleridge) 13:66, *67*, 73

'Christian' of *The Pilgrim's Progress* 1:63, 64, *64*, 65, *65*, 66, 67, 68, *68*, 69, 74, 75
Christianity in Victorian England 4:96-100, *96-100*
Christmas Carol, A (Dickens) 3:11, 24, *24*, 27, *27*
Christmas Holiday (Maugham) 5:67
Christophe, Henri 6:*97*, 98
Church, Christian, medieval 13:24-28, *24-28*
Church of England 4:96, *96-97*, 97, *98*
Churchill, Lady Randolph 7:33
Churchill, Winston 5:58, 92, 100; 7:33; 8:19, 20; 11:100; 12:82; 13:78, 79, 86
Cibber, Colley 1:*54*, 97
Circle, The (Maugham) 5:58, 66
Civil War, American 7:*6*, 7, 9, 14, 22, 24, *28*, 30, 78; 8:32, *34-35*, 35, *43*, 44, 45, 46, 48-52, *48-52*
Civil War, English 1:76-80, *76-80*
Civilisation (Bell) 8:99
'Civilised Man, A' (Leonard Woolf) 8:99
'Claggart, John' of *Billy Budd* 9:46
Clairmont, Charles 12:6
Clairmont, Claire (Jane) 12:6, 7, 8, *8*, 9, 10, 20
Clairmont, Claire 13:59, 60, 61
Clairmont, Mary Jane 12:6
'Clare, Angel' of *Tess of the D'Urbervilles* 3:61, 80, 81, 82, *82*, 83, *83*, 84, *84*, 85
Clarel (Melville) 9:43
Clarendon, Edward Hyde, Earl of 1:44, 45, *45*
Clark, Kenneth *see Index of Writers*
Clarke, Savile 10:*45*
'Claudius' of *I, Claudius* 6:35, *35*, 36, 37, *37*, 38, *38*, 39, *39*, 40, *40*, 41, 50, 52
'Claudius' of *Hamlet* 1:16, *16*, 17, 20
Claudius the God (Graves) 6:45
Clemens, Clara 7:*10*, 11
Clemens, Jane 7:*6*
Clemens, Jean 7:10, *10*, 11
Clemens, John Marshall 7:6
Clemens, Olivia (Livy) Langdon 7:8, *8*, 9, 10, *10*, 11, 20
Clemens, Orion 7:6, 7, *7*, 10
Clemens, Samuel Langhorne *see* Twain, Mark
Clemens, Susy 7:10, *10*
Clemm, Henry 12:32
Clemm, Maria 12:32, 33, *33*, 35, 45
'Clerval, Henry' of *Frankenstein* 12:12, 13, 16, *17*
Cleveland, Duchess of 1:54
Clockwork Orange, A (Burgess) 10:87
Clodd, Edward 3:58, *59*, 63
Cockburn, Alicia 11:*30*

Cockburn, Claude *see Index of Writers*
Cockburn, Lord 10:54
'Coffin, Peter' of *Moby-Dick* 9:36, *36*
'Coggan, Jan' of *Far from the Madding Crowd* 3:68
Cohen, Harriet 6:56
Cole, Horace 8:79
Coleridge, Samuel Taylor *see Index of Writers*
Coleridge, Sara Fricker 13:56, *57*
Collected Poems (Graves) 6:42, *44*
Collected Short Stories (Graves) 6:47, *47*
Collier, Jeremy 1:56, *56*
Collingwood, Mary Dodgson 10:31
Collingwood, Stuart 10:31
Collins, Charles 3:16; 12:*54, 55,* 56, *56*
'Collins, Mr' of *Pride and Prejudice* 8:12, 13, 14, 16, *16, 17*
Collins, Tom 7:63
Collins, William Wilkie *see Index of Writers*
Colonel Jack (Defoe) 11:11
Colonel Julian (Bates) 6:71
Columbus, Christopher 6:96, *96*
Colvin, Sidney 11:*56,* 57, 66
Combe, George 4:80
Comedians, The (Greene) 6:83, 84-89, *84-89,* 92, 93, 96
Coming of the Fairies, The (Conan Doyle) 12:*82*
Common Form (Kipling) 13:93
Common Objects of the Country (Wood) 9:26
Complete Poems (E. Brontë) 4:46
Comte, Auguste *see Index of Writers*
Condell, Henry 1:22, 24
Conduct of the Allies, The (Swift) 10:22, 23, *23*
Confessions of an English Opium Eater (De Quincey) 9:42; 13:73
Confidence Man, The (Melville) 9:43
Confidential Agent, The (Greene) 6:80, 90
Congo 9:72-76, *73-76*
Congreve, William 1:55, *55,* 56
Connecticut Yankee in King Arthur's Court, A (Twain) 7:18, 20, 21, 23, *23*
Conolly, John 12:75, 76
Conrad, Borys 9:58, *59*
Conrad, Jessie George 9:57, *58, 59*
Conrad, Joseph *see Index of Writers*
Constable, Archibald 11:34, 43
Conversion (Waugh) 10:66
Cooke, William 2:50
Cooper, Constance Fenimore 5:8, 9
Cooper, Lady Diana 10:57
Coppard, A. E. *see Index of Writers*
Coram, Thomas 1:91, *91*
'Cordelia' of *King Lear* 1:18, *18,* 19, *19,* 20, 21, 55

Coriolanus (Shakespeare) 1:22
Corke, Helen 6:8
Corsair, The (Byron) 13:59
Corsican Brothers, The (H. J. Byron) 2:*86*
Cortés, Hernán 6:28
Count Belisarius (Graves) 6:44
Counter-Attack (Sassoon) 13:81, 90
Country House, The (Galsworthy) 5:*90,* 92
Country Wife, The (Wycherley) 1:55
Court Duel, A (Collins) 12:56
Cousin Phillis (Gaskell) 4:69, 71, *71*
Couter, John 9:50
Couzens, James 10:98
Coward, Noel *see Index of Writers*
Cowper, William *see Index of Writers*
Cox, 'Ka' (Katherine) 13:78
Crabbe, George *see Index of Writers*
Crack-Up, The (Fitzgerald) 7:35, 44, 45, 47
'Craik' of *The Nigger of the 'Narcissus'* 9:69
Crane, Stephen 5:9, *11,* 27-28; 9:58
Crane, Walter 2:70; 11:70, *70*
Cranford (Gaskell)) 4:*55,* 57, 58, 60-65, *60-65,* 67, *67,* 69, 72
'Cratchit, Bob' of *A Christmas Carol* 3:27, *27*
'Crawley, Miss' of *Vanity Fair* 2:12, 16, *17*
'Crawley, Pitt' of *Vanity Fair* 2:12
'Crawley, Rawdon' of *Vanity Fair* 2:12, 13, 14, 15, *15,* 16, 17
'Crawley, Sir Pitt' of *Vanity Fair* 2:12, 16
Crease, Francis 10:55
'Creighton, Colonel' of *Kim* 11:84, 85, 87, 88, *88,* 89, *89*
Cricket on the Hearth, The (Dickens) 3:27
crime, 18th century England 1:100-104, *100-104*
Crime of the Congo, The (Conan Doyle) 12:*82*
Crimean War 2:10, 20, *21*
Crippen, Hawley Harvey 12:*97,* 100
Crome Yellow (Huxley) 10:80, 90, 94, *94*
Cromwell, Oliver 1:34, *35,* 36, 40, 62, 77, 78, *78,* 79, *79,* 80, *80*
Cromwell, Richard 1:40
'Cronshaw' of *Of Human Bondage* 5:*62,* 63, 64, *65*
Cross, John 4:*82,* 83
'Crowne, Lenina' of *Brave New World* 10:85, *85,* 86, *86,* 87, 88, *88,* 89
Crozier, Eric 9:83
Cruickshank, John 13:66
Cruikshank, George 2:11
Cruise of the Breadwinner, The (Bates) 6:68
'Crump, Lottie' of *Vile Bodies* 10:58,

60, *60,* 64, *64,* 65
'Cruncher, Jerry' of *A Tale of Two Cities* 3:20
'Crusoe, Robinson' of *Robinson Crusoe* 11:6, 9, *9,* 11, 12, *12,* 13, *13,* 14, *14,* 15, *15,* 16, 17, *17,* 19, 20, 24
'Cuff, Sergeant' of *The Moonstone* 12:66, 68, 70
Culloden, Battle of 11:*44,* 45
Cumberland, Duke of 11:*44*
Cunard, Nancy 10:*80,* 81
Cunningham, Alison 11:54-55, *54,* 71
Cup of Gold (Steinbeck) 7:56
'Curate' of *The War of the Worlds* 5:38, 39, *39,* 40, *41*
Currier, N. 9:*35*
Curzon, Lord 9:96, 99, *99*
'Cynthia' of *Wives and Daughters* 4:71, *71*
Cyrano de Bergerac *see Index of Writers*

D

D. H. Lawrence, Novelist (Leavis) 6:20
D'Albert Durade family 4:80, *81*
'D'Urberville, Alec' of *Tess of the D'Urbervilles* 3:80, 81, *81,* 82, 83, 84, 85, *85*
Daffodil Sky, The (Bates) 6:71
Daffodils (Wordsworth) 13:54, *65*
Daguerre, Louis 10:48; 12:48, *49,* 50
Dahl, Roald *see Index of Writers*
Dalkeith, Countess of 11:43
Dalton, John 12:49
Dampier, William *see Index of Writers*
Danger of the Protestant Religion Consider'd, The (Defoe) 11:*9*
Daniel Deronda (Eliot) 4:83, 92, *92,* 95, *95*
'Danny' of *Tortilla Flat* 7:67, 69, *69*
Danny Deever (Kipling) 11:94, 99
Dante Alighieri *see Index of Writers*
'Darcy' of *Pride and Prejudice* 8:12, 13, *13,* 14, *14,* 15, *15,* 16, *16,* 17, 20
Dark Flower, The (Galsworthy) 5:82
Dark Night's Work, A (Gaskell) 4:70
Darkling Thrush, The (Hardy) 3:87, 89
Darling, Malcolm 9:81
Darling Buds of May, The (Bates) 6:59, 68, 69, 70, *70*
Darlington, Lord 4:52
'Darlington, Lord' of *Lady Windermere's Fan* 2:66, 71, *71*

'Darnay, Charles' of *A Tale of Two Cities* 3:18, 19, 20, *20*, 21, *21*, 22, 23, *23*

Dartie, Montague 5:87

Darwin, Catherine 9:*6*

Darwin, Charles *see Index of Writers*

Darwin, Emma Wedgwood 9:8, *8, 9, 10*

Darwin, Erasmus *see Index of Writers*

Darwin, Henrietta 9:8

Darwin, Robert 9:6, 7, *7*

Darwin, Susannah Wedgwood 9:6, 7

'Dashwood, Marianne' of *Sense and Sensibility* 8:20, 22, *22*

Daughters of the Vicar, The (Lawrence) 6:20

Daughters of the Late Colonel (Mansfield) 8:70, 71, *71*

Davenant, Sir William *see Index of Writers*

David, Jacques-Louis 2:*24*

David Copperfield 2:22; 3:*6*, 8, *12, 13*, 15, *24*, 26, *41*, 43, *43*, 49, 50; 12:69

Davis, Bette 5:*61, 68*

Davis, Moll 1:52

Davis, Nuel 12:55

Davy, Sir Humphrey 12:49, *50*, 51

'Dawes, Gerald' of *The Longest Journey* 9:93

Dawn (Graves) 6:45

Dax, Alice 6:8

Day Lewis, Cecil *see Index of Writers*

'De Barral, Flora' of *Chance* 9:71

De Profundis (Wilde) 2:59, 66

De Quincey, Thomas *see Index of Writers*

De Ruyter, Michiel 1:37, *37*, 38, 42

De Witt, Johannes 1:*29*

Dead Man's Dump (Rosenberg) 13:93

'Dean, Ellen (Nelly)' of *Wuthering Heights* 4:34, 37, *37*, 38, 39, 40, 41, *41*

Dean, James 7:*58, 70*

'Deane, Lucy' of *The Mill on the Floss* 4:85, 87

Death in the Afternoon (Hemingway) 7:91

Decadence *see Aestheticism*

Decameron, The (Boccaccio) 13:*11*

Decline and Fall (Waugh) 10:56, 57, 66, 67, 69, *69*

'Decloud, Martin' of *Nostromo* 9:70

'Defarge, Madame' of *A Tale of Two Cities* 3:19, *18-19*, 20, 21, 22, *22*

'Defarge, Monsieur' of *A Tale of Two Cities* 3:18, *18-19*, 20, 22

Defence of Poetry (Shelley) 13:76

Defoe, Daniel *see Index of Writers*

Defoe, Mary Tuffley 11:8, *8*

Dejection: An Ode (Coleridge) 13:57

Dekker, Thomas 13:51, 52

Delacroix, Eugene 13:*59*

'*Delightful Day*' (Gauguin) 9:*48*

Dempsey, Jack 7:51

Denis Duval (Thackeray) 2:11

Departmental Ditties (Kipling) 11:93

Depression, The (Great) 6:62, *62*; 7:29, 43, 52, 56, 60, 72-76, *72-76*, 92, 94; 10:76, *76, 99*, 100

'Derriman, Festus' of *The Trumpet Major* 3:74

Descent into the Maelstrom, A (Poe) 12:33, *44*, 45, 50

Descent of Man, The (Darwin), 9:10, *22, 23*, 27

Despard, Charlotte 8:74

Desperate Remedies (Hardy) 3:53, 71

Dessalines, Jean-Jacques 6:98

Devils, The (Whiting) 10:95

Devils of Loudun, The (Huxley) 10:93, 95, *95*

Dew, Walter 12:*97*, 99-100

Diamond as Big as the Ritz, The (Fitzgerald) 7:44, 46

Diary (Pepys) 1:33, 34, *34*, 35, *35*, 36, *36*, 37, 38, *38*, 39, 40-45, *40-45*, 46, 47, *48*, 49, 50, 51, 52, 53

Dickens, Augustus ('Boz') 3:10

Dickens, Catherine Hogarth 3:*8-9*, 10, 11, *11, 13*, 15

Dickens, Charles *see Index of Writers*

Dickens, Elizabeth 3:6, *6*, 7, 8

Dickens, Fred 3:10

Dickens, Henry 3:17

Dickens, John 3:6, *6*, 7, 8, *10*

Dickens, Kate 3:*8-9, 14*, 15, 16

Dickens, Mary ('Mamie') 3:*8-9, 14*, 15, 16, 25

Dickens, Walter 3:*8-9*

Dickinson, Goldsworthy Lowes 9:79, 81

Dictionary of National Biography 8:78; 11:19

Did the Jesuits Write Shakespeare? (Johnson) 13:*31*

Diderot, Denis *see Index of Writers*

Digression on Madness (Swift) 10:22

Dill Pickle, A (Mansfield) 8:68

Dingley, Rebecca 10:9, 23

Dinner at Poplar Walk, A (Dickens) 3:10

'Director, The' of *Brave New World* 10:84, 85, 88

Disabled (Owen) 13:83

Disraeli, Benjamin *see Index of Writers*

Dissenters 11:7, 8, 10, 18, *18*, 20

Divine Comedy (Dante) 13:8, *20*

Divine Emblems (Bunyan) 1:72

Dobbin, William of *Vanity Fair*, 2:13, *13*, 14, 15, 16, *16*, 17

Dr Faustus (Marlowe) 13:50, *50*

Dr Fischer of Geneva (Greene) 6:92

Doctor Thorne (Trollope) 2:43, 45

Dodgson, Charles Lutwidge *see* **Carroll, Lewis**

Dodgson, Charles, senior 10:30, *30*, 34

Dodgson, Edwin 10:*32*

'Dodo' of *Alice in Wonderland* 10:36, *37*

'Dodson family' of *The Mill on the Floss* 4:84, *85*, 85-87, 88, *88*, 96

Defoe's young, would-be adventurer, *Robinson Crusoe, listens to his father's 'serious and excellent' counsel . . . counsel that cannot compete with the lure of the sea.*

Doll's House, A (Ibsen) 5:*96*, 97
Dombey and Son (Dealings with the Firm of Dombey and Son) (Dickens) 3:16, 24, 27, 29, *29*
Domestic Manners of the Americans (Frances Trollope) 2:31, 32, 42; 7:28
Don Fernando (Maugham) 5:67
Don Juan (Byron) 13:59, 64, 65, 67-68, *67*, *68*, 76
Don Quixote (Cervantes) 1:64, 96; 7:*19*; 11:49
'Donkin' of *The Nigger of the 'Narcissus'* 9:69
'Donnithorne, Arthur' of *Adam Bede* 4:93
Doors of Perception, The (Huxley) 10:82, 83, 93, 94
'Dorrit, Amy' ('Little Dorrit') of *Little Dorrit* 3:11, 45, *45*
Dorset 3:52, *53*, 54, *54*, 56, 57, *57*, 58, 65, 70, 76-79, *76-79*, 93, 94
Dorsetshire Labourer, The (Hardy) 3:94, 96
Doubleday, Nelson 5:59
Douglas, Lord Alfred ('Bosie') 2:58, *58-59*, 59, 63, 66, 70, 74, 76
Douglas, Norman 6:10
'Douglas, Widow' of *The Adventures of Huckleberry Finn* 7:12, *13*
Downing, George 1:36
Dowson, Ernest 2:*73*, 74, 76
Doyle, Alleyne Kingsley 12:81, 83

Doyle, Arthur Conan, Sir *see Index of Writers*
Doyle, Charles 12:78, *78-79*, 81
Doyle, Innes 12:80, 83
Doyle, Jean Leckie 12:81, *81*, 83
Doyle, Louise Hawkins 12:80, *80*, 81, *81*, 82
Doyle, Mary Foley (Ma'am) 12:78, *78*, 79, 81, 83
Doyle, Mary Louise 12:80
Dracula (Stoker) 12:28
Drake, Nathan 12:25
Drake, Sir Francis 6:96; 11:24
Drapier's Letters, The (Swift) 10:10, 18, 27, *27*
Drayton, Michael *see Index of Writers*
Dream is – Which?, The (Hardy) 3:89, 90
Dream-Woman, The (Collins) 12:70, 70-71
Dryden, John *see Index of Writers*
Duchenne, M.G.B. 12:*75*
'Duchess, The' of *Alice in Wonderland* 10:37, 38, 41, *41*
Duchess of Duke Street, The 10:58
Duchess of Padua, The (Wilde) 2:56
Duckworth, Jack 8:78
Duckworth, Robinson 10:30, *37*
Duckworth, Stella 8:78, *79*
Dugdale, Florence *see* Hardy, Florence Dugdale
'Duke, The' of *The Adventures of Huckleberry Finn* 7:13, 14, 15, *15*, 16, *16*, 17
Duke's Children, The (Trollope) 2:43, 46
Dulce et Decorum Est (Owen) 13:83, *90*, 91
Dumas, Lucie 2:80
'Dupin, C. Auguste' of *The Murders in the Rue Morgue* 12:36, 38, 39, *39*, 40, *41*, 90
'Durbeyfield, John' of *Tess of the D'Urbervilles* 3:80, 84, *85*
'Durbeyfield, Tess' of *Tess of the D'Urbervilles* 3:60, 61, 72, 78, 79, 80, *80*, 81, *81*, 82, *82*, 83, *83*, 84, *84-85*, 85, 95, 96
'Durham, Clive' of *Maurice* 9:95
Durning-Lawrence, Sir Edwin *see Index of Writers*
Duvalier, François ('Papa Doc') 6:84, 85, 86, 87, *91*, 92, *99*, 100
Duvalier, Jean-Claude ('Baby Doc') 6:100, *100*
Duvalier, Michele Bennett 6:100
Dyer, General 9:100

Dyer, Granny 8:54, 58
Dynasts, The (Hardy) 3:56, 74

E

Early Life of Thomas Hardy, The ('Biography') 3:56-57, *58*, 59, 61, 63
Early Success (Fitzgerald) 7:47
'Earnshaw, Hareton' of *Wuthering Heights* 4:37, *39*, 40
'Earnshaw, Hindley' of *Wuthering Heights* 4:37, *37*, 39, *39*, 40, *40*
'Earnshaw, Mr' of *Wuthering Heights* 4:37, *37*, 38, 40, 51
East India Company 9:96, *96*
East of Eden (Steinbeck) 7:*58*, 66, 67, 68, 69, 70, *70*
East of Suez (Maugham) 5:58
Eastman, Max 10:87
Eastward Hoe! 1:29
Ebb-Tide, The (Stevenson/Osbourne) 11:66
Eccles, Solomon 1:39, *39*
Echoes of the Jazz Age (Fitzgerald) 7:47
Economic Consequences of the Peace (Keynes) 8:99
Edalji, George 12:82
Eddison's Steam Plough Works 3:94
Edel, Leon 5:6
'Edgar' of *King Lear* 1:19, 55
Edinburgh, Picturesque Notes (Stevenson) 11:*72*, 76
Edinburgh 11:30, *30-31*, *32*, 33, 34, 44, 46, *46-47*, 50-51, *54*, 55, 56, 57, 72-76, *72-76*
Edison, Thomas 10:98
'Edmund' of *King Lear* 1:19, *19*
Edward, Prince of Wales 2:*96*, 97, 98; 3:*56-57*
Edward, the Black Prince 11:*51*
Edward III, King of England 11:*51*, 52; 13:6, *6*, 7, 8, *8*, *9*, 10, *11*, *25*, 26, 28
Edward VII, King of England 8:79; 12:82
Egg, Augustus 12:57, *57*, 66
Eglington Tournament 11:51-52, *51*
1880 (Beerbohm) 2:72
Eisenhower, Dwight D. 7:73
Elegy written in a Country Churchyard (Gray) 12:25
Eleonora (Poe) 12:44, *44*
Elephant's Child, The (Kipling) 11:95
'Elijah' of *Moby-Dick* 9:36, *37*, 38
'Elinor and Marianne' (Austen) 8:8
Eliot, George *see Index of Writers*
Eliot, T. S. *see Index of Writers*

Dicken's own experience of child labour was acquired at the age of 12 when, due to his family's destitution, he worked at Warren's Blacking Factory. He later called it 'the secret agony of my soul'.

Mansell Collection

'Elizabeth' of *Frankenstein* 12:12, *15,* *16, 17*

Elizabeth and her German Garden ('Elizabeth' – Countess von Arnim) 9:80

Elizabeth I, Queen of England 1:*11, 22-23,* 28, *28-29, 32;* 11:47, 49; 13:31, *32,* 33, *44-45,* 48, *48*

'Elizabeth-Jane' of *The Mayor of Casterbridge* 3:73

Ellington, Duke 7:51

'Elliot, Rickie' of *The Longest Journey* 9:93

Ellis & Blackmore 3:8

Ellis, Havelock *see Index of Writers*

Emerson, Ellen 8:45

'Emerson, George' of *A Room with a View* 9:91, 95

'Emerson, Mr' of *A Room with a View* 9:91, 95

Emerson, Peter Henry 10:51, *52*

Emerson, Ralph Waldo *see Index of Writers*

Eminent Victorians (Strachey) 8:99

Emma (Austen) 8:*10,* 11, *18, 21,* 22, 23, *23*

'Emmanuel, Paul' of *Villette* 4:22, *22*

'Emperor of Lilliput, The' of *Gulliver's Travels* 10:12, *12-13,* 14, 16

Empty House, The (Conan Doyle) 12:82, 92

Encantadas, The (Melville) 9:43

Enchantress, The (Bates) 6:71

enclosure movement 4:50, *51*

End of the Affair, The (Greene) 6:90, 93

End of the Chapter (Galsworthy) 5:93

Ends and Means (Huxley) 10:92

Endymion (Keats) 13:62, 63

Engels, Friedrich 4:76

English Bards and Scotch Reviewers (Byron) 13:58

English countryside, 20th century changes 6:72-76, *72-76*

English Humorists of the Eighteenth Century (Thackeray) 2:10, 20, *21*

Enquiry Concerning Political Justice, An (Godwin) 12:7

Entomologist's Weekly Intelligencer 9:26

Entertaining Naturalist, The (Mrs Loudon) 9:28

'Eppie' of *Silas Marner* 4:95, *95*

Epstein, Jacob 9:59

Erewhon (Butler) 2:80, 90, *92,* 94, *94;* 5:48

Erewhon Revisited (Butler) 2:93, 94, *94*

Ernst, Karl 5:73

Escaped Cock, The (Lawrence) 6:*20*

'Esmond, Henry' of *The History of Henry Esmond Esquire* 2:6, 21, 23

espionage, World War I 5:72-76, *72-76*

Esquirol, Jeanne 12:*74*

Essay in Autobiography (Wells) 5:42

Essex, Earl of 1:78

'Estella' of *Great Expectations* 3:35, *35,* 36, 37, 38, 39, *39*

Estimé, Dumarsais 6:100

Etherege, Sir George *see Index of Writers*

Euclid and his Rivals (Carroll) 10:42

Eugenie Granet (Balzac) 5:19

Euphrasia (M. Shelley) 12:*20*

Eureka! (Poe) 12:35, *42,* 45

Europeans, The (James) 5:19, 21, *21*

Eustace Diamonds, The (Trollope) 2:46, *46*

Evangelical movement 4:96, 97, *99*

Evans, Chrissey 4:79, 80

Evans, Christiana 4:79

Evans, Elizabeth 4:93, *97*

Evans, Isaac 4:79, 80, 82, *82,* 83, 90, 97, 99

Evans, Mary Ann/Marian *see* **Eliot George**

Evans, Mary 13:56

Evans, Robert 4:78, *78,* 79, *79,* 80, *81,* 82, *90,* 99

Eve of St Agnes, The (Keats) 13:63, *71*

Evelyn, John *see Index of Writers*

Evening Chronicle 3:10

'Everdene, Bathsheba' of *Far from the Madding Crowd* 3:56, 60, 64, 65, *65,* 66, *66,* 67, *67,* 68, *68,* 69, 72, 76, 93, 95

Every Man in His Humour (Jonson) 3:*16;* 13:52

Everyman 1:72

'Evremonde, Marquis St' of *A Tale of Two Cities* 3:18, *20,* 22, *31*

expatriates, American, in Europe 5:24–28, *24-28*

Exploits of Brigadier Gerard, The (Conan Doyle) 12:81, 92, 95, *95*

Expression of Emotions in Man and Animals, The (Darwin) 9:22

Eyeless in Gaza (Huxley) 10:81, 82, 92, 94, 95, *95*

The beautiful Estella *has been brought up to avenge by proxy Miss Havisham's jilting. Estella despises Pip and treats him badly, but the hero of* Great Expectations *still adores her.*

F

Factory Boy, The (Frances Trollope) 2:32, *32*

Facts in the Case of M. Valdemar (Poe) 12:36–37, 52

Fading Away (Robinson) 10:51

Faesch, Hans 2:83, *83*

'Fagin' of *Oliver Twist* 3:28, 47

Fair Haven, The (Butler) 2:80, 90, 91, *91,* 94

Fair Maid of Perth, The (Scott) 11:45

Fair Stood the Wind for France (Bates) 6:58, 59, 68, *68,* 69, *69*

Fairbanks, Douglas 7:52

Fairbanks, Douglas, Jr 7:*57*

'Fairfax, Gwendolen' of *The Importance of Being Earnest* 2:71, *71,*

Fairfax, Sir Thomas 1:*78,* 79

'Fairfield, Mrs' ('Grandmother') of *Prelude* 8:58, *58,* 61, 64, *64*

'Fairlie, Laura (Lady Glyde)' of *The Woman in White* 12:60, 61, *61*, 62, 63, *63*, 64, 65, *65*, 68, 72
'Faithful' of *The Pilgrim's Progress* 1:59, 65, 66, *66*, 68, 69, *69*
Falconer, William 8:24
Fall of the House of Usher, The (Poe) 12:34, 36, *36*, 37, *37*, 40, *41*
Fallen Idol, The (Greene) 6:80
Fallen Leaves, The (Collins) 12:58
Fallow Land, The (Bates) 6:58, 66, *67*, 73
False Rhyme, The (M. Shelley) 12:23
'Falstaff' of *Henry IV* 1:23, 25, *25*, 30, *32*
Far from the Madding Crowd (Hardy) 3:54, 60, 64-69, *64-69*, 71, 72, 75, 76, 77, 78, 79, *79*, 93, 94
Faraday, Michael 10:48; 12:49, *50*, 52
Farewell to Arms, A (Hemingway) 7:79, 91, 92, 93, 94, *94*
'Farfrae, Donald' of *The Mayor of Casterbridge* 3:73
farming, *see* agriculture
Farquhar, George *see Index of Writers*
'Father Victor' of *Kim* 11:85, 88, *88*
Fawcett, Henry 2:52
Fawcett, Millicent 8:74
'Fawley, Jude' of *Jude the Obscure* 3:75, *75*
'Fayaway' of *Typee* 9:45
'Fedallah' of *Moby-Dick* 9:36, 37, 40
Feilding, William 1:82
Felix Holt, the Radical (Eliot) 4:91, 92, 93, 94, *94–95*
Fenton, Leslie 6:59
'Fenwick-Symes, Adam' of *Vile Bodies* 10:60, *60*, 61, 63, 64, *64*, 65, 76
Ferguson, Sir Adam 11:50
'Fermor, Lord' of *The Picture of Dorian Gray* 2:64
Ferrers, Earl 1:104
Festing Jones, Henry 2:81, *81*, 83, *93*
Feuchtwanger, Lion 5:59
Feuerbach, Ludwig 4:82, 100
Feuillide, Eliza de 8:*9*
Field, Kate 2:34, *34*
Field, Richard 13:43
'Fielding' of *A Passage to India* 9:81, 84, 85, 87, 88, *88*
Fielding, Charlotte Cradock 1: 84-85, *85*, 86, *86*
Fielding, Edmund 1:82, 83
Fielding, Elizabeth 1:83
Fielding, Henry *see Index of Writers*
Fielding, Mary Daniel 1:87, *87*
Fielding, Sarah (mother of Henry) 1:82, 83
Fielding, Sarah (sister of Henry) 1:82
Fielding, Sir John 1:83, 87, 102, *102*
Final Problem, The (Conan Doyle) 12:81, 93, *93*

'Finn, Huckleberry' ('Huck') of *The Adventures of Huckleberry Finn* 7:12, *12*, 13, *13*, 14, 15, *15*, 16, *16-17*, 17, 21, 25, 28; 11:87
First Folio (Shakespeare) 1:13, 24, *30*
First Impressions (Austen) 8:8, *13*, 15
First Men in the Moon, The (Wells) 5:50
First Year in the Canterbury Settlement, A (Butler) 2:80
Fisher, James 11:7
Fisher Unwin 9:68
Fisherman and his Soul, The (Wilde) 2:67
Fitton, Mary 13:*32*, 33
Fitz Roy, Robert 9:*11*, *12*, 14
Fitzgerald, Edward 7:30, *30*
Fitzgerald, Frances ('Scottie') 7:33, *34*
Fitzgerald, Francis Scott Key *see Index of Writers*
Fitzgerald, Mollie 7:30, *30*
Fitzgerald, Zelda Sayre 7:31, 32, *32*, 33, *33*, 34, 35, 42, 43, 45, 46, 47, *47*, 48
'Fitzpiers, Edred' of *The Woodlanders* 3:75
'Flanders, Moll' of *Moll Flanders* 11:*10*, 18, 20, 22, *22*
Flappers and Philosophers (Fitzgerald) 7:42, 43
'Flask' of *Moby-Dick* 9:36
Flaubert, Gustave *see Index of Writers*
Fleming, Ann 10:59
Fletcher, John *see Index of Writers*
Fleurs de Mal, Les (Baudelaire) 2:72
Flower Fables (Alcott) 8:32, 42, 45, *45*
Flush (Woolf) 8:82, 91
Flynn, Errol 11:*28*
Fodger, Michael 9:50
Foe, Alice 11:6, *6*
Foe, Elizabeth 11:6
Foe, James 11:6, 7, *7*, 8
Foe, Mary 11:6
Foggi, Elise 12:8, 9, 10
Fonda, Henry 7:57, 59
For Whom the Bell Tolls (Hemingway) 7:78, 81, 82, 84-89, *84-89*, 92, 93, 98
Ford, Edsel 10:100
Ford, Ford Madox *see Index of Writers*
Ford, Henry 10:85, 96-100, *96-100*
Ford, Richard 3:50
Forest Lawn Cemetery 10:58, *58*
Forman, Simon 13:33
Forster, Edward Morgan *see Index of Writers*
Forster, Edward 9:78, *78*, 82
Forster, John 3:12, *14*, 15, 17, 36, 49; 4:67
Forster, Lily 9:78, *78*, 80, 82, 83

Huckleberry Finn and Tom Sawyer meet again at the farm of the latter's uncle. Their reunion is timely, since they unite to rescue the runaway slave Jim.

'Forsyte family,' members of, of *The Forsyte Saga* 5:78, 80, 82, 84-90, *84-89*, 92, 93, 94
Forsyte Saga, The (Galsworthy) 5:78, 80, 82, 84-89, *84-89*, 90, *90*, 91, 92, *92*, 93, 94
'Fosco, Count' of *The Woman in White* 12:60, 61, *61*, 62, *62*, 63, *63*, 64, *64*, 65, 66, 68, 75
Fountaine, Margaret 9:*24*, 25-26
Four Georges, The (Thackeray) 2:10, 20, *21*
Four Quartets, The (Eliot) 5:*28*
Fowler, Thomas 10:31
Fowler Steam Ploughing Tackle 3:*95*
Fox, The (Lawrence) 6:14-15
Fox Talbot, William Henry 10:48, 49
Framley Parsonage (Trollope) 2:43, *44*, 45
Francis I, King of France 11:*50*
Franco, Francisco 7:82, 96, *97*, 99, 100, *100*; 10:57
Frank Leslie's Illustrated Newspaper 8:33, 42-43
'Frankenstein, Victor' of *Frankenstein* 12:12, *12*, 13, *13*, 14, 15, *15*, 16, 17, *17*, 20
Frankenstein (M. Shelley) 12:5, 8, 10, 12-17, *12-17*, 19, *19*, 20, *21*, 22, 24, 28, 52
Franklin, Benjamin 9:47

Franz Ferdinand, Archduke of Austria 13:94, *94-95*
Fraternity (Galsworthy) 5:92
'Fray, Henerey' of *Far from the Madding Crowd* 3:68
'French Lieutenant' of *Lord Jim* 9:63, 64
French Revolution 3:30-33, *30-33*
French Revolution, The (Carlyle) 3:17, 18
Freud, Sigmund 8:80
'Friar Tuck' of *Ivanhoe* 11:*38-39*
Fricker, Edith 13:56
'Friday' of *Robinson Crusoe* 11:14, *14,* 15, *15,* 16, 17, *17*
Friend, The (Coleridge) 13:57
Frith, William 3:39
Froissart, Jean 13:7
From Cornhill to Grand Cairo (Thackeray) 2:18
From Sea to Sea (Kipling) 11:80
From the Earth to the Moon (Verne) 5:50
From the Four Winds (Galsworthy) 5:90
'Front-de-Boeuf, Sir Reginald' of *Ivanhoe* 11:37, *37, 38*
Frozen Deep, The (Collins and Dickens) 12:57, *58, 66,* 70, 71, *71*
Fry, Roger *see Index of Writers*
Furniss, Harry 10:45
Fuseli, Henry 12:9, *25,* 27-28

G

'Gabelle' of *A Tale of Two Cities* 3:19, 23
'Gabriel' of *Moby-Dick* 9:38
Gad's Hill 3:*10,* 11, *14,* 16, 17, *25, 26*
Gainsborough, Thomas 8:27
Galapagos Islands 9:8, 12, 14, 15, 20-21, 43
Galileo 3:87
Galsworthy, Ada 5:70, 80, *80,* 81, *81,* 82, *82,* 83, *90,* 91, 92
Galsworthy, Arthur 5:79, 80
Galsworthy, Blanche 5:78, *78*
Galsworthy, John *see Index of Writers*
Galsworthy, John, Senior 5:78, *78,* 79, 80, 92
Galsworthy, Mabel 5:80
Galvani, Luigi 12:52
Gandhi, Mohandas K. 9:*100*
Garbo, Greta 5:70, *70*
Garden of Eden (Hemingway) 7:91
Garden-Party, The (Mansfield) 8:70

'Gargery, Biddy (Mrs Joe)' of *Great Expectations* 3:35, 38
'Gargery, Joe' of *Great Expectations* 3:34, 35, 36, 37, 38, *38,* 39
'Garland, Anne' of *The Trumpet Major* 3:74
Garnett, David 6:58
Garnett, Edward 5:80, 90, *92,* 96, 99; 6:18, 19, 20, 56, 58, 59, *59,* 66, *67;* 9:66, 68
Garrard, Florence 11:93
Garrick, David 1:12
Garrison, William Lloyd 8:50, *51*
Gaskell, Elizabeth (Mrs) *see Index of Writers*
Gaskell, Florence Elizabeth (Flossy) 4:56, *57*
Gaskell, Julia Bradford 4:57
Gaskell, Marianne 4:56, *57*
Gaskell, Meta 4:56, *57,* 68
Gaskell, William (husband of Elizabeth Gaskell) 4:56, *56,* 57, *57,* 59, 66, *66,* 67, 68
Gaskell, William (son of Elizabeth Gaskell) 4:56-57, *57,* 66
Gate of the Hundred Sorrows, The (Kipling) 11:93
Gathering Waterlilies (Emerson) 10:*52*
'Gatsby, Jay' of *The Great Gatsby* 7:34, 36, *36,* 37, *37,* 38, *38,* 39, *39,* 40, *40-41,* 41, 43, 48, 50, 51
Gauguin, Paul 5:57, 69, *69;* 8:*98;* 9:*48,* 52; 11:*59*
Gautier, Theophile *see Index of Writers*
Gawthorpe, Mary 8:76
Gay, John *see Index of Writers*
Gay-Lussac, Joseph Louis 12:51
General History of the Robberies . . . of the Most Notorious Pirates, A (Defoe, probably) 11:19, 24, *25*
'General Preface to the Novels and Poems' (Hardy) 3:78
'Gentleman Brown' of *Lord Jim* 9:*62,* 64, *65*
Gentleman in the Parlour, The (Maugham) 5:67
'George' of *Of Mice and Men* 7:66, 71
George I, King of England 10:14, 16; 11:*26*
George II, King of England 1:*90, 96*
George III, King of England 8:27; 11:50; 12:76, *76*
George IV, King of England (Prince Regent) 8:*10,* 27, *28;* 11:34, *34-35,* 50-51
George V, King of England 9:96, *97;* 11:*83*
George Silverman's Explanation (Dickens) 3:26
George White's Scandals 7:49
'Gerard, Brigadier' of Conan Doyle stories 12:92, *92, 95, 95*

Gerin, Winifred 4:46
Gerlach, Max 7:34
'Germanicus' of *I, Claudius* 6:37, 38, 40
Gernsback, Hugo 5:52
Gershwin, George 7:*49,* 51
'Ghost, The' of *Hamlet* 1:12, 16, *16,* 17, *21,* 31
Ghost in the Garden Room, The (Gaskell) 4:70
Giaour, The (Byron) 13:59
'Gibson, Molly' of *Wives and Daughters* 4:71, *71*
Gielgud, John 1:12
Gifford, Emma *see* Hardy, Emma Gifford
Gifford, John 1:61, 63
Gift, The (Steinbeck) 7:69
Gilbert and Sullivan 2:56, *72*
Gilded Age, The (Twain) 7:18
Gillman, James 13:57
Gin Lane (Hogarth) 1:87, *100-101,* 102
Gioconda Smile, The (Huxley) 10:82
'Gipsy' of *The Virgin and the Gipsy* 6:12, 13, 16, *16,* 17
Gissing, George *see Index of Writers*
Gladstone, Herbert 5:100
Gladstone, William 2:50, 100; 11:60
'Glenmire, Lady' of *Cranford* 4:61, 63, 64, *64*
Glimpse, The (Hardy) 3:87
Globe Theatre 1:*23,* 28, *29,* 30-31, *31*
'Glumdalclitch' of *Gulliver's Travels* 10:12, 16, *16-17*
'Glyde, Sir Percival' of *The Woman in White* 12:60, 61, *62, 63,* 64, 65, *65*
'Godbole, Professor' of *A Passage to India* 9:84, 85, 86, 87, *87,* 88, *89*
Goddard, Paulette 10:*82*
Godwin, William *see Index of Writers*
Goebbels, Joseph Paul 5:59
Goering, Hermann 7:97
Goethe, Johann Wolfgang von *see Index of Writers*
Going, The (Hardy) 3:88
Gold-Bug, The (Poe) 12:*32, 43,* 46, 47, *47*
Golden Bowl, The (James) 5:10, 19, 20, 21, 22, *22*
Golden Fleece, The (Graves) 6:44
Goldsmith, Oliver *see Index of Writers*
'Golz, General' of *For Whom the Bell Tolls* 7:84, 85, 88
Gondal chronicles (E. and A. Brontë) 4:31, 34, 42, *44,* 46
Gone with the Wind 7:35
'Goneril' of *King Lear* 1:18, *18,* 19, 20, *21*
Good Wives see Little Women, Part II
Goodbye to All That (Graves) 6:34, 43, 45

'Goodwood, Caspar' of *The Portrait of a Lady* 5:12, 16, *16-17*
Gordon, Lord George 1:*104*
Gosse, Edmund *see Index of Writers*
Gosse, Philip 9:24
Gothic literature 12:24-28, *24-28*
'Gould, Charles' of *Nostromo* 9:70
Gould, Sir Henry 1:82
Gower, John 13:7
Grace Abounding to the Chief of Sinners (Bunyan) 1:46, 62, 70, 74, 75, *75*
'Gradgrind, Mr' of *Hard Times* 3:26
'Graham (Huntingdon), Helen' of *The Tenant of Wildfell Hall* 4:45, 47, *47*
Graham, Sheilah 7:35, *35*, 44
'Grandcourt, Henleigh' of *Daniel Deronda* 4:*92*, 93, 95
Grange, Red 7:52
'Grangerford family' of *The Adventures of Huckleberry Finn* 7:*12*, 13, *13*, 16
Grant, Duncan 8:79, *82*, *97*, 98, 99, *99*, 100, *100*
Grant, Ulysses S. 7:9
Grantchester (Brooke) 13:78
'Grantly, Dr' of *Barchester Towers* 2:36, *36*, 37, 38, 40, 44, 45, *45*
Granville-Barker, Harley 5:96, 97, *97*, 98, *98*, 99, 100
Grapes of Wrath, The (Steinbeck) 7:56, 57, 60-65, *60-65*, 66, 67, 68, 72, 76
Grapes of Wrath, The (Steinbeck) 1:64
Grattan, Henry 10:28, *28*
Graves, Alfred Perceval 6:30, *30*, 31
Graves, Amalie von Ranke 6:30, *30*
Graves, Beryl Hodge 6:34, *34*, 35, *35*
Graves, Caroline 12:56, 57, 59, *59*, 62
Graves, Lizzie 12:57, 59
Graves, Nancy Nicholson 6:31–32, *32*, 33, 34
Graves, Robert von Ranke *see Index of Writers*
Gray, Asa 9:9, 10
'Gray, Dorian' of *The Picture of Dorian Gray* 2:57, 60, *60*, 61, *61*, 62, *62-63*, 63, 64, *64*, 65, 72
Gray, John 2:74, 76
Gray, Thomas *see Index of Writers*
Great Boer War, The (Conan Doyle) 12:82
Great Exhibition of 1851 10:33, *33*
Great Exhibition of 1862 9:27
Great Expectations (Dickens) 3:*6*, 7, 9, *25*, 26, 34–39, *34-39*, 43, 46, 47, *50*
Great Fire of London 1:38, 40, *41*, 42, 43, 45, 47, *47*, 49

Gulliver is at first angry that the noble King of Brobdingnag regards Europeans as squabbling 'diminuitive insects', but he is later forced to admit that the King might be correct.

Mansell Collection

Great Gatsby, The (Fitzgerald) 7:33, 34, 36-41, *36-41*, 43, 44, 45, 46, 48, 51
'Great Glass Town Confederacy' (Brontës) 4:7, *9*, 18, 31, *42*
Great Hoggarty Diamond, The (Thackeray) 2:18
Great Mountains, The (Steinbeck) 7:69
Great Shadow, The (Conan Doyle) 12:92
Greaves, Walter 5:25
Greek Myths, The (Graves) 6:35, 52
Green Hills of Africa (Hemingway) 7:91
Greene, Barbara 6:80
Greene, Charles Henry 6:78, *79*
Greene, Elizabeth 6:80
Greene, Henry Graham *see Index of Writers*
Greene, Richard Tobias (Toby) 9:31, *32*, 45
Greene, Robert *see Index of Writers*
Greene, Vivien Dayrell Browning 6:79

'Grenfel, Henry' of *The Fox* 6:15, 16, 17
Grenfell, Julian *see Index of Writers*
Grey, Sir Edward 13:97
Grey Eminence (Huxley) 10:93
Grey Woman, The (Gaskell) 4:70
Groats-worth of Witte (Greene) 1:12; 13:48-49, 49
Gross, John 11:93
Grub-Street Opera, The (Fielding) 1:84
Guerin, Eddie 12:99
Guernica 7:*98-99*, 99-100
'Guest, Stephen' of *The Mill on the Floss* 4:85, 88, *88*, 89, 90
Guiccioli, Countess Teresa 13:59
Guide to the Lakes (Wordsworth) 13:55
'Guildenstern' of *Hamlet* 1:17
Guillotin, Joseph Ignace 3:21
guillotine 3:20, 21, *21*
'Gulliver, Lemuel' of *Gulliver's Travels* 10:6, 9, 12, *12-13*, 13, 14, *14*, 15, 16, *16*, 17, *17*, 18-19

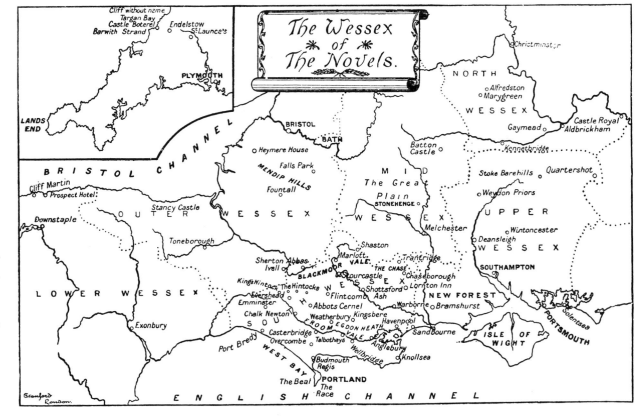

The Wessex
of
The Novels.

Thomas Hardy's novels *are set in Wessex (the name of one of the old Anglo-Saxon kingdoms in England). Hardy changed place names, but his fictional Wessex is clearly recognisable as his beloved county of Dorset.*

Gulliver's Travels (Swift) 5:48, *49*; 9:48; 10:5, 6, 11, 12-17, *12-17*, 19, 21, *21*, 22
Gun for Sale, A (Greene) 6:90
'Gunn, Ben' of *Treasure Island* 11:61, 62, 64, *65*
Gunn, Martha 8:28
Gurdjieff, George 8:59, *59*
Gustavus Adolphus, King of Sweden 11:21
Guy Domville (James) 5:9, 10
Gwyn, Nell 1:44, 52, *52-53*
gypsies 7:84, *84,* 87, *87, 88,* 89

H

Haig, Sir Douglas 13:100
Haile Selassie, Emperor of Ethiopia 10:57
Haiti 6:84, *84,* 86, 87, 88, 89, *91,* 92, 96-100, *96-100*
'Halcombe, Marian' of *The Woman in White* 12:60, 61, *62,* 63, 64, *65,* 66
'Haldin, Victor' of *Under Western Eyes* 9:71
'Hale, Margaret' of *North and South* 4:70
'Hall, Maurice' of *Maurice* 9:95
Hall, William 13:32

Halley's comet 7:11
'Hallward, Basil' of *The Picture of Dorian Gray* 2:60, *60,* 61, 63, 64, *64,* 65
Hamilton, Sir Ian 13:79
Hamlet (Shakespeare) 1:12, 14, 16-17, *16-17,* 20, *21,* 23, 24, 25, 30, 31, 32; 13:42-43, *50,* 52
'Hamlet, Prince of Denmark' of *Hamlet* 1:16, *16,* 17, *17,* 20, *21,* 31
'Hamley, Roger' of *Wives and Daughters* 4:71
Hammett, Dashiell *see Index of Writers*
Handel, George Frideric 1:91; 2:79, 83, *83*
Handful of Dust, A (Waugh) 10:*56,* 67
'Hands, Israel' of *Treasure Island* 11:61, *62,* 64, 65
'Hannah' of *Little Women* 8:36, *36,* 37, 40
Happy Prince and Other Tales, The (Wilde) 2:57, 66, 69, 70, *70*
Hard Times (Dickens) 3:13, 26, 41-42, 43, 44, *44*
Hardie, Keir 8:75
'Harding, Septimus' of *Barchester Towers* 2:36, *36,* 37, 38, 39, *39,* 40, *41,* 45
Hardy, Emma Lavinia Gifford 3:53, 54, *54-55,* 55, 56, 58, 60, *60,* 61, *61,* 62, 63, 87, 88, 89, 90
Hardy, Florence Dugdale 3:56, 57, *57,* 59, 60, *60-61, 62-63,* 63

Hardy, Jemima 3:52, *52,* 53, 55, 56, 58, *58,* 60
Hardy, Kate 3:58, *63*
Hardy, Mary 3:58
Hardy, Thomas, Senior 3:52, *52,* 55, 58, *58*
Hardy, Thomas *see Index of Writers*
Hardy's Wessex 3:65, 68, 72, 73, 76-79, *76-79,* 92, *96*
Hardy's Wessex (Lea) 3:79
'Harleth, Gwendolen' of *Daniel Deronda* 4:90, *92,* 95, *95*
Harley, Robert 10:9
Harlot's Progress, A (Hogarth) 1:87, 103
Hart, Charles 1:*53*
Hart, Joseph C. *see Index of Writers*
Harte, Bret *see Index of Writers*
'Hartright, Walter' of *The Woman in White* 12:60, 61, 62, 63, 64, *65*
Harvey, Gabriel 13:42
Harvey, Laurence 5:*68*
Hastings, Beatrice 8:56, 57, 76
Hatfield, C. W. 4:46
Hathaway, Anne 1:11, *11,* 13
Haunted Man, The (Dickens) 3:27
'Havisham, Miss' of *Great Expectations* 3:9, *9,* 26, 34, 35, 36, 37, 38, *38,* 39
Hawkins, Catherine 3:56
'Hawkins, Jim' of *Treasure Island* 11:60, 61, *61,* 62, *62,* 63, *63,* 64, *64,* 65, *65*
Haworth 4:6, *6-7,* 9, *9,* 10, 11, 24, 30, *30, 31,* 32, 33, *33,* 34, 35, 42, 48, 50, 51, 58

Hawthorne, Nathaniel *see Index of Writers*

Haxton, Gerald 5:57, *57,* 58, *58,* 59

Hazlitt, William *see Index of Writers*

Heart of Darkness (Conrad) 5:39; 9:57, 58, 68, 69, 70, 72, 75

Heart of Midlothian, The (Scott) 11:44, 45, 46, *46-47*

Heart of the Matter, The (Greene) 6:*80,* 81, 90, 93, 94, *94*

Hearts Insurgent (Hardy) 3:72

'Heaslop, Ronny' of *A Passage to India* 9:84, 85, 88

'Heathcliff' of *Wuthering Heights* 4:36, *36,* 37, *37,* 38, *38,* 39, *39,* 40, *40-41,* 41, 48, 50-51

Heatherley, Thomas 2:80

Heaven and Hell (Huxley) 10:83, 93, *93*

'Heep, Uriah' of *David Copperfield* 3:43

Heger, Claire 4:8, 9, 33

Heger, Constantin 4:8, 9, *10,* 11, 18, 27, *32,* 33, 34, 69

'Helstone, Caroline' of *Shirley* 4:19, 22, 23, *23*

Heminge, John 1:22, 24

Hemingway, Clarence (Ed) 7:78, *78,* 82

Hemingway, Elizabeth Hadley Richardson 7:79, *80,* 81, 82

Hemingway, Ernest *see Index of Writers*

Hemingway, Grace 7:78, *78,* 79

Hemingway, Gregory 7:82

Hemingway, John Hadley Nicanor ('Bumby') 7:*80,* 81

Hemingway, Martha Gellhorn 7:*80,* 82, 83

Hemingway, Marcelline 7:*78*

Hemingway, Mary Welsh 7:*80,* 83

Hemingway, Pauline Pfeiffer 7:*80,* 81, 82

Hemingway, Patrick 7:82

Hemingway, Ursula 7:*78*

'Henchard, Michael' of *The Mayor of Casterbridge* 3:73, *73*

Henley, William Ernest 11:57, 66

Hennell, Charles 4:79-80

Hennell, Sara 4:*79*

Henniker, Florence 3:55, *55, 63*

Henri I, King in northern Haiti *see* Christophe, Henri

Henrietta Maria, Queen Consort of Charles I of England 1:76, *76*

'Henry, Frederic' of *A Farewell to Arms* 7:92, 94

Henry, Sir Edward 12:99

Henry IV (Shakespeare) 1:23, 25, *25, 32*

Henry IV, King of England (Henry Bolingbroke) 13:*10,* 11

Henry V (Shakespeare) 1:23, 30; 11:96

Henry VI (Shakespeare) 1:12

Henry VII 13:7

Henry VIII (Shakespeare/ Fletcher) 1:22

Henry VIII, King of England 1:32, 50; 11:49, *50;* 13:*58*

Henslow, John 9:6, 8, 12

Henslowe, Philip 1:29, 30

'Hepburn, Philip' of *Sylvia's Lovers* 4:70-71

Herbert, Philip, Earl of Montgomery 13:32

Herbert, William, Third Earl of Pembroke 13:32, *32, 33*

'Herriton family' of *Where Angels Fear to Tread* 9:93

Herschel, Sir John 5:50

Herschel, Sir William 12:*52*

Hersey, Harold 5:52

Hervieu, Auguste 2:*32*

Hewer, William 1:39, *39,* 44

'Hexam, Gaffer' of *Our Mutual Friend* 3:45

Hiawatha (Longfellow) 10:47, 50

Hiawatha's Photographing (Carroll) 10:50

Hicks, John 3:53

Hide and Seek (Collins) 12:67

Hill, Sir Rowland 2:48, *48,* 49

Hill of Devi, The (Forster) 9:*92*

Hilton, Walter 13:24

Historical Register for the Year 1736, The (Fielding) 1:85, 94

History of Ears, A (Swift) 10:20

History of Great Britain (Hume) 11:*43,* 50

History of Henry Esmond Esquire, The (Thackeray) 2:18, 20-21, 22, 23, *23*

History of Mr Polly, The (Wells) 5:33, 43, 45, 47, *47*

Charles Dickens was bitterly critical of *theories of education that denied the importance of the imagination, and in* Hard Times *he shows their disastrous effects on two young people.*

Illustrated London News and Picture Library

History of Pendennis, The
(Thackeray) 2:*10,* 21, 22, *22*
Hitler, Adolf 7:74, 97; 8:82; 10:100
Ho Chi Minh 6:*82,* 83
Hobbema, Meindert 3:*70-71*
Hobbes, Thomas *see Index of Writers*
Hodge, Alan *see Index of Writers*
Hodges, Lucy 10:54
Hogarth, Catherine *see* Dickens,
Catherine Hogarth
Hogarth, Georgiana ('Aunt
Georgy') 3:11, *14,* 15, 16
Hogarth, George 3:*9,* 10
Hogarth, Mary 3:*8,* 10
Hogarth, William 1:84, *84,* 87, *87,*
91, *100-101,* 102, 103, *103*
Hogarth Press 8:58, 82, *82,* 86, 92,
92, 99
Hogg, Thomas 12:7, 11
'Holbrook, Thomas' of *Cranford*
4:62, 64, *65*
Holden, Molly *see Index of Writers*
'Holdsworth, Edward' of *Cousin
Phillis* 4:71
Holinshed, Raphael 1:23
'Holland, Nancy' of *Love for Lydia*
6:62, *62,* 63, 64
Holland, Peter 4:54, *55*
'Holland, Tom' of *Love for Lydia*
6:61, 62, *62,* 63, 64, *65*
Holloway, Harry and Rosa
11:78-79
'Holman, Phillis' of *Cousin Phillis*
4:71
'Holmes, Sherlock' of Sherlock
Holmes stories 12:47, 77, 80,
81, 82, 84, *84-85,* 85, 86, 87, *87,*
88, *88-89,* 89, 90, *90,* 91, *91,* 92,
93, *93,* 94, 96, 98, 99, 100
Holy War, The (Bunyan) 1:63, 70,
74, *74-75*
Holyoake, George 4:98
Home and Beauty (Maugham) 5:58
Homer *see Index of Writers*
'Honeychurch, Lucy' of *A Room
with a View* 9:90, 91, 95
Honorary Consul, The (Greene) 6:92,
93
Hood, Jacob 2:70
Hood, Thomas *see Index of Writers*
'Hook, Captain' of *Peter Pan* 11:*68*
Hooker, Joseph 9:8, 9, *11,* 22, 24
Hooker, Sir William 9:24
Hoover, Herbert 7:72, 73, 74, *74,* 75
Hopton, Sir Ralph 1:78
Horner, Gilpin 11:43
Hospital Sketches (Alcott) 8:*43,* 44,
45
Hound of the Baskervilles, The
(Conan Doyle) 12:92, 94, *94*
House of Fame, The (Chaucer) 13:9,
20
House of Pomegranates, A (Wilde)
2:67

House of Women, A (Bates) 6:76
Household Words 3:9, 11, 12, 13, *16,*
42, 44; 4:58, 67, 68, 70
'Houyhnhnms, The' of *Gulliver's
Travels* 10:13, *14-15,* 15, 16, *17*
How doth the little crocodile (Carroll)
10:45
How I Built Myself a House (Hardy)
3:53
How I Write My Books (Collins)
12:68
Howard, John 1:103
Howards End (Forster) 9:78, *79,* 81,
90, 91, 92, 93, 94, *94*
Howells, William Dean *see Index of
Writers*
Howitt, William 4:56, 57, 67
Hueffer, Ford Madox *see Index of
Writers*
Hughes, Arthur 10:*49,* 52
Human Condition, The (Huxley)
10:83
Human Factor, The (Greene) 6:81, 92
Humboldt, Alexander von *see Index
of Writers*
Hume, David *see Index of Writers*
'Hummel family' of *Little Women*
8:36, 37, *37*
Humphrey Clinker (Smollett) 8:27
Hunsdon, Henry Carey, Lord 1:*23*
Hunt, Henry 'Orator' 4:72
Hunt, Holman 5:*18*
Hunt, Leigh *see Index of Writers*
Hunt, Thornton 4:81, 82
Hunt, William Holman 2:100;
10:50, 52; 12:56, *69*
Hunting of the Snark, The (Carroll)
10:35, 39, 43, 44, 46, *46-47,* 47
'Huntingdon, Arthur' of *The Tenant
of Wildfell Hall* 4:45, *46,* 47
'Hurree Chunder Mookerjee'
('Hurree Babu') of *Kim* 11:86,
88, *89*
Hutchinson, Sara 13:57
Huxley, Aldous Leonard *see Index
of Writers*
Huxley, Julian 10:78, 79, *82*
Huxley, Julia Frances Arnold 10:78
Huxley, Leonard 10:78
Huxley, Margaret 10:78
Huxley, Maria Nys 10:79-80, 81,
81, 82, 83
Huxley, Matthew 10:80
Huxley, T. H. 4:80, 100, *100;* 5:*30,*
31; 9:9, *11;* 10:78, 79
Huxley, Trevenen 10:78, *78,* 79
Huysmans, J. K. *see Index of
Writers*
Hyde, Anne 1:*38*
Hymn to Intellectual Beauty (Shelley)
13:61
Hymn to the Pillory, A (Defoe) 11:11,
19
Hyperion (Keats) 13:63

I

I, Claudius (Graves) 6:34, 35, *35,* 36-
41, *36-41,* 44, 45, 49, 50, 51, 52
I Found Her Out There (Hardy) 3:87
I Spied for France (Richard) 5:74
'Iago' of *Othello* 1:23, 26, *26*
Ibsen, Henrik *see Index of Writers*
Icaromenippus (Lucian) 5:49
Ideal Husband, An (Wilde) 2:67, *67*
If (Kipling) 11:91
Iliad (Homer) 2:82, 91, 95; 6:50
Imlay, Gilbert 12:9
Importance of Being Earnest, The
(Wilde) 2:57, 67, *67,* 68, 69, 71,
71
Impressions of Theophrastus Such
(Eliot) 4:83
In a German Pension (Mansfield)
8:66, 70, *70*
In an Underground Dressing Station
(Sassoon) 13:*90*
In Chancery (Galsworthy) 5:82, 84,
85
In Dubious Battle (Steinbeck) 7:56,
66
In Flanders Field (McCrae) 13:87, *87*
In Memoriam (Mackintosh) 13:*86,* 87
In Our Time (Hemingway) 7:81, 92,
93, *93*
In Tenebris I (Hardy) 3:86
In the Days of the Comet (Wells)
5:42-43
In the Pink (Sassoon) 13:90
Independent Review, The 9:80, *91*
India, British 9:90, 96-100, *96-100*
Indian Camp (Hemingway) 7:93
Indian Mutiny of 1857 9:96, *96*
Indian National Congress 9:97, 99,
100
Indian Summer of a Forsyte
(Galsworthy) 5:92
Industrial Revolution 4:48, 50
Industry and Idleness (Hogarth) 1:87
Inferno (Dante) 5:49
'Ingram, Blanche' of *Jane Eyre* 4:13,
14, 16, *17,* 28
Inheritors, The (Ford and Conrad)
9:67
Innocents Abroad, The (Twain) 7:8,
9, 20, 21, 23, *23*
insane asylums, 19th century
12:72-76, *72-76*
International Brigades 7:84, 98, *98,*
99
International Red Cross 9:82
*Intimations of Immortality from
Recollections of Early Childhood*
(Wordsworth) 13:55, 64-65,
64-65
Into Battle (Grenfell) 13:87

Invisible Man, The (Wells) 5:31, 42, 45, 46, *46*, 51, *51*, 52
Ireland, England's governance of 10:24–28, *24-28*
Ireton, Henry 1:77, 80, *80*
'Isaac' of *Ivanhoe* 11:*36*, 37, 38, 39, 40
Isabella; or, the Pot of Basil (Keats) 13:62, 71
'Ishmael' of *Moby-Dick* 9:36, *36, 37*, 38, 39, 40, 41
Island (Huxley) 10:93, 94
Island of Dr Moreau, The (Wells) 5:31, 36, 42, 45, *45*
Island Pharisees, The (Galsworthy) 5:90, 94, *94*
Islands in the Stream (Hemingway) 7:91
Isle of Dogs, The (Jonson) 13:52
Israel Potter (Melville) 9:43, 45, 47
Ivancich, Adriana 7:*92*
Ivanhoe (Scott) 11:33, *33*, 34, 36–41, *36-41*, 44, 45, 48, *49*, 50, 51, 52
'Ivanhoe, Wilfred of' of *Ivanhoe* 11:36, 37, *37*, 38, 39, 40, 41, *41*, 48, *48*, 49

J

J'Accuse – The Dark Side of Nice (Greene) 6:83
Jabberwocky (Carroll) 10:34, 38, *38*, 39, 43
Jacaranda Tree, The (Bates) 6:59, 68
Jack the Ripper 12:96, 97-98, 99, *99*
Jackson, Holbrook 2:76
Jackson, John 1:50, 51
Jackson, Schuyler 6:34
Jackson, Stonewall 7:95
Jacob's Room (Woolf) 8:91, 93, *93*
Jacques I, Emperor of Haiti *see* Dessalines, Jean-Jacques
'Jaggers' of *Great Expectations* 3:*34-35*, 35, 36, 38, *38*, 47, *50*
James, Alice 5:7, 8, 9
James, Henry *see Index of Writers*
James, Henry, Sr 5:6, *6*, 8; 8:33
James, Mary 5:6, *6*, 8
James, Robertson 5:7, *10*
James, Wilky 5:7, 8
James, William 5:6, 10, *11*
James I, King of England and Scotland 1:12, 19, *19*, 23, 32; 13:32, 52
James II, King of England (Duke of York) 1:*38*, 39, 40, 43, *55*; 10:24, *24*; 11:*8*, 9
'Jamieson, Mrs' of *Cranford* 4:61, 64, *65*

Sir Walter Scott wrote vividly and convincingly – though not necessarily accurately – about the past. Ivanhoe is one of his most successful historical novels and its tale of medieval chivalry has enthralled generations of readers.

Mansell Collection

Jane Eyre (C. Brontë) 4:7, 10, 12-17, *12-17*, 20, *20*, 21, *21*, 22, 23, 25, 26, 28, 69; 12:*73*
Jazz Age 7:42, 43, 48-52, *48-52*
Je ne Parle pas Français (Mansfield) 8:68, 70, *70*
Jealousy (Brooke) 13:78
Jeffrey, Francis 11:42
'Jenkyns, Deborah' of *Cranford* 4:60, 63, 64, 72
'Jenkyns, Matilda (Miss Matty)' of *Cranford* 4:57, 60, 61, *61*, 62, *62*, 63, *63*, 64, 65, *65*, *67*, 72
'Jenkyns, Peter' of *Cranford* 4:57, 61, *62-63*, 64
Jerome, Jerome K. *see Index of Writers*
Jerrold, Douglas 12:55
Jesting Pilate (Huxley) 10:81, 91
Jew of Malta, The (Marlowe) 13:50
'Jewel' of *Lord Jim* 9:61, 64, *64*
'Jim, Lord' of *Lord Jim* 9:59, 60-65, *60*, *64*, 68
'Jim' of *The Adventures of Huckleberry Finn* 7:12, *12*, 13, 14, 15, *15*, 16, 17, *17*, 25; 11:87
Jim Smiley and His Jumping Frog (Twain) 7:8, *9, 18*, 21

Jo's Boys (Alcott) 8:35, 44, 45, 47, 47
'Joad, Grampa and Gramma' of *The Grapes of Wrath* 7:60, 64, *65*
'Joad, Ma' of *The Grapes of Wrath* 7:59, *59*, 61, 63, 64, *64*, 65, 66, 68
'Joad, Pa' of *The Grapes of Wrath* 7:63, 64, *64*
'Joad, Rose of Sharon' ('Rosasharn') of *The Grapes of Wrath* 7:64, *65*
'Joad, Ruthie' of *The Grapes of Wrath* 7:62, 64
'Joad, Tom' of *The Grapes of Wrath* 7:60, 61, 62, 63, 64, *64*
Joaquim, Martha 3:9
John, Augustus 3:57; 8:76
'John, Prince' of *Ivanhoe* 11:33, 36, *36*, 37, 39, *39*, 40
John Caldigate (Trollope) 2:*34*
John Marr and Other Sailors (Melville) 9:48
John of Gaunt, Duke of Lancaster 13:7, *7, 9*, 10, *10*, 11, 28
'Johnson, Blackie' of *Love for Lydia* 6:61, *61*, 64, *64-65*
Johnson, Dr Samuel *see Index of Writers*

Rudyard Kipling's own illustration conveys the magical qualities of his Just-So Stories. *Here, the cat that walks by himself displays the aloofness which means that, unlike the horse and the dog, he can never be totally tamed.*

Johnson, Esther ('Stella') 10:8, *8*, 9, 10, 11, 20, 22, 23, *23*
Johnson, Harold *see Index of Writers*
Johnson, Lionel 2:*73*, 74, 75, 76
Johnson, Lyndon 7:59
Jonathan Wild (Fielding) 1:86, 97, 98, *98*
Jones, Bobby 7:51
Jones, Ernest 4:76
Jones, Inigo 1:32; 13:*52*
Jones, John Paul 9:47
'Jones, Major' of *The Comedians* 6:84, 85, *86, 87*, 88, *88*
'Jones, Tom' of *Tom Jones* 1:88, *88*, 89, *89*, 90, *90*, 91, *91*, 92, *92*, 93, 97
Jonson, Ben *see Index of Writers*
'Jordan, Robert' of *For Whom the Bell Tolls* 7:84, *84-85*, 85, 86, 87, *87*, 88, *88*, 89, *89*, 98
Joseph, Lily Delissa 13:84
'Joseph' of *The Comedians* 6:*84*, 88
'Joseph' of *Wuthering Heights* 4:34, 38, 40, *41*
Joseph Andrews (Fielding) 1:86, 95, *95*, 96, *96-97*, 97, 98, *98*
Josephine, Empress of the French 2:*25*
Journal (Scott) 11:42, 44
Journal from This World to the Next, A (Fielding) 1:96, 98, *98*

Journal of a Voyage to Lisbon, The (Fielding) 1:97, 99, *99*
Journal of the Plague Year (Defoe) 11:11, *18-19*, 19, 21, 22, *22-23*
Journal to Stella (Swift) 10:8, 9, 20, 22, 23, *23*
Journey Without Maps (Greene) 6:80, *80*
Joyce, James *see Index of Writers*
Jude the Obscure (Hardy)3: 55, *57*, 61, 62, 63, 71, 72, 73, 75, *75*, 77, 78, 87
'Julia' of *I, Claudius* 6:37, 40
Julian and Maddalo (Shelley) 13:61
'Juliet' of *Romeo and Juliet* 1:14, *14*, 15, *15*, 20, *20*, 31
Julius Caesar (Shakespeare) 1:22, 26, *26* 90, 92, 93, 94, *94*
Jungle Books, The (Kipling) 11:81,
Juno 6:41, 49, 50, *50, 51*, 52, *52*
Jupiter 6:41, 49, *49*, 50, *50*, 51, 52, *52*
Just So Stories (Kipling) 11:82, 92, *92*, 93, 95, *95*
justice, administration of, 18th century England 1:100–104, *100-104*
Justice (Galsworthy) 5:81, *91*, 92, 94, 95, *95, 99*, 100
Justification of the Censorship of Plays, A (Galsworthy) 5:99
Juvenal *see Index of Writers*

K

Kangaroo (Lawrence) 6:10, 19, *19*
Karloff, Boris 12:28, *28*
Karori (Mansfield) 8:66
'Katharina' ('Kate') of *The Taming of the Shrew* 13:36, 37, *37*, 40, 41, *41*
Keats, John *see Index of Writers*
Kelly, Gerald 5:56
Kelyng, Justice 1:59, *59, 62*
Kemble, Fanny 5:19
Kempe, Will 1:12, *30*
Kenilworth (Scott) 11:45, 47, *47*
Kenney, Annie 8:73
Kerensky, Alexander 5:58, 75, *75*, 76
Kern, Jerome 7:51
Kew Gardens (Woolf) 8:92
Kew Gardens 9:*9*, 24, *28*
Keynes, John Maynard *see Index of Writers*
Kidd, William 11:27
Kidnapped (Stevenson) 11:58, 67, 68, 69, *69*
Killigrew, Thomas 1:52, *52*
Kim (Kipling) 11:77, *78*, 83, 84–89, *84-89*, 90, 91, *92*
'King, The' of *The Adentures of Huckleberry Finn* 7:13, *13*, 14, 15 *15*, 16, *16*, 17
King Jesus (Graves) 6:43, 45, 47, *47*
King John (Shakespeare) 1:23
King Lear (Shakespeare) 1:14, 18-19, *18-19*, 20, 21, *21*, 22, 23, 24, *24*, 25, 30, 55
'King of Brobdingnag, The' of *Gulliver's Travels* 10:13, *13*, 14, 16, *17*
King of Pirates, The (Defoe) 11:19, 24, 27
'Kinraid, Charley' of *Sylvia's Lovers* 4:70-71
Kipling, Alice Macdonald 11:78, *78*, 79, *80*
Kipling, Caroline 'Carrie' Balestier 11:81, *81*, 82, 83, 93
Kipling, Elsie 11:*83*
Kipling, John 11:83, *83*, 100, *100*
Kipling, John Lockwood 11:78, *78*, 80, *80*, 97
Kipling, Joseph Rudyard *see Index of Writers*
Kipling, Josephine 11:81, 82, *83*
Kipling, Trix 11:78, 79
Kipps (Wells) 5:43, 45, 46, *46*
Kirke, Walter 5:73
Kitchener, Lord 11:*97*; 12:82
Kitchenmaid, The (Vermeer) 4:*91*
Kitchin, Xie 10:52
Klimt, Gustav 2:*74-75*

Knickerbocker Magazine 9:42
Knight, Catherine 8:7, *8–9*
Knight, Edward *see* Austen,
    Edward
'Knight, Henry' of *A Pair of Blue*
    Eyes 3:61
Knight, Thomas 8:7, *8–9*
Knipp, Mrs 1:52
Koch, Robert 12:80
Korda, Alexander 6:59, 80, 82, *82*
Korzeniowski, Apollo 9:54, *54*, 55
Korzeniowski, Eva 9:54, *54*
Korzeniowski, Jozef Teodor
    Konrad, *see* Conrad, Joseph
Korzeniowski, Thadeus 9:55, *55*,
    56, 57, 58
'Krook' of *Bleak House* 3:15, *15*, 26,
    41
Kropotkin, Sasha 5:*75*
Kubla Khan (Coleridge) 13:57, 66,
    66-67, 73
Kyd, Thomas *see Index of Writers*
'Kulu woman' of *Kim* 11:*85*, 88
'Kurtz' of *Heart of Darkness* 9:68, 70
Kyd, Thomas 1:32

L

The spirit of India
was captured for
many readers by
Kipling's novels and
short stories. Perhaps
the most successful is
Kim, *which has*
been described as the
best portrait of India
by an English writer.

L'Avare (The Miser) (Moliere) 1:84
La Coranto (Frith) 3:39, *39*
'Ladislaw, Will' of *Middlemarch* 4:90,
    94
Lady Chatterley's Lover (Lawrence)
    6:11, 13, 18, 19, 21, 23, *23*
Lady Frederick (Maugham) 5:56
Lady of the Lake, The (Scott) 11:32,
    32-33, 33, 50
Lady Windermere's Fan (Wilde) 2:57,
    66, 67, 69, 71, *71*
Lady with Lilacs, The (Hughes) 10:*49*
'Laertes' of *Hamlet* 1:17, *17*
Laetitia (Lawrence) 6:19
Lake District (English) 13:54, 55,
    55, 57, 62
Lamarck, Jean Baptiste 2:95
Lamb, Charles *see Index of Writers*
Lamb, Lady Caroline 13:58, *58*
Lamb House 5:9, *10-11, 18,* 20, *20*
Langdon, Charles 7:8
Langland, William *see Index of*
    Writers
Langtry, Lily 2:*97*, 98
Lanier, Emilia Bassano 13:33
Lardner, Ring *see Index of Writers*
Larkin, Philip *see Index of Writers*
Last Chronicle of Barset, The
    (Trollope) 2:43, 44, 45
Last Man, The (M. Shelley) 12:11,
    19, *19*, 20, 21, *21*, 22, 23, *23*

Last Poems (Lawrence) 6:19
Last Stagecoachman, The (Collins)
    12:55
Last Tycoon, The (Fitzgerald) 7:35,
    44, 45, 47, *47*
Laud, William 1:76, 77
'Laurence, Mr' of *Little Women* 8:36,
    37, *37*, 40, *41*
'Laurie' of *Little Women* 8:36, *36*, 37,
    37, *39*, 40, *41*, 46, 47
law enforcement, 19th century
    Britain 12:96-100, *96-100*
Lawless Roads, The (Greene) 6:80
Lawrence, Arthur 6:6, 7
Lawrence, David Herbert
    Richards *see Index of Writers*
Lawrence, Frieda von Richthofen
    Weekley 6:8, *8*, 9, 10, 11, *11*,
    18, *18*, 19, *19*, 20; 8:57, 76;
    10:81, 92
Lawrence, Lydia 6:6, 7, *7*, 8
Lawrence, T. E. (Lawrence of
    Arabia) 6:43, *43*, 45, 56
Lawrence and the Arabs (Graves) 6:43,
    43
Lay of the Last Minstrel, The (Scott)
    11:32, 43
Laycock, Bob 10:58
Le Carré, John *see Index of Writers*

Le Gallienne, Richard 2:68, *73*
Le Neve, Ethel 12:*97*, 100
Lea, Hermann *see Index of Writers*
Leacock, Stephen *see Index of*
    Writers
Leader of the People, The (Steinbeck)
    7:69
Lean, David 6:59, 68
Lear, Edward *see Index of Writers*
'Lear, King' of *King Lear* 1:18, *18*,
    19, *19*, 20, *21*
Leavis, F. R. *see Index of Writers*
Lecount, Peter 12:48
Lee, Nathaniel 1:56
Lees of Happiness (Fitzgerald) 7:46
Lefroy, Thomas 8:*9*, 10
Legend of Good Women (Chaucer)
    13:20
Legend of Montrose, The (Scott)
    11:42
Leicester, Robert Dudley, Earl of
    1:28, *28-29*
Leighton, Lord Frederick 2:*19*
Lenin, V. I. 5:34, *34*, 75, 76, *76*
'Lennie' of *Of Mice and Men* 7:66,
    71, *71*
Leopold, Prince 10:48
Leopold II, King of Belgium 9:72,
    72, 73, *73*, 74, *75*, 76, *76*

GENERAL INDEX

'Lestrade, Inspector' of *Sherlock Holmes* stories 12:91
Leviathan (Hobbes) 1:56
Lewes, Agnes 4:81, 82
Lewes, George Henry 4:*80,* 81, 82, *82,* 83, 90, 92, 99, 100; 12:50
Lewis, Maria 4:79, 97
Lewis, Matthew 12:*25,* 27, 28
Lewis, Rosa 10:58, *58*
Lewis, Wyndham *see Index of Writers*
Leyland, Frederick 5:26
Liberator, The 8:50, 51, *51*
Liddell, Alice 10:30, 32, *34-35, 39,* 42, *42,* 43, *43,* 48, 52
Life and Death of Tom Thumb the Great, The (Fielding) 1:84, *84,* 94, *96*
Life and Death of Mr Badman, The (Bunyan) 1:63, 70, 74, *74*
Life and Habit (Butler) 2:94, 95
Life and Letters of Dr Samuel Butler, The (Butler) 2:*93*
Life of Charlotte Brontë, The (Gaskell) 4:11, 58-59, *59,* 67, 69
Life of Samuel Johnson, The (Boswell) 11:*34*
Life of Sir Walter Scott (Lockhart) 11:*34*
Life of William Shakespeare, The (Rowe) 1:13
Life on the Mississippi (Twain) 7:*18,* 19, 21, 22, *22,* 25
Life's Handicap (Kipling) 11:90
Liggins, Joseph 4:83
Light That Failed, The (Kipling) 11:79, 81, 90, 93, *93*
Limbo (Huxley) 10:80, 90
'Lime, Harry' of *The Third Man* 6:94, *94*
Lincoln, Abraham 8:*49, 50,* 51, 52
Lindbergh, Charles 7:*51,* 52
Lingard, Jim 9:59

Linnaean Society 9:9, 10
Linnaeus, Carolus 9:*26*
'Linton, Catherine' of *Wuthering Heights* 4:36, *39,* 40
'Linton, Edgar' of *Wuthering Heights* 4:37, *37,* 38, 40, *41*
'Linton, Isabella' of *Wuthering Heights* 4:37, 39, 40, *40*
Liszt, Franz 4:*92*
Little Dorrit (Dickens) 3:14, 40, 42, 43, 45, *45*
Little Dream, The (Galsworthy) 5:81
Little Governess, The (Mansfield) 8:63, 68
Little Learning, A (Waugh) 10:66, 69
Little Men (Alcott) 8:34, 42, 44, 45, 46, *46*
Little Mexican (Huxley) 10:90
'Little Nell' of *The Old Curiosity Shop* 3:11, 16, 24, 25, *28-29,* 29
Little Women (Alcott) 8:30, 33, *33,* 34, 36-41, *36-41,* 42, 43, 44, 45
Little Women, Part II (Good Wives) (Alcott) 8:44, 45, 46, *46*
Littlejohn, H. D. 11:76
Lives of the Most Eminent Literary and Scientific Men (M. Shelley) 12:19
'Livesey, Dr' of *Treasure Island* 11:61, 62, 64, *64,* 65
'Livia' of *I, Claudius* 6:36, *36,* 37, 38, 39, 40, 41, *41*
Living Room, The (Greene) 6:*91*
Livingstone, David 4:14
Livy, Titus 13:*42*
Liza of Lambeth (Maugham) 5:56, 66, *66-67,* 69, *69*
Lizzie Leigh (Gaskell) 4:67
Lloyd George, David 5:82; 13:100
'LM' *see* Baker, Ida Constance
Lochinvar (Scott) 11:43
Lock Up Your Daughters 1:84
Locke, John 13:75

Lockhart, John Gibson *see Index of Writers*
Lockhart, Sophia Scott 11:34
'Locksley' (Robin Hood) of *Ivanhoe* 11:33, *33,* 37, *38-39,* 40
'Lockwood, Mr' of *Wuthering Heights* 4:36, *36,* 40, 41, 48
Lodore (M. Shelley) 12:19, *19,* 20
Lois the Witch (Gaskell) 4:70
London, 19th century 3:46-50, *46-50*
London Foundling Hospital 1:91
London Labour and the London Poor (Mayhew) 2:98; 3:47
'Long Ben' *see* Avery, John
Long Weekend, The (Graves/ Hodge) 6:44, 45, 46, *46*
Longest Journey, The (Forster) 9:90, 91, 93, *93*
Longfellow, Henry Wadsworth *see Index of Writers*
Looney, J. Thomas 13:31
Loos, Anita *see Index of Writers*
Lord Arthur Savile's Crime and Other Stories (Wilde) 2:66, 69, *69*
Lord Jim (Conrad) 9:58, 60–65, *60-65,* 69, 72, *76*
Lord of the Rings, The (Tolkien) 10:34
'Lorry, Jarvis' of *A Tale of Two Cities* 3:18, 19, *20,* 21, 22, 23, *23*
Loser Takes All (Greene) 6:82
Lost Love (Hardy) 3:88
Lost World, The (Conan Doyle) 5:49 12:92, 95, *95*
Loti, Pierre 9:52
Loudon, Mrs *see Index of Writers*
Louis Napoleon Bonaparte 4:75, 76
Louis XI, King of France 11:47
Louis XIV, King of France 1:*38,* 39; 2:20–21; 3:30
Louis XV of France 3:30, 31

The young Alice Liddell was the inspiration for Lewis Carroll when he wrote Alice in Wonderland. *Here, the fictional Alice has grown to immense size after eating a cake labelled, 'EAT ME'.*

Louis XVI of France 3:30, 31, *31, 32, 33*
Louis XVIII, King of France 2:27
'Louisa, Aunt' of *Of Human Bondage* 5:60, 61, 62, 64, *65*
Louse Hunting (Rosenberg) 13:92
Love and Mr Lewisham (Wells) 5:43, *43*
Love and Self-love (Alcott) 8:42
Love for Love (Congreve) 1:*55*
Love for Lydia (Bates) 6:59, 60–65, *60-65,* 68, 71, 72, 75, 76
Love in Several Masques (Fielding) 1:84
Love's Labours Lost (Shakespeare) 13:44, *44*
Loved One, The (Waugh) 10:58, *58,* 67, 69, 70, *70*
'Loveday, John and Bob' of *The Trumpet Major* 3:74
Lowell, James Russell *see Index of Writers*
Loyalties (Galsworthy) 5:94, 95, *95*
'Lucas, Charlotte' of *Pride and Prejudice* 8:13, 16, 17
Luck of Barry Lyndon, The (Thackeray) 2:18, 22, *22*
Lucy, Sir Thomas 1:12
Luddite riots 4:23, 50
Luhan, Tony 6:11
Lumb, Hannah 4:54, *55,* 56, 72
'Lurgan Sahib' of *Kim* 11:85, 87, 88
Lusitania 13:*96,* 98
Lutwidge, Skeffington 10:32, 43
'Lydgate, Dr' of *Middlemarch* 4:*91,* 94
Lyell, Charles 9:6, 7, 8, 9, 10, 12, 13; 12:49
Lygon, Hugh 10:56
Lyly, John 13:48
'Lyon, Esther' of *Felix Holt* 4:94
Lyrical Ballads (Wordsworth/ Coleridge) 13:54, 57, 66, 76
Lyttelton (or Lyttleton), George 1:83, 87, *94,* 95
Lytton, Lady Constance 8:74
Lytton, Lord 2:90

M

MacArthur, Douglas 7:73
Macaulay, Thomas Babington *see Index of Writers*
Macbeth (Shakespeare) 1:23, 24, 25, 27, *27,* 55
MacDonald, George *see Index of Writers*
MacDonald, Greville 10:34
Macdermots of Ballycloran, The (Trollope) 2:33, *43*

Macdonald, Ramsay 3:57
Mackail, Angela 11:*92*
Mackenzie, Sir Compton *see Index of Writers*
Mackintosh, E. A. *see Index of Writers*
Maclean, Donald 6:81
Maclise, Daniel 3:*14*
Macmillan, Alexander 2:35; 3:70
'Mad Hatter, The' of *Alice in Wonderland* 10:33, *33, 36,* 37, 39, 41, *41,* 43
Mademoiselle de Maupin (Gautier) 2:72
'Magiot, Doctor' of *The Comedians* 6:85, 87, 88, *88*
Magloire, Paul 6:100
'Magwitch' (alias 'Provis') of *Great Expectations* 3:34, *34,* 36
Maharajah of Dewas State Senior 9:81, 82, *82,* 83, 98
'Mahbub Ali' of *Kim* 11:84, 85, 87, *87,* 88, 89, *89*
Mallarmé, Stephane *see Index of Writers*
Mallorca 6:34, *34,* 35, *35, 42, 44,* 47
Malthus, Thomas Robert 9:8
'Maltster, The' of *Far from the Madding Crowd* 3:68
'Malvolio' of *Twelfth Night* 13:38, *38,* 39, *39,* 40, 41, *41*
Man and Superman (Shaw) 5:98
Man of Honour, A (Maugham) 5:56
Man of Mode (Etherege) 1:55
Man of Property, The (Galsworthy) 5:80, 84, 86, 87, 90, 91, 92, 94

Magwitch, an escaped convict helped by the young Pip, returns years later to shatter the illusions of the adult hero of Dickens' *Great Expectations*.

Man That Corrupted Hadleyburg, The (Twain) 7:20, 21, 22, *22-23*
Man Who Would Be King, The (Kipling) 5:39
Man Within, The (Greene) 6:79
Man Without a Temperament, The (Mansfield) 8:68, 70, 71, *71*
Man with the Twisted Lip, The (Conan Doyle) 12:85–86, *85,* 88, 89, *89*
Manchester, Earl of 1:78
Manchester 4:55, 56, 57, *57,* 58, 67, 68, 72, 73, *73,* 74, 75, 76
Mandalay (Kipling) 11:91, *91,* 94
'Manette, Doctor' of *A Tale of Two Cities* 3:18, *18,* 19, 20, *20,* 21, 22, 23, *23*
'Manette, Lucie' of *A Tale of Two Cities* 3:18, *18,* 19, 20, *20,* 21, 22, *22,* 23
Mann, Thomas *see Index of Writers*
Manning, George 3:48
'Manning, Paul' of *Cousin Phillis* 4:71
Mansfield, Katherine *see Index of Writers*
Mansfield Park (Austen) 8:11, 22, *22*
'Marabar Caves' of *A Passage to India* 9:84, 86, *87,* 91
Maracot Deep, The (Conan Doyle) 12:92
Marble Woman, The (Alcott) 8:33
'March, Amy' of *Little Women* 8:36, *36,* 37, 38, 39, 40, *41, 46,* 47
'March, Aunt' of *Little Women* 8:37, 40, 46

Mansell Collection

'March, Beth' of *Little Women* 8:36, *36*, 37, 38, *38*, 39, 40, 41, *41*, 46

'March, Jo' of *Little Women* 8:36, *36*, 37, *37*, 38, 39, *39*, 40, *40-41*, 41, 44, 46, 47

'March, Meg of *Little Women* 8:36, *36*, 37, 38, 39, *39*, 40, *40*, 46, 47

'March, Mr' of *Little Women* 8:36, *36*, 37, 38, 40, 41, 46, 47

'March, Mrs' ('Marmee') of *Little Women* 8:36, *36*, 37, 38, 40, *40*, 41, 47

'March' of *The Fox* 6:14, 15, *15*, 16, *17*

Mardi (Melville) 9:32, 42, 43, 45, 46, 48

'Maria' of *For Whom the Bell Tolls* 7:82, *82*, 84, *84*, 85, *85*, 87, 88, *88*, 89

Marie–Antoinette, Queen of France 3:*31*, 33

'Markham, Gilbert' of *The Tenant of Wildfell Hall* 4:45, 47

Marlborough, Duke of 2:23; 10:23; 11:98

'Marley' of *A Christmas Carol* 3:27

'Marlow' of *Lord Jim* 9:61, *61*, 62, 63, 64, *65, 66*, 68, 70, 76

Marlowe, Christopher *see Index of Writers*

Marmion (Scott) 11:32, 43

Marquesas Islands 9:31, *32*, 45, 48, 49, 51, 52

Marsden, Dora 8:76

Marsh, Edward 6:9, 42; 13:78, 79, 84, 85

Marshalsea Prison 3:7, *7*

Marston, John 13:51, 52

'Martha' of *Cranford* 4:*61*, 62, 63, 64, 65

'Martians' of *The War of the Worlds* 5:37, *37*, 38, *38-39*, 39, 40, *40-41*, 41

Martin, John 12:*50*; 13:74

Martin, Julia 3:52–53

Martineau, Harriet 4:20

Marvels of Pond Life, The 9:26

'Marx, Bernard' of *Brave New World* 10:85, 86, *86*, 88, *88*, 89

Marx, Karl 4:76

Mary Barton (Gaskell) 4:*56*, 57, *57*, 66, 67, 68, 69, *69*, 72, 76

Mary, Queen of England 9:96, *97*

Mary Queen of Scots 13:31, *31*

Masefield, John *see Index of Writers*

Mask of Anarchy, The (Shelley) 13:61, 64, 69-70, *69*

Mason, A. E. W. 5:76

'Mason, Bertha' ('Mrs Rochester') of *Jane Eyre* 4:11, 16, 25

'Mason, Richard' of *Jane Eyre* 4:12, 13

Masood, Syed Ross 9:80, 81, *81*, 82

Masque of Blackness, The (Jonson) 13:*52*

***Siegfried Sassoon writes vividly** in* Memoirs of an Infantry Officer *of his experiences during World War I.*

Masque of the Red Death, The (Poe) 12:44, *45*, 46, 47, *47*

Master of Ballantrae, The (Stevenson) 11:58, 66, *67*, 68, *68*, 69

Mata Hari 5:74, *74*

Mathilda (M. Shelley) 12:20, 22, *22*

Matisse, Henri 8:98, 99

Maturin, Charles 12:28

Maugham, Edith Mary 5:54, *54*

Maugham, Harry 5:58

Maugham, Henry MacDonald 5:55, *55*, 56

Maugham, Liza 5:57, *58-59*, 59

Maugham, Robert Ormond 5:54

Maugham, Syrie Barnardo Wellcome 5:57, *57*, 58, 73

Maugham, William Somerset *see Index of Writers*

Maupassant, Guy de *see Index of Writers*

Maurice (Forster) 9:82, 90, 91, 92, 93, 95

Maxse, Kitty 8:96, 97

May Day (Fitzgerald) 7:44, 46

May We Borrow Your Husband? (Greene) 6:92, 95, *95*

Mayan Indians 6:24, *24*, 25, *25*

Mayhew, Henry *see Index of Writers*

Mayor of Casterbridge, The (Hardy) 3:73, *73*, 94

Mayward, Robert 11:27

Mazzini, Giuseppe 4:80

McCrae, John *see Index of Writers*

McIntosh, Mavis 7:56

McIntosh and Otis 7:56

McPherson, Aimee Semple 10:62

Meditations (Boyle) 10:18

Meditations on a Broomstick (Swift) 10:18

'Medullina' of *I, Claudius* 6:37

Mejans, Maurice *see Index of Writers*

Melbourne, Lord 11:51

'Melbury, Grace' of *The Woodlanders* 3:75

Melvill, Allan 9:30, *30*

Melvill, Maria Gansevoort 9:30, *30*

Melville, Allan 9:32

Melville, Elizabeth 9:*35*

Melville, Elizabeth Shaw 9:31, *32*, 35

Melville, Frances 9:*35*

Melville, Herman *see Index of Writers*

Melville, Leonard 9:30

Melville, Malcolm 9:32, 35, *35*

Melville, Stanwix 9:*35*

Memoir (Collins) 12:55

Memoires Relating to the State of the Royal Navy (Pepys) 1:47, *49*

Memoirs (Grant) 7:9

Memoirs of a Cavalier (Defoe) 11:19, 20, 21, *21*

Memoirs of a Fox-Hunting Man (Sassoon) 13:80, 81
Memoirs of an Infantry Officer (Sassoon) 13:81
Memoirs of Sherlock Holmes, The (Conan Doyle) 12:93, *93*
Men at Arms (Waugh) 10:58, 69, 71
Men Like Gods (Wells) 10:92
Menuhin, Yehudi 10:81, 83, *83*
'Mercutio' of *Romeo and Juliet* 1:14, *14*, 20
Meredith, George *see Index of Writers*
Meredith, H. O. 9:78, 80
Meres, Francis *see Index of Writers*
'Merle, Madame' of *The Portrait of a Lady* 5:12, 13, 14, 15, 16, *16*, 19
Merrill, George 9:82, *95*
Merry Wives of Windsor, The (Shakespeare) 1:*32*
Mesmer, Anton 12:52
Mesmeric Revelation (Poe) 12:52
Mesopotamia (Kipling) 13:93
Messiah (Handel) 1:91
Metamorphoses, The (Ovid) 6:49
Metternich, Prince von 4:76
Mexico 6:10, 11, 13, *14, 20, 23, 24-28, 24-28*
Meyrick, Kate 10:74
Micah Clarke (Conan Doyle) 12:80
'Micawber, Mr' of *David Copperfield* 3:24, 43, *43*
Middlemarch (Eliot) 4:78, 83, 90, 91, *91, 92, 93, 94, 94*, 97
Middleton, Thomas *see Index of Writers*
Midsummer Night's Dream, A (Shakespeare) 1:52, 55; 11:95; 13:34, *34*, 40, *40*, 44, *44-45*
'Mildred' of *Of Human Bondage* 5:61, *61, 62, 62*, 64, *64*
Mill, John Stuart *see Index of Writers*
Mill, The (Bates) 6:58
Mill on the Floss, The (Eliot) 4:80, 82, 83, 84-89, *84-89*, 90, 91, 93, 96, *97, 100*
Millais, John Everett 2:34, *44*; 10:32, 48, 50, 52; 12:56, *56*
Millar, Andrew 1:87
Miller, Arthur *see Index of Writers*
Miller, Henry *see Index of Writers*
Millet, Francis Davis 5:27, *28*
Milton, John *see Index of Writers*
Ministry of Fear, The (Greene) 6:92
Minster, York 9:14
Minstrelsy of the Scottish Border (Scott) 11:32, 43
Mirror of Parliament 3:9, 12
Mirror of the Sea, The (Conrad) 9:57
Misanthrope, Le (Moliere) 1:56
Miscellanies (Fielding) 1:96, 98
Misery (Chekhov) 8:67
Miss Brill (Mansfield) 8:66

Mississippi River 7:6, 7, *9*, 11, 12, 15, 16, *18*, 21, 22, *22*, 24-28, *24-28*, 51
Missouri Compromise 49, 51
Mitford, Nancy *see Index of Writers*
Moby-Dick (Melville) 9:30, 33, 34, 35, *35*, 36-39, 40-41, *40-41*, 43, *43*, 45, 48, 52
'Moby Dick' of *Moby-Dick* 9:36, 37, 38, 39, *39*, 40
Mocha Dick 9:34, *42*
Model Millionaire, The (Wilde) 2:69
Modern Comedy, A (Galsworthy) 5:*92*, 93, 94, *94-95*
Modern Husband, The (Fielding) 1:84
Modern Times 10:87, *99*, 100
Modern Utopia, A (Wells) 5:42
Modest Defence of the Proceedings of the Rabble in All Ages (Swift) 10:20
Modest Proposal, A (Swift) 10:19, 22, 23, *23*, 26
Mola, Emilio 7:96, 99
Moliere, Jean Baptiste Poquelin *see Index of Writers*
Moll Flanders (Defoe) 11:11, 20, 21, 22, *22*
Molloy, Charles 3:9
'Mond, Mustapha' ('Controller') of *Brave New World* 10:85, 86, 87, 88, *88-89*, 89
Monday or Tuesday (Woolf) 8:91
Monk, The (Lewis) 12:*25*, 27, *27*
'Monmouth, Duchess of' of *The Picture of Dorian Gray* 2:*62*, 64
Monmouth, Duke of 11:8-9, *8*
Monro, Thomas 12:74
Monsignor Quixote (Greene) 6:92, 95, *95*
'Monster' of *Frankenstein* 12:12, 13, *13*, 14, *14*, 15, *15*, 16, *16*, 17, *19*
Montagu, Edward, Earl of Sandwich 1:36, 37, *38*, 39, 44, 45, *45*
Montagu, Lady Mary Wortley 1:83, 84, *94*
'Montero, General' of *Nostromo* 9:70
Montes, Lola 12:*90*
Montesquiou, Robert de 2:*61*
Moods (Alcott) 8:33, 43, 45
Moon and Sixpence, The (Maugham) 5:57, 58, 66, 68, 69, *69*
Moon is Down, The (Steinbeck) 7:*57*, 66
Moonstone, The (Collins) 12:59, 66, 67, 68, 69, 70, *70*
Moore, G. E. *see Index of Writers*
Moore, George *see Index of Writers*
Moore, Lesley *see* Baker, Ida Constance
'Moore, Louis' of *Shirley* 4:23
'Moore, Mrs' of *A Passage to India* 9:84-85, *85*, 86, 87, *87*, 88, *89*, 99
'Moore, Robert' of *Shirley* 4:23, *23*

Moran, Lois 7:34
Morel, E. D. 9:76
Morgan, Henry 11:*24*, 25
'Moriarty, Professor' of *Sherlock Holmes* stories 12:81, 91, 93, *93*
'Morland, Catherine' of *Northanger Abbey* 8:*19*, 23, *23*, 26, 27
Morning Chronicle 3:9, 10
Morning Clouds (Carroll) 10:*32*
Mornings in Mexico (Lawrence) 6:26
Morrell, Lady Ottoline 6:9, *19*; 8:58, 76, 99, 100, *100*; 10:79, *90*
Morrell, Sir Philip 10:79
Morris, Jane 10:*50-51*
Morris, Margaret 5:81, *81*, 82
Morris, William 10:*51*
Morse, Samuel 2:50; 12:48
Mortal Coils (Huxley) 10:80, 90
Mortal Immortal, The (M. Shelley) 12:21, 22, 23, *23*
Mortimer, Raymond *see Index of Writers*
Mortmain (Greene) 6:95, *95*
Morton, Charles 11:7
Morton, Jelly Roll 7:51
'Moss, Ada' of *Pictures* 8:63, *63*, 64, 65
Motte, Benjamin 10:11
Moule, Horace 3:53, *53*, 54, 72
Mountbatten, Lord Louis 9:*100*
Moveable Feast, A (Hemingway) 7:91
Movements in Modern History (Lawrence) 6:18
Mr Britling Sees it Through (Wells) 5:34
Mr Noon (Lawrence) 6:18
Mrs Craddock (Maugham) 5:66
Mrs Dalloway (Woolf) 8:91, 93, 94, *94*
Mrs Eglantine (Bates) 6:71
Mrs Gaskell's Tales of Mystery and Horror 4:69, 70, *70*
Mrs Warren's Profession (Shaw) 5:99
MS Found in a Bottle (Poe) 12:33
Much Ado About Nothing (Shakespeare) 13:*44*
Muggeridge, Malcolm 10:59
Muralto, Onuphrio 12:25
Murders in the Rue Morgue, The (Poe) 12:36, 38, 39, *39*, 40, 41, *41*, 78
'Murdstone, Edward' of *David Copperfield* 3:43
Murphy, Arthur 1:94
Murray, Gilbert 5:99, 100
Murray, John 8:*21*; 9:42
Murry, John Middleton *see Index of Writers*
Mussolini, Benito 7:97; 10:57
My Heart Leaps Up (Wordsworth) 13:65, *65*
My Lost City (Fitzgerald) 7:47
Myconian, The (Graves) 6:47
Myers, F. W. H. 4:100

Mysteries of Udolpho, The (Radcliffe) 8:*20*, 23; 12:*25*, 26-27, *27*
Mysterious Stranger, The (Twain) 7:20
Mystery of Edwin Drood, The (Dickens) 2:63; 3:11, 17, 26, 43, 45, *45*, 48

N

'Nancy' of *Oliver Twist* 3:16, *26*, 28
Napoleon Bonaparte 2:*13*, *17*, 24-28, *24-28*; 3:33; 6:98; 11:32, 35, 42, 50
Napoleonic Wars 2:24-28; 8:8, 15, *15*, 19, 28; 11:*96-97*, 98
'Narborough, Lady' of *The Picture of Dorian Gray* 2:*62*, 64
Narrative of Arthur Gordon Pym, The (Poe) 12:38, 45, 46, *46*, 51
'Narrator' of *The War of the Worlds* 5:36, 37, *37*, 38, 39, *39*, 40, *40*, 41
Narrow Corner, The (Maugham) 5:67
Nash, Paul 13:99
Nash, Richard (Beau Nash) 8:27
Nashe, Thomas *see Index of Writers*
National Council for Civil Liberties 9:83
natural history
    literature on 9:26-28
    Victorian interest in 9:24-28
Natural History of Selborne (White) 9:26
Nazarene Gospel Restored, The (Graves) 6:43
Necessity of Atheism (Shelley) 13:60, 76
Necker, Jacques 3:32
Needham, Mother 1:103
Nelson, Horatio 2:25, 26
Nesbitt, Cathleen 13:79
Neutral Tones (Hardy) 3:86
New Age, The 8:56, 57, 66, *66*, 76, 76
'New Deal' 7:*74*, 75, *75*, 76
New Machiavelli, The (Wells) 5:33, 43
New Orleans 7:*24-25*, 25, *28*, *50*, 51
New York Herald 9:68
New Zealand 8:54, 55, *56*, 60, 61, 66, *66*, 68, 70, 72
Newby, T. C. 4:10
Newcastle, Duchess of 1:52
Newcomes, The (Thackeray) 2:10, 18, 19, *19*, *20*, 21, 22, 23, *23*
Newgate Prison 11:10, *10*, 11, 28
Newman, John Henry 4:97, *97*

Newport, Andrew 11:19
'Newson' of *The Mayor of Casterbridge* 3:73
Newton, Sir Isaac 1:47, *48* ; 13:75, 75
Nicholas II, Tsar of Russia 13:96
Nicholas Nickleby (Dickens) 3:*8*, 26, 27, 29, *29*
Nicholls, Arthur Bell 4:10, *10-11*, 11, 26, 59, 66
Nichols, Gove 12:35
Nichols, Robert *see Index of Writers*
Niepce, Joseph Nicephore 12:*49*
Nigger of the 'Narcissus', The (Conrad) 9:58, 69
Night and Day (Woolf) 8:91
Night and Day (Rosenberg) 13:84
Night Scene in London A (Dickens) 3:47
Nightingale and the Rose, The (Wilde) 2:70
Nightingale, Florence 4:26, *28*, 58, 59, 80; 11:99
Nightmare, The (Fuseli) 12:*24–25*, 28
Nightmare Abbey (Peacock) 12:28
1984 (Orwell) 10:87
1914 Sonnets (Brooke) 13:79, 86
No Name (Collins) 12:69, 70, 71
Noel, Baptist 2:*100*
'Norman, Henry' of *The Three Clerks* 2:47, *47*
Norris, James 12:74, *76*
North, Marianne 9:25, *28*
North, Sir Thomas 1:22, *22*, 23
North and South (Gaskell) 4:58, 59, 68, 69, 70, *70*
Northanger Abbey (Austen) 8:8, *19*, 20, *20*, 22, 23, *23*, 24, *24*, 26, 27; 12:28
Northcliffe, Lord 2:*38*; 10:62
Norton, Charles Eliot 4:59, *59*

*Dickens' last, **unfinished novel*** *was* The Mystery of Edwin Drood. *Here heroine Rosa Bud receives some unwelcome attentions.*

Nostromo (Conrad) 9:58, 68, 69 70, 76
Not so Bad as We Seem (Bulwer-Lytton) 12:58
Notebooks (Butler) 2:92
Nussey, Ellen 4:7, *7*, 11, 26, 33, 34, 42
Nussey, Henry 4:8, 25

O

O'Connell, Daniel 3:24
O'Connor, Feargus 4:*73*, *74*, 75, 76
'O'Hara, Kim' of *Kim* 11:84, *84*, 85, *85*, 86, *86*, 87, *87*, 88, *88-89*, 89, 92
O'Rourke, May 3:59
'Oak, Gabriel' of *Far from the Madding Crowd* 3:59, 64, 65, *65*, 66, *66*, 68, 69, *69*, 76, 78, 79, *79*, 94, 95
Oastler, Richard 4:51
Ober, Harold 7:32
'Oberon' of *A Midsummer Night's Dream* 13:34, *34*, 35, 40, *40*, *44-45*
Ode on a Grecian Urn (Keats) 2:73; 13:71
Ode on Melancholy (Keats) 13:71, 73
Ode to a Nightingale (Keats) 13:63, 64, 65, 70-71, *70-71*, 73, 76
Ode to Psyche (Keats) 13:*71*

Ode to the West Wind (Shelley) 13:*60,* 61, *69,* 76

Odyssey (Homer) 2:82, 91, *91,* 95, *95*

Of Human Bondage (Maugham) 5:55, 60-65, *60-65,* 66, 67, *68,* 69

Of Mice and Men (Steinbeck) 7:56, 57, 66, 69, 71, *71*

Officers and Gentlemen (Waugh) 10:58, 69, 71

Old Curiosity Shop, The (Dickens) 3:24, 27, *28-29,* 29

Old Huntsman, The (Sassoon) 13:81, 83, 91

Old Man and the Sea, The (Hemingway) 7:92, 93, 95, *95*

Old Mortality (Scott) 11:44, 45, *46,* 47

Old Nurse's Story, The (Gaskell) 4:70

Oldcastle, Sir John 1:30

Oliver Twist (Dickens) 3:*8,* 26, *26,* 27, 28, *28,* 46, 47, 49

'Olivia' of *Twelfth Night* 13:38, 39, *39,* 40, 41

Omega Workshops 8:*98-99,* 99

Omoo (Melville) 9:31, 42, 43, 45, 48

On a Chinese Screen (Maugham) 5:67

On First Looking into Chapman's Homer (Keats) 13:62

On Forsyte 'Change (Galsworthy) 5:93

On the Margin (Huxley) 10:90

'Ophelia' of *Hamlet* 1:17, *17,* 20

Orage, Alfred Richard 8:56, 57, *66,* 76

Ordeal of Gilbert Pinfold, The (Waugh) 10:59, 69, 71

Origin of Species, The (Darwin) 4:100, *100;* 9:9, 10, *11,* 15, 22, 23, 27, 28

Orlando (Woolf) 8:81, 91, 92, 93, 95, *95,* 100

Oroonoko (Behn) 1:*53*

Orpen, William 13:*99*

Orphan, The (Otway) 1:56

Orwell, George *see Index of Writers*

'Osborne, George' of *Vanity Fair* 2:12, 13, *13, 14,* 15, 16, *17,* 27

Osbourne, Lloyd *see Index of Writers*

Osgood, Frances 12:35

'Osmond, Gilbert' of *The Portrait of a Lady* 5:13, *13,* 14, *14,* 15, *15,* 16, 17, *17,* 19

Othello (Shakespeare) 1:23, 25, 26, *26,* 30, 52

Otis, Elizabeth 7:56

Otway, Thomas *see Index of Writers*

Our Betters (Maugham) 5:57, 58, 66

Our Man in Havana (Greene) 6:91-92

Our Mutual Friend (Dickens) 3:40, 43, 45, *45*

Outcast of the Islands, An (Conrad) 9:57, 69

Outline of History, The (Wells) 5:34, 44

'Overton, Edward' of *The Way of All Flesh* 2:84, 85, 86-87, 88, *88,* 89

Ovid *see Index of Writers*

Owen, Orville Ward 13:*31*

Owen, Robert 4:79, *80*

Owen, Sir Richard 12:49-50

Owen, Wilfred *see Index of Writers*

Owl and the Pussycat, The (Lear) 10:38

Oxford, Edward de Vere, 17th Earl of 13:31

P

'Pablo' of *For Whom the Bell Tolls* 7:84, *84,* 85, 86, 87, 88, *88,* 89, 97

Paige, James W. 7:9

Painted Veil, The (Maugham) 5:67, 69, 70, *70*

Pair of Blue Eyes, A (Hardy) 3:61

'Palencia, Finito de' of *For Whom the Bell Tolls* 7:*85,* 87

Paley, William 9:6

Palladis Tamia: Wit's Treasury (Meres) 1:13

'Palliser, Plantagenet' of Palliser novels 2:44, 46

Palliser novels (Trollope) 2:43, *43,* 44, 45, 46, *46*

Palmer, John 2:*49*

Palmerston, H. J. T. 4:75

Pamela (Richardson) 1:86, 94, 95, *95,* 98

Pamplona 7:81, 93

Pankhurst, Christabel 8:72, 73, *74,* 75

Pankhurst, Emmeline 8:72, 73, *73,* 74, 75, 99

Pankhurst, Sylvia 8:72, 75, *75*

Paradise Lost (Milton) 12:15

Parliament of Fowls, The (Chaucer) 13:20, 22, 23, *23*

Parry, Edward 4:31

Parson, John R. 10:*51*

Partridge, John 10:19

'Partridge' of *Tom Jones* 1:88, 89, 92, 93, *93*

Pasquin (Fielding) 1:85, 94

Passage to India, A (Forster) 9:81, 82, 83, 84-89, *84-89,* 91, 92, 93, *96,* 100; 11:87

Passionate Friends, The (Wells) 5:33

'Patch, Anthony and Gloria' of *The Beautiful and Damned* 7:43, 45, *45*

Patience (Gilbert and Sullivan) 2:56, *56,* 72

Patrician, The (Galsworthy) 5:92

Paul Morel (Lawrence) 6:19

Pauli, Charles Paine 2:79-80, 81, *81,* 83

Pauline's Passion and Punishment (Alcott) 8:33, *42,* 43, 45

Payne, Walter 5:56

Peace (Brooke) 13:79, 86

Peace, Charlie 12:99

Peacock, Thomas Love *see Index of Writers*

A local dancing girl disguises Kim O'Hara, the eponymous hero of Kipling's novel, as a low-cast Hindu to help him to escape from school.

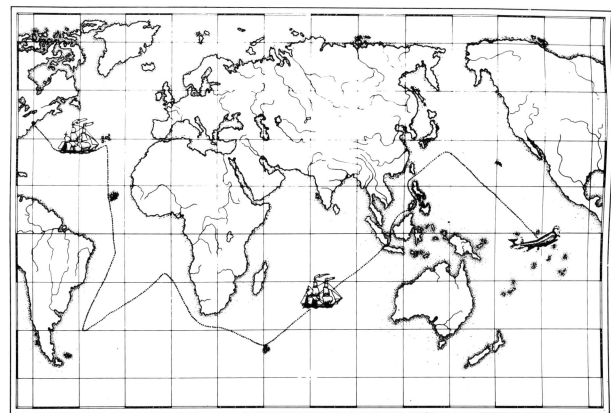

In Herman Melville's novel, *the ill-fated whaling ship* Pequod *sails to the Pacific ocean on her captain's obsessional quest for the white whale,* Moby Dick.

Pearl, The (Steinbeck) 7:66, 67
Pears, Abijah 4:*79*
Pears, Elizabeth 4:79, *79*
Peck, Gregory 6:*58*, 59
Peel, Frank 4:48
Peel, Sir Robert 3:47; 12:50, 96
Peele, George *see Index of Writers*
'Peggotty, Clara' of *David Copperfield* 3:26, 43
'Peleg' of *Moby-Dick* 9:36, 39
'Pembroke, Agnes' of *The Longest Journey* 9:93
PEN Club 5:83, *83*
'Pendennis, Arthur (Pen)' of *The History of Pendennis* 2:22
'Pennyways' of *Far from the Madding Crowd* 3:68
Pepys, Elizabeth St. Michel 1:35, 36, 37, 39, 41, 42, *43*, 44, 45, *45*, 47, 48, 52
Pepys, John 1:34
Pepys, Margaret Kite 1:34
Pepys, Samuel *see Index of Writers*
'Pequod, The' of *Moby-Dick* 9:36, 37, *37*, 38, 39, *39*, 40
Perceval, John 12:75-76
Perceval, Spencer 12:75
Perennial Philosophy, The (Huxley) 10:92-93
Perkins, Maxwell 7:32, 33, 35
Perrers, Alice 13:8
Personal Narrative (Humboldt) 9:*25*
Persse, Jocelyn 5:10
Persuasion (Austen) 8:20, 21, 22, 23, *23*, 24, 26, 28

Peter Pan (Barrie) 11:*68*; 12:81
Peterloo Massacre 4:*52*, 72-73, *72*; 13:69, *69*
Pethick-Lawrence, Emmeline 8:74
Petrarch *see Index of Writers*
'Petruchio' of *The Taming of the Shrew* 13:36, *36*, 37, *37*, 40, 41, *41*
Phantasmagoria (Carroll) 10:46, 47, *47*
Phantom Horsewoman, The (Hardy) 3:87
Pharos and Pharillon (Forster) 9:93
Phibbs, Geoffrey 6:33, 34
Phibbs, Norah 6:33
Philby, Kim 6:81, *81*, 92
'Philipot junior' of *The Comedians* 6:85, 86, *87*
Philippa, Queen of England 11:52; 13:7, 8
Philips, Katherine *see Index of Writers*
Phineas Finn (Trollope) 2:43, 46
Phineas Redux (Trollope) 2:46
Picasso, Pablo 7:*98-99*, 100; 8:67, 98, 99
Pickford, Mary 7:52
Pickwick Papers, The (Dickens)3: *8*, 10, *12*, 26, 27, 28, *28*, 48, 49, 50
Picture of Dorian Gray, The (Wilde) 2:55, 60-65, *60-65*, 66, 67, 69, 72, 73
Pictures (Mansfield) 8:60, 63, *63*, 64, 65, *65*, 68, 70
Pier-Glass, The (Graves) 6:45, *45*

Pierre or The Ambiquities (Melville) 9:43
Pigeon, The (Galsworthy) 5:*82*
'Pilar' of *For Whom the Bell Tolls* 7:84, *84*, 85, *85*, 86, 87, 88, *88*, 89, 97
Pilgrim's Progress, The (Bunyan) 1:57, 58, 62, 63, 64-69, *64-69*, 70, *70-71*, 72, *72*, 73, *73*, 74; 8:33, *33*
Pilgrim's Progress, The, Part II (Bunyan) 1:70, 73, 74, 75, *75*
Pillow Problems (Carroll) 10:33, 46
'Pineda, Angel' of *The Comedians* 6:84, *85*, 88, *89*
'Pineda, Martha' of *The Comedians* 6:84, 85, *85*, 86, 87, 88, *89*
'Pinfold, Gilbert' of *The Ordeal of Gilbert Pinfold* 10:54, 68, 69, 71
'Pip' ('Philip Pirrip') of *Great Expectations* 3:7, 34, *34*, 35, *35*, 36, *36*, 37, 38, 39, *39*, 50
'Pip' of *Moby-Dick* 9:40, 41
Piranesi, Giambattista 12:26, *26*
pirates/buccaneers 11:24-28, *24-28*, 60, 61, *61*, 62, *62*, 63, *63*
Pit and the Pendulum, The (Poe) 12:46, *46-47*
Pitmen at Play 4:*50*
Pitt, William 2:24
Pitt, William, the Elder 1:83
plague *see* Black Death
Plain Dealer, The (Wycherley) 1:*55*, 56
Plain Tales from the Hills (Kipling) 11:80, 90, 93, *93*

Plaine Man's Pathway to Heaven, The 1:61

Plays Pleasant and Unpleasant (Shaw) 5:98

Plots and Counterplots (Alcott) 8:45, 47, *47*

Plumed Serpent, The (Lawrence) 6:10, 11, 19, 20, *20*, 21, 23, *23*, 24, 28

Plutarch *see Index of Writers*

Poacher, The (Bates) 6:66, 76

'Pocket, Herbert' of *Great Expectations* 3:37, 38, 39, *39*

Poe, David 12:30, *30*, 34

Poe, Edgar Allan *see Index of Writers*

Poe, Elizabeth 12:30, *30-31*, 33, 34

Poe, Henry 12:30, 32, 34

Poe, Rosalie 12:30

Poe, Virginia Clemm 12:32, *32*, 33, *33*, 34, 35, *42*, 44, 47

Poems (Owen) 13:91

Poems (Wilde) 2:56

Poems (Brontës) 4:10, 22, 35, 44, 46

Poems 1912-13 (Hardy) 3:87

Poetical Bath Guide 8:*25*

Point Counter Point (Huxley) 8:68-69; 10:*81*, 91, 92, 94, *94*

'Poll the parrot' of *Robinson Crusoe* 11:14, *15*, 16, 20

'Polly, Alfred' of *The History of Mr Polly* 5:43, 47

Pomare, Queen of Tahiti 9:49

Pompey (Philips) 1:52

Ponder, Nathaniel 1:63

'Pontifex, Alethea' of *The Way of All Flesh* 2:85, 88, *88*,

'Pontifex, Christina' of *The Way of All Flesh* 2:84, *84*, 85, 86, 87, 88, *88*

'Pontifex, Ernest' of *The Way of All Flesh* 2:79, 83, 84, *84*, 85, *85*, 86, *86*, 87, *87*, 88, *88*, 89

'Pontifex, George' of *The Way of All Flesh* 2:84, 86, 88

'Pontifex, Theobald' of *The Way of All Flesh* 2:84, *84*, 85, *85*, 86, 87, 88, *88-89*

Poor Man and the Lady, The (Hardy) 3:70

'Poorgrass, Joseph' of *Far from the Madding Crowd* 3:68

Popay, William 12:96

Pope, Alexander *see Index of Writers*

Pope-Hennessy, James 2:44

Poradowska, Marguerite 9:56

Porteous, John 11:46

Portinari, Beatrice 13:*20*

Portman, Eric 6:*91*

Portrait of a Lady, The (James) 5:8, 9, 12-17, *12-17*, 19, 20, 21, 24

Post Office (British) reform of 2:48-52

'Postumus' of *I, Claudius* 6:37, 38, 40

Pound, Ezra *see Index of Writers*

Power and the Glory, The (Greene) 6:80, 90, 93, *93*

Poynter, Sir Edward 11:80

Poyntz Hall (Woolf) 8:83

Prabhavananda, Swami 10:*82*

Practice of Piety, The 1:61

Pratt, John 8:42

Prelude (Mansfield) 8:58, 60, *60*, 61, *61*, 62, *62*, 64, *64*, 66, 68, 70

Prelude, The (Wordsworth) 13:55, *55*, *73*, 76

Premature Burial, The (Poe) 12:*43*

'Preparing for Market' (Currier) 9:*34-35*

'Price, Fanny' of *Of Human Bondage* 5:58, 60, 64

Pride, Thomas 1:80

Pride and Prejudice (Austen) 4:25; 8:8, 10, 11, 12-17, *12-17*, 18, 19, 21, 22; 10:*82*, *92*

Priestley, J. B. *see Index of Writers*

Prime Minister, The (Trollope) 2:43, 46

Prince Regent *see* George IV

Princip, Gavrilo 13:94

Principia Ethica (Moore) 8:96-97

Prinsep, Sarah 10:52

Pritchard, George 9:49

Proceed, Sergeant Lamb (Graves) 6:44

Proctor, Mother 1:104

Professor, The (C. Brontë) 4:10, 18, *18*, 22, 26

Prohibition 7:38, *48*, 49, 50

Prometheus Unbound (P. B. Shelley) 12:14; 13:61

Promise, The (Steinbeck) 7:69

Prophetic Books (Blake) 13:72

Proposal for Making an effectual Provision for the Poor, A (Fielding) 1:100

'Pross, Miss' of *A Tale of Two Cities* 3:20, 21, 22

prostitution, Victorian 2:96-110, *99-100*

'Proudie, Dr' of *Barchester Towers* 2:36, *36*, 37, 40, 44, 45

'Proudie, Mrs' of *Barchester Towers* 2:36, *36*, 37, 39, *39*, 40, *40*, 41, 44, 45

Prussian Officer, The (Lawrence) 6:20

'Puck' of *A Midsummer Night's Dream* 13:34, *34*, 35, 40, *44-45*

Puck of Pook's Hill (Kipling) 11:90, 93, 95, *95*

Pudd'nhead Wilson (Twain) 7:11, 19, 21, 22, *22*

Purple Plain, The (Bates) 6:*58*, 59, 68, *68*

Put Out More Flags (Waugh) 10:58, 69

Putnam's magazine 9:43

Pygmalion (Shaw) 5:98, *100*

'Pym, Arthur Gordon' of *The Narrative of Arthur Gordon Pym*

Splendidly appalling, Mrs Proudie dominates both the characters and reader of Anthony Trollope's Barchester Towers.

Q

'Quarles, Philip' of *Point Counter Point* 10:91, 94

Queen Mab (Shelley) 13:60

'Queen of Hearts' of *Alice in Wonderland* 10:37, *37*, 39, 41

Queen of Hearts, The (Collins) 12:57, 70

Queen's College, London 4:28, *28*

Queensberry, Marquess of 2:58

'Queequeg' of *Moby-Dick* 9:36, 37, *37*, 39, 40, 41, *41*

Quentin Durward (Scott) 11:45, 47, *47*, 50

'Quested, Adela' of *A Passage to India* 9:84, 85, 87, 88, *88*, 89, 91, *96*

Quetzalcoatl, the Plumed Serpent 6:24, *24*, 25, 26, *27*, 28

Quiet American, The (Greene) 6:91, 93, *94-95*, 95

'Quilp, Daniel' of *The Old Curiosity Shop* 3:29

Quiney, Thomas 1:13

'Quiverful, Mr' of *Barchester Towers* 2:37, *39*, 40

GENERAL INDEX

R

Racine, Jean *see Index of Writers*
Rackham, Jack 'Calico Jack' 11:28
Radcliffe, (Mrs) Ann *see Index of Writers*
Raeburn, Sir Henry 11:72
Rafinesque-Schmaltz, Constantine 9:25
Raikes, Alice 10:*39*, 43
Rain (Maugham) 5:66, 69, 70, *70*
Rain on a Grave (Hardy) 3:88
Rainbow, The (Lawrence) 6:9, 13, 18, 19, 20, 21, 22, *22*
Rainsborough, Colonel 1:80
Raj, *see* India, British
Rake's Progress, A (Hogarth) 1:87, *103*
Raleigh, Sir Walter *see Index of Writers*
Ralph, James 1:86
Rambles Beyond Railways (Collins) 12:56
Rambles in Germany and Italy (M. Shelley) 12:19
Ramsay, Allan 11:72
'Ramsay, Cam' of *To the Lighthouse* 8:*84*, 86, *87*, 88, *89*
'Ramsay, James' of *To the Lighthouse* 8:84, *84*, 85, *85*, 86, *87*, 88, 89, *89*
'Ramsay, Mr' of *To the Lighthouse* 8:82, 84, 85, *85*, 86, *87*, 88, 89, *89*
'Ramsay, Mrs' of *To the Lighthouse* 8:82, 84, *84*, 85, *85*, 86, 87, *87*, 88, 89, *89*
Ranji 9:98
Rape of Lucrece, The (Shakespeare) 1:12; 13:32, *33*, 42, *42–43*
Rape upon Rape (Fielding) 1:84, *95*
Ravagli, Angelo 6:8
Raven, The (Poe) 12:*34*, 35, *35*, 43, *43*, 46, *46*
Razor's Edge, The (Maugham) 5:67, 68, 69, 71, *71*
'Razumov, Kirylo' of *Under Western Eyes* 9:68, 71
Read, Mary 11:27, 28, *28*
Read, William 11:*26*
Reade, Charles *see Index of Writers*
Reader over Your Shoulder, The (Graves/Hodge) 6:44
'Rebecca' of *Ivanhoe* 11:*36*, 37, *37*, 38, *38*, 39, 40, *40*, 48, 49
Recessional (Kipling) 11:91
Recollections of the Lake Poets (De Quincey) 13:55
Recruiting (Mackintosh) 13:*86*, 87
Recueil des Causes Célèbres (Mejans) 12:68

Red and White Roses, The (Cameron) 10:*48-49*
Red-headed League, The (Conan Doyle) 12:84
Red Pony, The (Steinbeck) 7:69, *69*
Redburn (Melville) 9:32, *32*, 42, 45, 47, 48
Redgauntlet (Scott) 11:*44*, 45, 46, *46*
'Reed, Aunt' of *Jane Eyre* 4:12, 13, 15, 16
Reed, Carol 6:*92*
'Reed family' of *Jane Eyre* 4:12, *12*, 16, *16*, *17*, 24
Reeves, Amber 5:33
Reform Act of 1832   3:9
Refugees, The (Conan Doyle) 12:92
'Regan' of *King Lear* 1:18, *18*, 19, 20, *21*
Regent's Park Zoo 9:24
Rejlander, Oscar 10:51, 52
religion
   Moby-Dick and 9:36, *37*, 38
   theory of evolution and 9:11, *11*, 13, 14, 18, 20, 22, 23, *26*, 28
Remote People (Waugh) 10:57
Report on the Sanitary Conditions of the City of Edinburgh (Littlejohn) 11:76
Reproach (Graves) 6:45
Requiem (Stevenson) 11:59
Rescue, The (Conrad) 9:57, 58, 59, 67
Rescuer, The (Conrad), *see Rescue, The*
Restoration Drama 1:52-56, *52-56*, 84
Retirement (Cowper) 8:28
Return of the Native, The (Hardy) 3:61, 73, 74, 93
Returning, we hear the Larks (Rosenberg) 13:92, *93*
Reverie (Rossetti) 10:*51*
Reynolds, J. N. 12:46, 51
Rhodes, Cecil 11:82
Rhythm 8:57, 67
Richard, Marthe *see Index of Writers*
'Richard I (The Lionheart)' of *Ivanhoe* 11:36, 37, *38-39*, 39, 40, 41, *48*, 49
Richard II, King of England 13:*9*, 10, *10*, 11
Richard III (Shakespeare) 1:23, 25, *25*, 30
Richards, Frances 2:57
Richardson, Samuel *see Index of Writers*
'Richardson' of *Love for Lydia* 6:60, *60-61*, 61, 62, *62-63*, 63, 64, *64*, 65
Richmond, Duchess of 2:27, 28
Richmond, Kenneth 6:78
Ricketts, Ed 7:56, 57, *57*, 58, 68
Riding, Laura 6:*32*, 33, *33*, 34, *34*, *42*

Rime of the Ancient Mariner, The (Coleridge) 12:46; 13:57, 64, 66–67, *66*, 73, 76
Ringrose, Basil 11:25
Rita, Dona 9:57
'Rival Prima Donnas, The' (Alcott) 8:42
Rivera, Diego 6:*26-27*
'Rivers, St John' of *Jane Eyre* 4:14, 15, 16, *16*, *17*, 25
Road from Colonus, The (Forster) 9:91, 94
Roaring Twenties, The 10:72-76, *72-76*
Rob Roy (Scott) 11:42, *44*, 45, *45*
Robbins, Amy Catherine 'Jane' *see* Wells, Amy Catherine 'Jane' Robbins
Roberts, Bartholomew 11:28
Roberts, Frederick Sleigh 12:*82*
Roberts, Lord 11:*98*, 99
Robertson, Sir William 11:97
Robespierre, Maximilien 3:33
'Robin, Fanny' of *Far from the Madding Crowd* 3:65, *66*, 67, 68, *68*, 71
Robin Hood 11:33, *33*, *38-39*, 40
Robinson, Henry Peach 10:*50-51*, 51, 52
Robinson Crusoe (Defoe) 5:49; 9:48; 11:5, 11, 12-17, *12-17*, 20, 21, 24; 12:74
'Rochester, Edward' of *Jane Eyre* 4:*11*, 12, *12*, 13, *13*, 14, 15, *15*, 16, *16*, *17*, 20, 21, 25, *26*, 28
Rock, The (Forster) 9:91
Rodin, Auguste 11:*58*
Rodney Stone (Conan Doyle) 12:94, *94*
Rogue's Life, A (Collins) 12:54
Rolle, Richard *see Index of Writers*
Roman gods and heroes 6:48-52, *48-52*
Romance (Ford and Conrad) 9:67
Romance of the Rose, The 13:20, *21*
Romance of Yachting, The (Hart) 13:31
Romantic Egotist, The (Fitzgerald) 7:31
Romantic Poets, *see Index of Writers*
Romanticism 13:72-76, *72-76*
'Romeo' of *Romeo and Juliet* 1:14, *14*, 15, *15*, 20, *20*, 31
Romeo and Juliet (Shakespeare) 1:14–15, *14-15*, 20, *20*, 25, 31, 55
Romola (Eliot) 4:90, 92, 93, *93*
Room of One's Own, A (Woolf) 8:81, 91, *91*, 92, 99, 100
Room with a View, A (Forster) 9:81, 90, 91, 93, 95, *95*
Roosevelt, Franklin Delano 5:35; 7:57, 74, 75, *75*, 76
Roosevelt, Theodore 5:35
Rosa, Salvator 12:26

Rose and the Ring, The (Thackeray) 2:21
Rosenberg, Barnett 13:*84*
Rosenberg, Isaac *see Index of Writers*
'Rosencrantz' of *Hamlet* 1:17
Ross, James 12:*52*
Ross, Robert 2:57, 59; 13:*81, 83*
Rossetti, Dante Gabriel 2:75, 100; 4:83; 10:48, *51,* 52, 56, 57, 66, 67; 12:28
Rossetti: His Life and Works (Waugh) 10:57
Rostand, Edmond 5:49
'Rothschild, Father' of *Vile Bodies* 10:63, 64, *65*
Rothstein, Arnold 7:34, *34*
Roughing It (Twain) 7:*6-7, 7,* 9, 21
Rousseau, Jean-Jacques *see Index of Writers*
Rover, The (Behn) 1:53
Rowe, Nicholas 1:13, *32*; 13:*33*
Rule Britannia! (Arne) 1:83
Rowell, Ellen 10:31
'Rowena' of *Ivanhoe* 11:36, 37, 40, 41, *41*
Rowse, A. L. 13:*33*
Roxana, or The Fortunate Mistress (Defoe) 11:19, 20, 21, 23, *23*
Roxburgh, J. F. 10:55
Royal Academy 2:*57, 80,* 81
Royal Commission on the Employment of Children, Young Persons and Women in Agriculture, A 3:78, 94, 96
Royal Court Theatre 5:92, 96, 97, *97,* 98, *98*
Rudd, Martha 12:58, *59*
Ruined Maid, The (Hardy) 3:88, *88*
'Runcible, Agatha' of *Vile Bodies* 10:60, *62-63,* 63, 64, *65*
Rupert, Prince 1:*43*
Ruskin, John *see Index of Writers*
Russell, Bertrand *see Index of Writers*
Russell, Richard 8:27
Ruth (Gaskell) 4:67, 68, 69
Ruth, Babe 7:51
Rutland, William *see Index of Writers*

S

Sackville-West, Vita *see Index of Writers*
Sacred Fount, The (James) 5:28
Sainsbury, George 2:74
Salisbury, Lord 10:35
Salome (Wilde) 2:*68,* 69, 70, *70,* 75
Salt, Sir Titus 4:51
Salvation of Swithin Forsyte, The (Galsworthy) 5:90, *91*

'Sanderson, Alex' of *Love for Lydia* 6:61, 62, 63, 64, *64*
Sandinistas 6:83, *83*
'Santiago' of *The Old Man and the Sea* 7:92, 95, *95*
Sargent, John Singer 5:10, 25, *26-27*; 11: *56-57*; 13:*99*
Sassoon, Siegfried Loraine *see Index of Writers*
Saturday Evening Post 7:32, *42,* 44
Saussure, Cesar de 1:102
Sauter, Georg 5:79
Sauter, Lilian Galsworthy 5:79, 80
Sauter, Rudolf 5:*78*
Savage, Eliza 2:80, 81, *81,* 83, 91, *92,* 93
'Savage, John' of *Brave New World* 10:85, *85,* 87, *87,* 88, 89, *89*
Save Me the Waltz (Zelda Fitzgerald) 7:35
Savile, Henry 1:54
Savoy, The 2:74, 75
'Sawyer, Tom' of *The Adventures of Tom Sawyer* and *The Adventures of Huckleberry Finn* 7:12, 13, 15, 16, 19-20, 21 *21*
Scandal in Bohemia (Conan Doyle) 12:84

scarlet fever 8:32, 37, 38
Scarlet Letter, The (Hawthorne) 9:33
Scarlet Sword, The (Bates) 6:68, 69, 70, *70*
Scenes of Clerical Life (Eliot) 4:*81,* 82, 90, *90*
'Schlegel, Helen' of *Howards End* 9:94
'Schlegel, Margaret' of *Howards End* 9:90, 94
'Schwert, Archie' of *Vile Bodies* 10:58, 60, 64
science fiction 5:48-52, *48-52*
Science of Life, The (Wells) 5:44
Scoop (Waugh) 10:*57,* 66, 69, *69*
Scott, Anne Rutherford 11:30, *31*
Scott, Charlotte Carpenter (or Charpentier) 11:31, *33,* 35
Scott, Jane Jobson 11:34
Scott, Sir Walter *see Index of Writers*
Scott, Walter, Senior 11:30, 31, *31*
Scott, Walter (son of Sir Walter Scott) 11:34, 35
Scott-King's Modern Europe (Waugh) 10:66
Scouting for Boys (Baden-Powell) 11:52

Mary Evans Picture Library

In the balcony scene, *one of the most famous passages from Shakespeare, Romeo and Juliet pledge their love. But, because of their families' enmity, tragedy is inevitable.*

Scriblerus Club 10:11
Scribners 7:32, 34
'Scrooge, Ebenezer' of *A Christmas Carol* 3:27, *27*
Sea and Sardinia (Lawrence) 6:19
Sea Child, The (Mansfield) 8:67
Sea of Cortez (Steinbeck/ Ricketts) 7:57
'Seagrim, Molly' of *Tom Jones* 1:88, *88-89*, 92, *92*, 102
Searle, Alan 5:59, *59*
Second-Fated, The (Graves) 6:35
Secret Agent, The (Conrad) 5:42; 9:58, 67-68, 69, 71
Sedgwick, Adam 9:6
'Sedley, Amelia' of *Vanity Fair* 2:12, 13, *13*, *14*, 15, 16, *17*, 24
'Sedley, Jos' of *Vanity Fair* 2:12, *12*, 13, 15, 16, *16*, 24
Sedley, Sir Charles 1:54
Sejanus (Jonson) 1:13
Selfish Giant, The (Wilde) 2:70

Selkirk, Alexander 11:9
Sense and Sensibility (Austen) 8:8, 11, 18, 19, 20, *21*, 22, *22*
Sensible Thing, The (Fitzgerald) 7:46, *46*
Sergeant Lamb of the Ninth (Graves) 6:44
Settle, Elkanah 1:56
Seven by Five (Bates) 6:71, *71*
Severn, Joseph 13:*62*, 63
Shaftesbury, Lord 4:97, *99*
Shakespeare, William *see Index of Writers*
Shakespeare, Hamnet 1:11, 13
Shakespeare, John 1:*10*, 11, 13
Shakespeare, Judith 1:11, 13
Shakespeare, Mary Arden 1:11, 13
Shakespeare, Susanna 1:11, 13
Shamela (An Apology for the Life of Mrs Shamela Andrews) (Fielding) 1:86, 95, *95*, 96
Shape of Things to Come, The (Wells) 5:*35*, 44, *44*

'Sharp, Rebecca (Becky)' of *Vanity Fair* 2:12, *12*, 13, *13*, 14, *14*, 15, *15*, 16, *16-17*, 24, *27*
Shaw, George Bernard *see Index of Writers*
Shelley, Charles 12:8
Shelley, Clara 12:8
Shelley, Elena Adelaide 12:9, 10
Shelley, Eliza Ianthe 12:6, 8
Shelley, Harriet 12:6, 8
Shelley, Harriet Westbrook 13:60, 61
Shelley, Mary Godwin *see Index of Writers*
Shelley, Percy Bysshe *see Index of Writers*
Shelley, Percy Florence 12:10, *10*, 11, 19; 13:*60*
Shelley, Sir Timothy 12:*10*, 11
Shelley, William 12:7, 9, 10, *10*, 22
Shelton, Sarah Elmira Royster 12:31, *34*, 35
Shelton, Thomas *see Index of Writers*
'Shepherdson family' of *The Adventures of Huckleberry Finn* 7:13
Sherston's Progress (Sassoon) 13:81
Ship of Death, The (Lawrence) 6:19
Shirley (C. Brontë) 4:19, 20, *20*, 21, *21*, 22, 23, *23*
Short Happy Life of Francis Macomber, The (Hemingway) 7:82, 92
Short History of the World (Wells) 5:44
Short View of the Immorality and Profaneness of the English Stage, A (Collier) 1:56, *56*
Shortest Way with the Dissenters, The (Defoe) 11:10, 11, *18*
Shout, The (Graves) 6:44
Sick Rose, The (Blake) 13:75
Sidney, Sir Philip *see Index of Writers*
Siege of Rhodes (Davenant) 1:52, 56
Siegfried's Journey (Sassoon) 13:81
Sign of Four, The (Conan Doyle) 12:80
'Sikes, Bill' of *Oliver Twist* 3:26, 28
Silas Marner (Eliot) 4:91, 92, 93, 95, *95*
'Silver, Long John' of *Treasure Island* 11:61, *61*, 62, *62*, 63, 64, *64-65*, 68
Silver Box, The (Galsworthy) 5:80, 92, 94, 96, 98, *99*
Silver Spoon, The (Galsworthy) 5:94
Silverado Squatters, The (Stevenson) 11:58, *66*
Simond, Louis 11:50
'Singleton, Adrian' of *The Picture of Dorian Gray* 2:64
'Singleton' of *The Nigger of the 'Narcissus'* 9:69
'Singleton, Robert' of *Captain Singleton* 11:21

Long John Silver *was one of Robert Louis Stevenson's most vivid creations. And, like the young Jim Hawkins, the reader of* Treasure Island *is both attracted and repelled by the pirate's character.*

"Dick's square" said Silver

Somerset, Countess of 10:18, *18*
Somerville, Alexander *see Index of Writers*
Something of Myself (Kipling) 11:79, 83, 90, 100
Something Tapped (Hardy) 3:*88*, 89, 91
Somme, Battle of the 13:85, 86, 87, 90, 98
Somoza Debayle, Anastasio 6:83, *83*
Song of Songs (Owen) 13:83
Songs of Experience (Blake) 13:75, *75*
Songs of Innocence (Blake) 13:75, 76
Sonnets (Shakespeare) 13:31–33, *32, 33*, 42, 43–44, *43*, 46–47
Sons and Lovers (Lawrence) 6:6, 7, 8, 19, 21, *21*; 8:57, 58
'Sordo, El' of *For Whom the Bell Tolls* 7:85, 87, 88
'Sorrell, Hetty' of *Adam Bede* 4:93, *93*
Sort of Life, A (Greene) 6:92
'South, Marty' of *The Woodlanders* 3:75
South Seas 9:48–52, *48-52*
Southampton, Henry Wriothesley, Third Earl of 1:12; 13:32, *33*, 42, 43, *43*
Southey, Robert *see Index of Writers*
Spanish Civil War 7:82, *82*, 84, 85, 91, 96–100, *96-100*
Spanish Gypsy, The (Eliot) 4:92
Spanish Tragedy, The (Kyd) 13:*50*, 51
Sparks, Martha 3:61
Sparks, Rebecca 3:61
Sparks, Tryphena 3:53, 55, *55*, 56, *59*, 60, 61, 63, 86
spas and sea-bathing resorts of England 8:24–28, *24-28*
Speckled Band, The (Conan Doyle) 12:84–85, *85*, 88, *88*
Spella Ho (Bates) 6:58, 76
Spencer, Herbert 2:90; 4:80, 81, *98*, 100
Spencer, Stanley 13:*99*
'Spenlow, Dora' of *David Copperfield* 3:43
Spenser, Edmund *see Index of Writers*
Sphinx without a Secret, The (Wilde) 2:69
'Squeers, Wackford' of *Nicholas Nickleby* 3:26, 29, *29*
'St Clair, Mrs' of *The Man with the Twisted Lip* 12:*85*, 86, 88,
'St Clair, Neville' of *The Man with the Twisted Lip* 12:*85*, 86, 88, 89
St George and the Dragon 1:59
St Ives (Stevenson) 11:66
St John, Jane 12:11
'Stackpole, Henrietta' of *The Portrait of a Lady* 5:12, 13, 14, *14*, 16
Stalin, Joseph 5:35
Stalky & Co. (Kipling) 11:93, *94-95*, 95

When acting in Shakespeare's comedies, tragedies or history plays, contemporary actors did not wear period costume, but the Elizabethan dress that was familiar to them. This tradition has been revived in recent years, and Shakespeare is often acted in modern dress – with varying degrees of artistic success.

Sir Gawain and the Green Knight 13:20
Sir John Oldcastle 1:30
Sir Nigel (Conan Doyle) 12:*92*
Sir Thomas More 1:22
Sister of the Baroness, The (Mansfield) 8:70, *70*
Sisters, The (Lawrence) 6:19
Sisters, The (Conrad) 9:57
Sitwell, Frances 11:56–57, *56*
Sitwell, Osbert and Edith *see Index of Writers*
Sketches by "Boz" (Dickens) 3:10, 27, 28, 50
'Skiffins, Miss' of *Great Expectations* 3:37
Skinner, Mollie *see Index of Writers*
Skynner, Mary 1:39
Slater, Oscar 12:82
slavery 6:96, *96*, 97, *97*, 98; 7:6, 12–13, 14, *14*, 20, 22, *22*, 25, 26, *26*, 27, *27*; 8:31, 48, *48*, 49, *49*, 50, *50*, 51, *51*; 9:*9*, *12*, 13, *16*, 50, *51*, 73, *73*; 11:12, 14, 15, *15*, 16, 27
Sleeping and Waking (Fitzgerald) 7:47
Sleepless Moon, The (Bates) 6:59
'Slope, Obadiah' of *Barchester Towers* 2:36, *36*, 37, *37*, 38, *38*, 39, *39*, 40, *40*, 41, 44
Small Boy and Others, A (James) 5:6
Small House at Allington, The (Trollope) 2:43, 44, 45
'Smallbury, Liddy' of *Far from the Madding Crowd* 3:*65*, 68
'Smike' of *Nicholas Nickleby* 3:29
Smith, Adam 11:44, 73
Smith, Bessie 7:51
Smith, Elder 4:10, 11, *21*
Smith, George 4:11, 68, 92
Smith, John 1:43
'Smith, Mary' of *Cranford* 4:60, 62, 63, 64, *64*, 65
'Smith, Mr and Mrs' of *The Comedians* 6:84, *85*, 86, 87, 88, 89
Smith-Cumming, Mansfield 5:73
Smithers, Leonard 2:74
'Smollett, Captain' of *Treasure Island* 11:61, *61*, 63, 64, *64*
Smollett, Tobias George *see Index of Writers*
Smyth, Dame Ethel 8:74, 82
Snodgrass, Dr 12:35
'Snowe, Lucy' of *Villette* 4:19, 22, *22*, 27
Snows of Kilimanjaro, The (Hemingway) 7:82, 91, *91*
Sobieniowski, Floryan 8:56, 59
soldier, British, life of 11:96–100, *96-100*
Soldier, The (Brooke) 13:79, 86
Soldier's Declaration, A (Sassoon) 13:81, *81*
Soldier's Memories in Peace and War, A (Younghusband) 11:96
Soldiers Three (Kipling) 11:90, *91*, 93, *97*
Some Words with a Mummy (Poe) 12:52

GENERAL INDEX

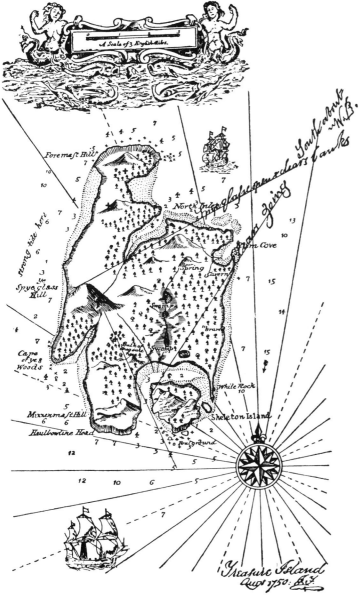

Robert Louis Stevenson's most famous novel is Treasure Island – *a potent tale that both draws upon and inspires young dreams of freedom, sailing ships, pirates, brave deeds . . . and treasure maps.*

Stamboul Train (Greene) 6:80, 90, *90*
Stanard, Jane 12:30, 42
'Stanhope, Bertie' of *Barchester Towers* 2:37, *38*, 40
'Stanhope, Charlotte' of *Barchester Towers* 2:37
'Stanhope, Madeline' of *Barchester Towers* 2:*36*, 37, 38, 39, 40, *40-41*
Stanley, Henry 9:72, *73*
'Starbuck' of *Moby-Dick* 9:36, 39, 40, 41
Stead, Sam 4:34
steamboats 7:*25*, 26-28
Steele, Richard 1:*55*, 86; 10:9, *20*
Steevens, Mrs G. W. 5:56

Stein, Gertrude *see Index of Writers*
'Stein' of *Lord Jim* 9:61, *62*, 63, 64, *65*
Steinbeck, Carol Henning 7:*55*, 56, *56*, 57
Steinbeck, Elaine Scott 7:*58*, 59
Steinbeck, Gwyndolyn Conger 7:56, 57, *57*, 58
Steinbeck, John (son of Steinbeck) 7:*57*, 58
Steinbeck, John Ernst *see Index of Writers*
Steinbeck, John Ernst, Sr 7:54, *54*, 56
Steinbeck, Olive 7:54, *54*, 56
Steinbeck, Thom 7:58, 59

Stephen, Adeline Virginia *see* Woolf, Virginia
Stephen, Adrian 8:79, 96, 97, *97*
Stephen, Julia Duckworth 8:82, *82*, 86, 78, *78*, 79
Stephen, Leslie 3:54, 65, 71, 72
Stephen, Minny Thackeray 8:78
Stephen, Sir Leslie 8:78, 79, 82, *82*, 92, 97
Stephen, Thoby 8:78, 79, *80*, 96, 97
Sterne, Mabel Dodge 6:10, 11, *11*
Stevenson, Adlai 7:59
Stevenson, Bob 11:55, 56, 57
Stevenson, Catherine 4:55
Stevenson, Fanny Van de Grift Osbourne 11:*56-57*, 57, 58, *58*, 59, *66*, 67, 70
Stevenson, John 4:54, 55, 57
Stevenson, Margaret (Maggie) 11:54, *54-55*, 57, 58, *58*, 59
Stevenson, Robert Louis *see Index of Writers*
Stevenson, Thomas 11:54, *54-55*, 55, 56, 57, 58, 66
Stevenson, William (father of Elizabeth Gaskell) 4:54, 55
Stevenson, William (half-brother of Elizabeth Gaskell) 4:55
'Stevie' of *The Secret Agent* 9:71
Stewart, Frances, Duchess of Richmond 1:*40*
Stoker, Bram *see Index of Writers*
Stonehenge 3:77, *83*
'Stoner, Helen' of *The Speckled Band* 12:85, *85, 88, 88*
Stopes, Marie 10:76
Story of a Panic, The (Forster) 9:80, 91, 94
Stowe, Harriet Beecher *see Index of Writers*
Strachey, Lytton *see Index of Writers*
Strafford, Thomas Wentworth, Earl of 1:76, 77
Strange Case of Dr Jekyll and Mr Hyde, The (Stevenson) 11:58, 67, 68, 69, 71, 71
Strange Meeting (Owen) 13:83, 92, *92*
Strange Story, A (Bulwer-Lytton) 12:52
Stranger, The (Mansfield) 8:70, 71, *71*
Stratford-upon-Avon 1:9, 10, *10*, 11, *11, 12*, 13, *13*; 13:29, 30, 31, 33, 43, 52
Stratton, Alfred and Albert 12:99
Strauss, David Friedrich 4:99
Strauss, Richard 2:70
Strife (Galsworthy) 5:92, *92-93*, 94, 99
Strong, Belle Osbourne 11:57, *58*, 68, *68*
Strudwick, John 1:*63*
'Stryver, Mr' of *A Tale of Two Cities* 3:18, 22

'Stubb' of *Moby-Dick* 9:36, 40, 41
Studies in Classic American Literature (Lawrence) 6:18
Study in Scarlet, A (Conan Doyle) 12:80, 84, *90*, 96
Suffragette/suffragist movement 8:34, 35, *35*, 56, 72-76, *72-76*, 99
Sullavan, Margaret 7:35
Summing Up, The (Maugham) 5:54, 68
Sun Also Rises, The (Fiesta) (Hemingway) 7:81, 93, *93*
Susan (Austen) 8:8
Swainson, William 9:25
Swan Song (Galsworthy) 5:94
Sweet Thursday (Steinbeck) 7:70
Swift, Abigail Erick or Herrick 10:6, 7, 9
Swift, Jonathan *see Index of Writers*
Swift, Jonathan, Senior 10:6
Swinburne, Algernon C. *see Index of Writers*
Swinnerton, Frank 5:42
Sword of Honour (Waugh) 10:59, 68, 69, 71, *71*
Swynford, Katherine 13:7, *7*
'Sybil, The' of *I, Claudius* 6:36, *37*, 39
Sylvia's Lovers (Gaskell) 4:57, 59, *68*, 69, 70-71, *70-71*
Sylvie and Bruno (Carroll) 10:44, 45, 46, *46*
Symons, Arthur *see Index of Writers*

T

Tables Turned, The (Wordsworth) 13:76
Tahiti 9:31, 45, 48, *48*, 49, 51, *51*, 52
Tailhade, Laurent 13:83
'Taji' of *Mardi* 9:46
Tale of a Tub, A (Swift) 10:8, 9, 18, 19, 20, 21, *21*, 22, *22*
Tale of Two Cities, A (Dickens) 3:13, 17, 18-23, *18-23*, 30, 42, 43; 12:71
Tale of the Ragged Mountains, A (Poe) 12:52
Tales and Stories (M. Shelley) 12:23, *23*
Tales of Mystery and Imagination (Poe) 12:30
Tales of Terror and the Supernatural (Collins) 12:70, *70-71*
Tales of the Jazz Age (Fitzgerald) 7:42, 45, 46, *46*
Talisman, The (Scott) 11:45, 50
Talks with Elizabethans 13:31

'Tall, Laban' of *Far from the Madding Crowd* 3:68
Tamburlaine (Marlowe) 13:49-50
Tamerlane and other Poems (Poe) 12:31
Taming of the Shrew, The (Shakespeare) 13:36-37, *36-37*, 40, 41, *41*
Tangled Tale, A (Carroll) 10:45, 46, *46*
'Tansley, Charles' of *To the Lighthouse* 8:84, 86, 88
Tarzan (Burroughs) 5:52
Tate, Nahum 1:55
Tatler, The 10:9, *20, 81*
Taylor, A. J. P. *see Index of Writers*
Taylor, Alfred 2:58
Taylor, James 4:11
Taylor, Mary 4:7
Taylor, Robert 7:35
Teach, Edward 'Blackbeard' 11:*25*, 26, *26*, 27
Tell-Tale Heart, The (Poe) 12:45
Tempest, The (Shakespeare) 1:25, 55; 10:85, 86, *86*; 13:30, *45*
Temple, Mary 'Minny' 5:6, 9, *9*
Temple, Shirley 6:80, *90*
Temple, Sir William 10:7, *7*, 8, 22
Tenant of Wildfell Hall, The (A. Brontë) 4:11, 32, 45, *45*, 46-47, 47
Tender is the Night (Fitzgerald) 7:35, 44, 45, *46-47*, 47
Tenniel, John 10:*30*, 33, *43*, 45
Tennyson, Alfred, Lord *see Index of Writers*
Ternan, Ellen 3:11, *11*, 15, 16, *16*

Terry, Ellen 10:32, *32*, 33
'Teshoo Lama' of *Kim* 11:84, *84*, 85, *85*, 86, *86-87*, 87, 88, *88*, 89, 91-92
Tess of the D'Urbervilles (Hardy) 3:53, 55, 57, 60, 61, 71, 72, 77, 78, 79, 80-85, *80-85*, 87, 94, 95, 96
'TH' (Holden) 3:*61*
Thackeray, Anne (Anny) (daughter of W. M. Thackeray) 2:8, *9*, 9-10, 11, 18, 19, 20
Thackeray, Anne (mother of W. M. Thackeray) 2:6, *6-7*, 9, *9*, 11, *20*
Thackeray, Harriet (Minny) 2:8, *9*, 9-10, 11, 18, 20
Thackeray, Isabella Shawe 2:7, 8, 9, *9*, 18, 20
Thackeray, Jane 2:8, 11
Thackeray, Richmond 2:6, *6-7*
Thackeray, William Makepeace *see Index of Writers*
Theatre, Elizabethan 1:28-32, *28-32*
Theatre, Elizabethan/Jacobean 13:48-52, *48-52*
Theatre, Restoration 1:52-56, *52-56*
'Theatre of Ideas' 5:96-100, *96-100*
They (Kipling) 11:82
They Hanged My Saintly Billy (Graves) 6:44
Third Man, The (Greene) 6:80, 81, 93, 94, *94*
This Side of Paradise (Fitzgerald) 7:30, 31, 32, 42, 45, *45*, 47
Thomas à Becket, Saint 13:12, 15, *15*, 28
Thompson, E. Gertrude 10:33

When her husband Rawdon is taken to the baliff's plunging-house to await imprisonment for his debts, Becky is slow to bail him out. Her reluctance leads eventually to the end of their marriage, and the heroine of Vanity Fair *must again fend for herself.*

An unusual version of the eternal triangle is enacted in H. E. Bates' The Triple Echo *when a woman disguises an army deserter as her sister.*

Thoreau, Henry David *see Index of Writers*
Thoreau, John 8:30
'Thornton, John' of *North and South* 4:70
Thornton, Marianne 9:78, 83
Thorpe, Thomas 13:32, *33*
Those Barren Leaves (Huxley) 10:90
Thoughts on the Education of Daughters (Wollstonecraft) 12:9
Thousand-and-second Tale of Scheherezade, The (Poe) 12:48–49
Three Clerks, The (Trollope) 2:44, 45, 47, *47*
Three Comrades, The (co-written by Fitzgerald) 7:35, *44*
Threepenny Opera, The (Brecht) 5:*100*
Through the Looking-Glass see Alice in Wonderland
Thrown Away (Kipling) 11:93
Tiare Tahiti (Brooke) 13:79
'Tiberius' of *I, Claudius* 6:36, 37, 38, 39, 40, 41
Tick of the Clock, The (Greene) 6:78
Tilden, Bill 7:*50*, 51
Time Machine, The (Wells) 5:31, 36, 42, 45, *45*

Time Must Have a Stop (Huxley) 10:92
Tintern Abbey (Wordsworth) 13:54, *64*, 76
'Tiny Tim' of *A Christmas Carol* 3:27, *27*
Tipoo-Tib 9:73
Tiredness of Rosabel, The (Mansfield) 8:63
'Titania' of *A Midsummer Night's Dream* 13:34, *34*, 35, *35*, 40, *40*, *44-45*
Titus Andronicus (Shakespeare) 1:24, *24*
To Arms (Conan Doyle) 12:82
To Autumn (Keats) 13:71
To a Skylark (Shelley) 13:*70*
To Have and Have Not (Hemingway) 7:92, 93, 94, *94*
To Helen (Poe) 12:31
To Imagination (E. Brontë) 4:43
To Let (Galsworthy) 5:82, 84
To Solitude (Keats) 13:62
To the Lighthouse (Woolf) 8:81, 82, 84-89, *84-89*, *90*, 91, 93
To the Warmongers (Sassoon) 13:88–89
Toast to Ava Gardner, A (Graves) 6:47

Tolkien, J. R. R. *see Index of Writers*
Tolstoy, Leo *see Index of Writers*
'Tom' of *Typee* and *Omoo* 9:45
Tom Jones (Fielding) 1:*84*, 85, 87, 88-93, *88-93*, *94*, 95, 97, 102, 104
Tom Sawyer, Detective (Twain) 7:21
Tom Sawyer Abroad (Twain) 7:21
Tomson, Rosamund 3:55
Tone, Wolfe 10:28
Tono-Bungay (Wells) 5:43, 45, 46, *47*
Tontons Macoutes 6:84, *84*, 85, *86*, 89, 100, *100*
Torrents of Spring, The (Hemingway) 7:81
Torrijos Herrera, Omar 6:83, *83*
Tortilla Flat (Steinbeck) 7:56, *56*, 66, 69, *69*
'Touchett, Lydia' of *The Portrait of a Lady* 5:12, 14, 16, 24
'Touchett, Ralph' of *The Portrait of a Lady* 5:12, 13, *13*, 14, 15, 16, *16*, 17, 19
Tour Through the Whole Island of Great Britain, A (Defoe) 11:11, 21, 22, *22-23*
Toussaint L'Ouverture 6:*96*, 97, 98
Townshend, Chauncey Hare *see Index of Writers*
Tracy, Spencer 7:*56*, 57
Traitor, The (Maugham) 5:73
'Transome, Harold' of *Felix Holt* 4:91, 94
'Transome, Mrs' of *Felix Holt* 4:91, 94
Travels with Charley (Steinbeck) 7:69, 71, *71*
Travels with a Donkey in the Cevennes (Stevenson) 11:69, 70, *70*
Travels with my Aunt (Greene) 6:92
Treasure Island (Stevenson) 9:48; 11:58, 60-65, *60-65*, 66, *67*, 68, 69, 76
'Trelawney, Squire' of *Treasure Island* 11:61, 63, 64, *64*
Trelawny, Edward John 12:10, *10*
Trespasser, The (Lawrence) 8:57
Trevelyan, G. M. *see Index of Writers*
Trial from Pickwick (Dickens) 3:16
Triple Echo, The (Bates) 6:59, 68, 69, 71, *71*
Troilus and Criseyde (Chaucer) 13:9, *9*, 20, *21*, 22, 23, *23*
Trollope, Anthony *see Index of Writers*
Trollope, Frances (Fanny) *see Index of Writers*
Trollope, Frederick 2:33, 34, *34*
Trollope, Henry (brother of Anthony Trollope) 2:30, 32
Trollope, Henry (son of Anthony Trollope) 2:33
Trollope, Rose Heseltine 2:33, *33*, 34, *34*

Trollope, Thomas (father of
    Anthony Trollope) 2:30, 32
Trollope, Tom (brother of Anthony
    Trollope) 2:30, 32, 34
Trowell, Garnet 8:55, *57, 66*
'Troy, Sergeant Frank' of *Far from
    the Madding Crowd* 3:65, 66, *66,*
    67, *67,* 68, *68,* 69, 71, 93
True-Born Englishman (Defoe) 11:18,
    19
True History, The (Lucian) 5:49
True Sun 3:9
Trumpet Major, The (Hardy) 3:72,
    73, 74, 78
Tucker, Frederick 11:100
'Tudor, Alaric' of *The Three Clerks*
    2:47, *47*
'Tudor, Charley' of *The Three
    Clerks* 2:44, 47, *47*
'Tulliver, Maggie' of *The Mill on the
    Floss* 4:84, *84,* 85, *85,* 86, 87, *87,*
    88, 89, *89,* 90, 91
'Tulliver, Mr' of *The Mill on the
    Floss* 4:84, 85, 86, *86,* 87, 88, 89,
    89
'Tulliver, Mrs (Bessy)' of *The Mill
    on the Floss* 4:84, 86, 87, 88
'Tulliver, Tom' of *The Mill on the
    Floss* 4:84, *84,* 85, *85,* 86, *86,* 87,
    87, 88, 89, *89,* 90
Tumble-Down Dick (Fielding) 1:85
Turgenev, Ivan *see Index of Writers*
Turn of the Screw, The (James) 5:19,
    21, 23, *23*
Turner, Anne 4:55
Turner, J. M. W. 10:*35*; 13:*76*
Turner, Mary 4:55
Turner, Nat 8:50, *50*
Turner, Saxon Sydney 8:96
Turner, William 4:55
Tutin, Dorothy 6:*91*
*Tutor to Tachygraphy, or Short-
    Writing* (Shelton) 1:35, 47
Twain, Mark *see Index of Writers*
'Tweedledum and Tweedledee' of
    Alice in Wonderland 10:37, 38,
    40, *40,* 41, *45*
Twelfth Night (Shakespeare) 1:22,
    56; 13:38-39, *38-39,* 40, 41, *41*
Twentieth Century-Fox 6:*90*
Two Gentle People (Greene) 6:95, *95*
Two Lips (Hardy) 3:89, 91
Two Noble Kinsmen, The
    (Shakespeare/Fletcher) 1:22
Two Sisters, The (Bates) 6:55, 56,
    66, 67
Two Ways of Life, The (Rejlander)
    10:51
'Tybalt' of *Romeo and Juliet* 1:14, *14,*
    20
Tyler, Wat 13:*9*
Typee (Melville) 5:24; 9:31, *32,* 33,
    42, 43, 45, 48, 50, 52
Typhoon (Conrad) 9:69

**Sergeant Troy's
military glamour**
*captures female
hearts, but he refuses
to take responsibility
for his conquests –
with fatal results for
some of the characters
in* Far From the
Madding Crowd.

U

Ulalume (Poe) 12:42
Ulysses (Joyce) 8:86
Uncle Tom's Cabin (Stowe) 5:100;
    7:*26*
Unconditional Surrender (Waugh)
    10:59, 69, 71
Under the Greenwood Tree (Hardy)
    3:73, 74, 86
Under the Hill (Beardsley) 2:74
Under Western Eyes (Conrad) 9:68,
    69, 71
'Underground Railway' 7:14; 8:31,
    50
Universal Gallant, The (Fielding)
    1:85
Unknown, The (Maugham) 5:58
Unloved Wife, The (Alcott) 8:32
*Unparalleled Adventure of one Hans
    Pfaall, The* (Poe) 5:50
Upbraiding, An (Hardy) 3:89, 90
'Uriah Heep' of *David Copperfield*
    3:*24,* 26
Useful and Instructive Poetry (Carroll)
    10:42
'Usher, Madeline' of *The Fall of the
    House of Usher* 12:*36,* 37, 40, *41,*
    44, *44,* 45
'Usher, Roderick' of *The Fall of the
    House of Usher* 12:*36,* 37, 40, *41*

V

Valentino, Rudolph 7:*50,* 52
Vallon, Annette 13:54
Valperga (M. Shelley) 12:10, 19, *19,*
    20, 22, *22*
Van Gogh, Vincent 8:*98*
Vanbrugh, John *see Index of Writers*

'Vane, James' of *The Picture of
    Dorian Gray* 2:61, 62, *62,* 64, *65*
'Vane, Sybil' of *The Picture of Dorian
    Gray* 2:*60,* 61, 64, *65*
Vanhomrigh, Esther (or Hester)
    10:9-10, *10*
Vanished World, The (Bates) 6:59,
    72, 73, 76
Vanity Fair (Thackeray) 2:6, 9,
    12-17, *12-17,* 16-21, *16-21,* 22,
    24, *27,* 28; 10:91
'Varens, Adele' of *Jane Eyre* 4:12, 16
*Variations in Flesh Colour and Green:
    The Balcony* (Whistler) 5:*26*
Vathek (Beckford) 12:25, 26, *26,* 27
Vaughan Williams, Ralph 9:*91*
Vedrenne, J. E. 5:96
Venice Preserv'd (Otway) 1:56, *56*
Venus and Adonis (Shakespeare) 1:12;
    13:32, *33,* 42, *42,* 43
'Verloc, Adolf' of *The Secret Agent*
    9:71
Verne, Jules *see Index of Writers*
Vestal Virgins 6:37, *37,* 51
Vicar of Bullhampton, The (Trollope)
    2:45, 47
Victoria, Queen of England 2:50,
    97-98; 3:11, 77, 78: 4:29, 76;
    9:96, *96;* 10:*39,* 51; 11:51, *52,*
    71, 98; 12:96
Victoria County History of Dorset 3:78
Victorian morality 2:96-100
Victory (Conrad) 9:67
Vile Bodies (Waugh) 10:58, 60-65,
    60-65, 66, 67, *67,* 69, 72, 75, 76
Villalta, Nicanor 7:81
Villeneuve, Admiral Pierre de 2:26
Villette (C. Brontë) 4:*10,* 11, 18, *18,*
    19, 20, 21, 22, *22,* 26, 27
Vindication of the Rights of Woman, A
    (Wollstonecraft) 12:9
Virgil *see Index of Writers*
Virgin and the Gipsy, The (Lawrence)
    6:12, 13, 16, *16,* 20
Virginians, The (Thackeray) 2:20
Vision and Design (Fry) 8:99
Vision of Piers Plowman (Langland)
    13:20, 26

Visits to Remarkable Places (Howitt) 4:56

Voice, The (Hardy) 3:87, 89, 90

Volpone (Jonson) 13:*51*, 52, *52*

Voltaire (François Marie Arouet) *see Index of Writers*

Von Kurowsky, Agnes Hannah 7:79, *79*

Voodoo 6:87, *87*, 89, 97, 100, *100*

Voyage Out, The (Woolf) 8:79, 80, 91, 93, *93*

Voyage of the 'Beagle', The (Darwin) 9:12-15

Voyage Round the World, A (Dampier) 10:15

Voyagers, The (Bates) 6:56

Voyages Extraordinaires (Verne) 5:50

'Vye, Eustacia' of *The Return of the Native* 3:74

'Vyse, Cecil' of *A Room with a View* 9:90, 95

W

'Wait, Jimmy' of *The Nigger of the 'Narcissus'* 9:69

Wakefield, Edward 12:74

'Wakem, Mr' of *The Mill on the Floss* 4:84, *86, 87,* 89

'Wakem, Philip' of *The Mill on the Floss* 4:80, 84, 85, 87, *87,* 88, *88,* 89

Walden (Thoreau) 8:*32*

Wall Street Crash of 1929 7:34, 43, 47, 52, *52,* 72, *73;* 10:76

Wallace, Alfred 9:9, 10, 25, *25*

Wallinger, Sir John 5:57, 73, 74

Walpole, Horace *see Index of Writers*

Walpole, Hugh *see Index of Writers*

Walpole, Sir Robert 1:84, 85, 86, 94, *96,* 97, 98; 10:10, 11, 16; 12:25

Walrus and the Carpenter, The (Carroll) 10:37, 41, *41,* 43

Walters, Catherine 2:98

Walters, Philadelphia 8:7

'Walters, William' of *Captain Singleton* 11:21

'Walton, Robert' of *Frankenstein* 12:12, *12,* 13, *15,* 16, 17

'Wamba the Witless' of *Ivanhoe* 11:37, 40, 41, *41*

War in South Africa, The (Conan Doyle) 12:82

War in the Air, The (Wells) 5:42

War of the Worlds, The (Wells) 5:31, 35, 36-41, *36-41,* 42, 45, 50

War Poets, The *see Index of Writers*

War Prayer, The (Twain) 7:20

Warburg, Max 5:75

Ward, Basil 2:57, *57*

Ward, John 1:13

Ward, Mrs Humphrey *see Index of Writers*

Warden, The (Trollope) 2:33, 35, 43, 44, 45

Warner, Charles Dudley 7:18

Warren, Sir Charles 12:98

Warren's Blacking Factory 3:7-8, *7*

Washington Square (James) 5:8, 19, 21, 22, *22*

Waste (Granville-Barker) 5:99

Wasteland, The (Eliot) 5:28

Watch and Ward (James) 5:7

Waterloo (Conan Doyle) 12:82

Waterloo, Battle of 2:*12-13,* 15, 27, 28, *28*

'Waters, Mrs' of *Tom Jones* 1:89, 92, 93, *93*

Waterton, Charles 9:25, 27

Watkins-Pitchford, D. J. ("BB") 6:72

'Watson, Dr John' of *Sherlock Holmes* stories 12:84, 85, 86, 87, *87,* 88, *88-89,* 89, 90, *90,* 91, *91,* 93, 94, 99

'Watson, Helmholtz' of *Brave New World* 10:85, *86,* 88, *88-89*

'Watson, Miss' of *The Adventures of Huckleberry Finn* 7:12, 14, 15

Watts, G. F. 10:52

Waugh, Alec *see Index of Writers*

Waugh, Arthur 10:54, *54*

Waugh, Catherine 10:54, *54*

Waugh, Evelyn Gardner (She-Evelyn) 10:56-57, *56*

Waugh, Evelyn *see Index of Writers*

Waugh, Laura Herbert 10:58, *58,* 59, *59*

Waugh, Margaret 10:59

Waugh in Abyssinia (Waugh) 10:57

Waverley (Scott) 11:33, 42, *44,* 45, *45*

Waves, The (Woolf) 8:82, 90, 93, 94, *94*

Way of All Flesh, The (Butler) 2:78, 80, 81, 82, 83, 84-89, *84-89,* 93, 96

Way of the World (Congreve) 1:55, *55*

Way We Live Now, The (Trollope) 2:45, 46, *46*

Wayward Bus, The (Steinbeck) 7:67, 69, 71, *71*

Webster, John *see Index of Writers*

Wedding Ring, The (Lawrence) 6:19

Wedgwood, Josiah, I 9:6, 7, 8, *9*

Wedgwood, Josiah, II 9:6, 7, *9*

Wedgwood, Julia 9:*8*

Wedgwood, Sarah 9:7

Wedgwood, Thomas 9:*9*

Wee Willie Winkie (Kipling) 11:90

Weekley, Ernest 6:8

Weightman, William 4:32, 44, 46

Weir of Hermiston (Stevenson) 11:59, 66, 68, *68,* 69, 70, *70*

Weld, Mary 5:19

Wellcome, Henry 5:57

Wellcome, Syrie *see Maugham, Syrie Barnado Wellcome*

Weller, Mary 3:6

Welles, Orson 5:35, *35,* 50

Wellington, Duke of 2:26, 27, 28, *28,* 98; 4:7, *18,* 75; 11:96, 98

Wellington House Academy 3:8

Wells, Amy Catherine 'Jane' Robbins 5:31, 32, *32,* 34, 35, *42*

Wells, Frank (brother of H. G. Wells) 5:36

Wells, Frank (son of H. G. Wells) 5:32

Wells, George 5:32

Wells, Herbert George *see Index of Writers*

Wells, Isabel Mary 5:31, *31, 32*

Wells, Joseph 5:30, *30*

Wells, Sarah 5:30, *30, 31, 43*

'Wemmick' of *Great Expectations* 3:36-37, *37,* 38, 46

Wescott, Glenway 5:57, 58

Wesley, John 4:96, *97*

'Wessex' *see Hardy's Wessex*

West, Anthony 5:33, 34, 35

West, Benjamin 9:*43*

West, Rebecca *see Index of Writers*

West Indies and the Spanish Main, The (Trollope) 2:43, 44

'Western, Sophia' of *Tom Jones* 1:85, 89, *89, 90,* 91, *91,* 92, *93*

Westminster Abbey 1:*36,* 41; 3:11, *11,* 17, 57; 11:83

'Weston, Edmund' of *Agnes Grey* 4:47

whaling 9:30-31, *34,* 36-39, *36-39,* 51-52

Wharton, Edith *see Index of Writers*

What Maisie Knew (James) 5:21, 22, *22*

Wheatstone, Charles 2:50

Wheelwright, Laetitia 4:33, 34

When the Going Was Good (Waugh) 10:66

When the Lamp is Shattered (Shelley) 13:61, *61*

Where Angels Fear to Tread (Forster) 9:80, *80,* 90, 91, 93, *93*

Whistler, James McNeill 2:67, 73; 5:25, 26, *26,* 27

Whistler at the Plough, The (Somerville) 3:78

White, George 7:49

White, Gilbert *see Index of Writers*

White Company, The (Conan Doyle) 12:80, 92, *92,* 94, *94*

White Goddess, The (Graves) 6:35, 43, 45, 47, *47*

White-Jacket (Melville) 9:32, 42, 45, 47, 48

White Monkey, The (Galsworthy) 5:94, *94-95*

White Peacock, The (Lawrence) 6:8, 19, 21, *21*

'White Rabbit' of *Alice in Wonderland* 10:36, 41, *41*, 43

Whiting, John *see Index of Writers*

Whitman, Helen 12:35

Whitman, Walt *see Index of Writers*

Whittier, John Greenleaf 8:*51*

Who's Who 3:58

'Wickham' of *Pride and Prejudice* 8:13, *13*, 14, *15*, 16, *16*

'Wife of Bath' of *The Canterbury Tales* 13:12, 13, 14, 16, 18

Wife to Mr Milton (Graves) 6:44

Wilberforce, Samuel 4:100, *100*; 9:11

Wilberforce, William 4:96-97, *98*

'Wilcox family' of *Howards End* 9:94

Wilde, Constance Mary Lloyd 2:*56*, 57, 59

Wilde, Cyril 2:*56*, 57

Wilde, Lady Jane Francesca Elgee 2:54, *54*

Wilde, Oscar *see Index of Writers*

Wilde, Sir William 2:54, *54*

Wilde, Vyvyan 2:*56*, 57

'Wildeve, Damon' of *The Return of the Native* 3:93

'Wilfer, Bella' of *Our Mutual Friend* 3:45

Wilhelm II, Kaiser of Germany 13:94, *95*, 100

Wilkie, Sir David 11:*32*; 12:*55*

Wilkinson, Lily Gair 8:75

'Willems' of *An Outcast of the Islands* 9:69

William III, King of England (William of Orange) 1:39; 10:24, *24*; 11:9, *9*, 10, 18, *19*

William of Wykeham 13:26

William Wilson (Poe) 12:36, 37-38, *37*, 40, 41, *41*

Williams, A. P. 9:59

Williams, Edward 12:10, *10*, 11; 13:61, *61*

Williams, Jane 12:10, 11; 13:61, *61*

Williams, John 9:33

'Willoughby, John' of *Sense and Sensibility* 8:20, 22, *22*

Wills, Helen 7:*50*, 51

Wills, William Henry 3:13

Wilmot, John, Earl of Rochester *see Index of Writers*

Wilson, Carus 4:6-7, *20*

Wilson, Edmund *see Index of Writers*

Wilson, Harriet 2:98

'Wilson, Jem' of *Mary Barton* 4:69, 76

'Wilson, Myrtle' of *The Great Gatsby* 7:36, 40, *41*

'Wilson' of *The Great Gatsby* 7:*39*, 40, *41*

Windsor Prophesy, The (Swift) 10:18

Wings of a Dove, The (James) 5:10, 20

Winstanley, Gerard 1:80

Winter's Tale, The (Shakespeare) 13:49

Winter Words (Hardy) 3:88

'Winterbourne, Giles' of *The Woodlanders* 3:75

Wiseman, Sir William 5:75-76

Witcop, Milly and Rose 8:75

Wives and Daughters (Gaskell) 4:59, 69, 71

Wolfe, Lilian 8:75

'Wolfsheim, Meyer' of *The Great Gatsby* 7:34, 40

Wollstonecraft, Mary *see Index of Writers*

Woman in White, The (Collins) 3:9, *9*, 13; 12:*55*, 56, *56*, 60-65, *60-65*, 66, *66*, 67, 68, 69, 70, 72, 75, 76

Woman of No Importance, A (Wilde) 2:67, 68

Woman's Vengeance, A 10:82

Woman's World, The 2:57, 66, 67

Woman Who Rode Away, The (Lawrence) 6:11, 13-14, *14*, 16, *16*, 20, 25, 26

Women in Love (Lawrence) 6:13, 18, 19, 21, 22, *22*

women's rights 8:72-76, *72-76*
    see also Suffragette/suffragist movement

Women's Social and Political Union (WSPU) 8:72, 73, *73*, 74, 75

women, Victorian 24-28, *24-28*

'Wonham, Stephen' of *The Longest Journey* 9:93

Wood, Reverend J. G. 9:26

Wood, William 10:18, *19*, 27, *27*, 28

Woodlanders, The (Hardy) 3:73, 75, *75*, 79, *79*

'Woodward family' of *The Three Clerks* 2:47

Wooler, Miss 4:7, 8, 11

Woolf, Leonard *see Index of Writers*

Woolf, Virginia *see Index of Writers*

Woolner, Thomas 4:81-82

Worcester, Earl of 1:28

Wordsworth, Dorothy *see Index of Writers*

Wordsworth, Mary Hutchinson 13:55, *55*

Wordsworth, William *see Index of Writers*

Work (Alcott) 8:43

Work, Wealth and Happiness of Mankind, The (Wells) 5:44

World in Ripeness, The (Bates) 6:59

World Set Free, The (Wells) 5:42

World War I 5:10, 28, 33, 34, 43-44, 52, 57, 58, 70, 71, 72-76, 82, *82*, 83, 92, 99; 6:9, 18, 23, 31, 43, *43*, 45, 46, 73, 79; 7:31, 42, 48, 73, 78, *79*, 93, 94, *94*, 95; 8:58, 66, 68, 72, 74, 100; 9:59, *81*, 82, 92, 100; 10:54, *55*, 62, 72, 79, 97, *98*, 99; 11:52, 83, *83*, 100, *100*; 13:77, *77*, 78, 79, 80, *80-81*, 81, 86, *86*, 90, 93, 94-100, *94-100*

The young men of Europe greeted the outbreak of World War I as a chance to prove themselves. They were soon disillusioned, and their feelings were encapsulated by poets like Brooke, Owen and Sassoon – the War Poets.

Courtesy of the Trustees of Imperial War Museum, London

World War II 5:*34-35*, 35, 59; 6:42, 58, 68, *68*, 69, 71, *76*, 80, 81; 7:57, *57*, 58, 66, 69, 74, 76, 82–83, 97; 8:82, 83; 9:83; 10:58, 67, 69, 70; 11:99

'Worlds in the Moon' (Defoe) 5:49

Worthies (Fuller) 1:34

'Worthing, Ernest' of *The Importance of Being Earnest* 2:71

'Worthing, Jack' of *The Importance of Being Earnest* 2:71, *71*

'Wotton, Lady Henry' of *The Picture of Dorian Gray* 2:64

'Wotton, Lord Henry' of *The Picture of Dorian Gray* 2:60, 61, *61*, 62, 63, 64, *64*, 65, 67, 72

Wrecker, The (Stevenson/ Osbourne) 11:66

Wren, Sir Christopher 1:43, *43*, 52, 53

Wrong Box, The (Stevenson/ Osbourne) 11:66

Wuthering Heights (E. Brontë) 4:10, 30, 34, *34-35*, 35, 36–41, *36-41*, 43, 46, 48, 50, 52

Wycherley, William *see Index of Writers*

Wyclif, John 13:*27*, 28

Wynfield, David Wilkie 10:52

'Xury' of *Robinson Crusoe* 11:12, 14, 16

'Yahoos, The' of *Gulliver's Travels* 10:13, *14-15*, 15, 16, 17

Yates, Edmund 10:34, 42

Years, The (Woolf) 8:91

Yeats, W. B. *see Index of Writers*

Yellow Book, The 2:74, 75, *75*

Yellowplush Papers, The (Thackeray) 2:18

'Yeobright, Clym' of *The Return of the Native* 3:61, 74

'Yillah' of *Mardi* 9:46

Yonge, Charlotte M. *see Index of Writers*

Yorkshire life, nineteenth century 4:48-52, *48-52*

You are old, Father William (Carroll) 10:45

Young, Arthur 3:32

Younghusband, Sir George *see Index of Writers*

Youth (Conrad) 9:58, 69

Youth (Rosenberg) 13:85

'Yvette' of *The Virgin and the Gipsy* 6:12, *12-13*, 13, 16, *16*, 17, *17*

Zanetti, Isabella 2:80

Ziegfeld Follies 7:*49*

Zola, Emile *see Index of Writers*

Zoonomia (Erasmus Darwin) 9:6

INDEX OF WRITERS

INDEX OF WRITERS

Note Page numbers in italic type refer to illustrations.

A

Alcott, Louisa May 8:29, *29*
  adoption of niece Lulu 8:35, *35*
  as abolitionist 8:*33*, 50, 51
  as nurse in Civil War 8:32, 33, *34-35*, 35, *43*, 44, 45
  as supporter of women's suffrage movement 8:34, 35
  birth 8:30, *30*, 48
  'blood and thunder' stories 8:33, 42-43
  career 8:42-44, *42-44*
  characters 8:38, *39*, 40-41, *40-41*
  childhood 8:30, *31*
  death 8:35, 44
  death of mother 8:34-35
  early writings 8:32, 42, 45
  family responsibilities 8:31, 32, 33, 34, 35, *35*, 42, 45
  ill health 8:33, *34*, 35, 44
  income from writing 8:33, 34, 42
  poem to John Brown 8:51
  poem for father 8:35
  pseudonym (A. M. Barnard) 8:33, 42, *42*, 43, 47
  trips to Europe 8:33, 34, *34*
  views on *Little Women* 8:37, 39
  views on work 8:42
  works in outline 8:45-47, *45-47*
    Captive of Seville, The 8:32
    Flower Fables 8:32, 42, 45, *45*
    Hospital Sketches 8:*43*, 44, 45
    Jo's Boys 8:35, 44, 45, 47, *47*
    Little Men 8:34, 42, 44, 45, 46, *46*
    Little Women 8:30, 33, *33*, 34, 36-41, *36-41*, 42, 43, 44, 45
    Little Women, Part II (Good Wives) 8:44, 45, 46, *46*
    Marble Woman, The 8:33
    Moods 8:33, 43, 45
    Pauline's Passion and Punishment 8:33, *42*, 43, 45
    Plots and Counterplots 8:45, 47, *47*
    Unloved Wife, The 8:32
    Work 8:43
Aldiss, Brian 5:52
Amis, Kingsley 11:99
Anderson, Sherwood 7:80
Arnim, Countess von 9:80
    Elizabeth and her German Garden 9:80
Arnold, Matthew 4:20, 46, 99; 10:78
    Dover Beach 4:99

Austen, Jane 2:43; 4:25, 66, 72; 8:5, *5*, 12, *12*, 14, 16, 25; 10:82, *92*; 11:33, 44; 12:28
  Addison's Disease 8:11
  birth 8:6, 18
  career 8:18-21, *18-21*
  characters 8:16-17, *16-17*
  death 8:11, *11*, 19
  dedication of *Emma* 8:10
  early writings 8:7-8
  education 8:7
  introduction to society 8:8
  key dates 8:6
  marriage proposal 8:9
  maturation of art 8:10
  moral code 8:20
  mother's views on 8:*6*
  move to Bath 8:8, 9, *10*, 24, *25*, 27
  possible love affair 8:8-9, *9*, 28
  putrid fever 8:7
  themes of novels 8:10, *10-11*, 23
  Thomas Lefroy and 8:*9*, 10
  views on Bath 8:*24*
  views on Hampshire countryside 8:7, *7*
  views on *Mansfield Park* 8:22
  works in outline 8:22-23, *22-23*
    Elinor and Marianne 8:8
    Emma 8:*10*, 11, *18*, *21*, 22, 23, *23*
    First Impressions 8:8, *13*, 15
    Mansfield Park 8:11, 22, *22*
    Northanger Abbey 8:8, *19*, 20, *20*, 22, 23, *23*, 24, *24*, 26, 27; 12:28
    Persuasion 8:20, 21, 22, 23, *23*, 24, 26, 28
    Pride and Prejudice 4:25; 8:8, 10, 11, 12-17, *12-17*, 18, 19, 21, 22; 10:82, *92*
    Sense and Sensibility 8:8, 11, 18, 19, 20, *21*, 22, 22
    Susan 8:8

B

Bacon, Francis 13:*30*, 31, *31*
Baden-Powell, Sir Robert 11:52
    Scouting for Boys 11:52
Bagehot, Walter 11:36
Balzac, Honoré
    Eugenie Granet 5:19
Barnard, A. M. *see* Alcott, Louisa May
Barrie, J. M. 5:6, 99; 6:54; 11:*68*; 12:81
    Peter Pan 11:*68*; 12:81
Bates, Herbert Ernest 5:90; 6:53, *53*, *55*, 58, 60, *67*, 68

art lessons 6:54
as clerk in leather factory 6:54
as junior reporter 6:54
as literary editor of the *Spectator* 6:58
as RAF short-story writer 6:*57*, 58, 68
autobiography 6:56, 59, 66
biography of Edward Garnett 6:59, 66
birth 6:54
career 6:66-68, *66-68*
CBE (Commander of the British Empire) 6:59, *59*
characters 6:64-65, *64-65*
childhood 6:54, 72, 73, *73*, 74, *75*, 76, *76*
children 6:56, 57
death 6:59
description of Rushden, Northamptonshire 6:*54*
essay on Shakespeare 6:54
film adaptations 6:*58*, 59
first novel 6:66
Flying Officer X stories 6:58, 59, 68, *68*
gardening 6:57, *57*
ill health 6:57, 58, 59
key dates 6:55
marriage 6:56
radio plays 6:59
school 6:54
travels abroad 6:56, 58, 59
views on short story 6:66
views on writing 6:67
visits to London 6:56
works in outline 6:69-71, *69-71*
    Across the Bay 6:71, *71*
    Blossoming World, The 6:59
    Breath of Fresh Air, A 6:59
    Charlotte's Row 6:69, *69*
    Colonel Julian 6:71
    Cruise of the Breadwinner, The 6:*68*
    Daffodil Sky, The 6:71
    Darling Buds of May, The 6:59, 68, 69, 70, *70*
    Enchantress, The 6:71
    Fair Stood the Wind for France 6:58, 59, 68, *68*, 69, *69*
    Fallow Land, The 6:58, 66, 67, 73
    House of Women, A 6:76
    Jacaranda Tree, The 6:59, 68
    Love for Lydia 6:59, 60-65, *60-65*, 68, 71, 72, 75, 76
    Mill, The 6:58
    Mrs Eglantine 6:71
    Poacher, The 6:66, 76
    Purple Plain, The 6:*58*, 59, 68, *68*
    Scarlet Sword, The 6:68, 69, 70, *70*
    Seven by Five 6:71, *71*

Sleepless Moon, The 6:6, 7, 8, 19, 21, *21*

Spella Ho 6:58, 76

Triple Echo, The 6:59, 68, 69, 71, *71*

Two Sisters, The 6:55, 56, 66, 67

Vanished World, The 6:59, 72, 73, 76

Voyagers, The 6:56

World in Ripeness, The 6:59

Baudelaire, Charles 2:72; 12:42

Fleurs de Mal, Les 2:72

Beardsley, Aubrey 2:74

Beauchamp, Kathleen Mansfield *see* Mansfield, Katherine

Beaumont, Francis 1:55; 13:51

Beckford, William 12:25

Vathek 12:25, 26, *26*, 27

Beerbohm, Max 2:72

Behn, Aphra 1:52-53, *53*

Oroonoko 1:*53*

Rover, The 1:53

Bell, Clive 5:56; 8:76, 79, 82, *82*, *83*, 96, *96*, 97, *97*, 98, 100

Civilisation 8:99

Bell, Currer, Ellis and Acton 4:10, 11, 35, 46

see also Brontë, Anne, Emily and Charlotte

Belloc, Hilaire 5:*43*

Bennett, Arnold 5:10, 56, 58; 6:9; 8:90; 13:83

Benson, A. C. 5:20

Bentham, Jeremy 9:97

Betjeman, John 3:88; 10:58

Binyon, Laurence 13:92

Blake, William 2:75; 12:*21*, 27; 13:*44-45*, 72, 73, 75, *75*, 76

Prophetic Books 13:72

Sick Rose, The 13:75

Songs of Experience 13:75, *75*

Songs of Innocence 13:75, 76

Bloomsbury group 8:58, 59, 76, 79, 81, 96-100, *96-100*; 9:78-79, *80*; 10:79

Boccaccio, Giovanni 13:8, *11*, 20, *21*

Decameron, The 13:*11*

Boswell, James 1:*83;* 11:*34*

Life of Samuel Johnson, The 11:*34*

Boyle, Robert 10:18

Meditations 10:18

Brecht, Bertolt 5:*100*

Threepenny Opera, The 5:*100*

Brontë, Anne 4:6, *9,* 10, 11, *18*, 24, 28, 29, *29*, 30, 31, *31*, 32, *32*, 33, 34, 35, 42, *42*, *43*, 44-45, *45*, 46, 58

Agnes Grey 4:10, 24, 28, 32, 44, 47, *47*

Gondal chronicles 4:31, 34, 42, *44*, 46

Tenant of Wildfell Hall, The 4:11, 32, 45, *45, 46-47*, 47

This sketch of Haworth parsonage, the home of the Brontë family, was drawn by Elizabeth Gaskell for her Life of Charlotte Brontë.

Brontë, Charlotte 2:20; 4:5, *5, 9;* 8:20; 12:*73*

as governess 4:8, 11, 19, 27, 28, 32, 33

as impoverished gentlewoman 4:24, 52

as teacher 4:8, 9, 27

birth 4:6

career 4:18-21

characters 4:12, 16-17, *16-17*

Constantin Heger and 4:8, 9, *10*, 11, 18

death 4:11, 58

description of 4:6, 7

description of Anne 4:44

Emily and 4:30, 31, 32, 33, 34-35, *35*, 46, 48

first drafts 4:20

heroines 4:18-20, *18-19*

in London 4:21

Jane Eyre preface 4:15

journal 4:8

key dates 4:7

marriage 4:11, 26, 58, 66

marriage proposals 4:8, 11, 25

Mrs Gaskell and 4:58, 59, *59, 67, 69*

natural imagery 4:21

poetry 4:9-10, 22

portrait of Anne 4:*32*

pseudonyms 4:10, 11, 20, 27, 35, *43*

Robert Southey and 4:27

school 4:6-7, *7,* 8, *10, 32*

story-telling 4:7, 18, *18*

views on Sir Walter Scott 4:*35*

views on White family 4:27

views on *Wuthering Heights* 4:39

works in outline 4:22-23, *22-23*

Jane Eyre 4:7, 10, 12-17, *12-17*, 20, *20,* 21, *21,* 22, 23, 25, 26, 28, 69; 12:*73*

Professor, The 4:10, 18, *18*, 22, 26

Shirley 4:19, 20, *20,* 21, *21,* 22, 23, *23*

Villette 4:*10,* 11, 18, *18,* 19, 20, 21, 22, *22,* 26, 27

Brontë, Emily 4:*9,* 29, *29*

as governess 4:33, *34*

as impoverished gentlewoman 4:24

as model for Charlotte's *Shirley* 4:23

as teacher 4:27

birth 4:6, 30, *31*

characters 4:38-39

creation of 'Gondal' 4:42

death 4:11, 35, 42, 45, 58

diaries 4:32, 42

Great Glass Town Confederacy and 4:*42*

in Brussels with Charlotte 4:18

influence of moors 4:45

key dates 4:31

pets 4:32, *33*, 35

physical courage 4:32

poetry 4:9-10, 29, 30, 33, 34, 42, 43, *43,* 44, 46

pseudonym 4:10, 35, *43*

school 4:7, *7,* 8, *10,* 30, 32, *32*

self-criticism 4:32-33

story-telling 4:*18*

temperament 4:30, *30*

views on Sir Walter Scott 4:*35*

visions 4:30, 43

writing of *Wuthering Heights* 4:10

Yorkshire people and 4:48, 50, 52

Complete Poems 4:46

Gondal chronicles 4:31, 34, 42, *44,* 46

INDEX OF WRITERS

Mary Evans Picture Library

The Way of All Flesh *describes Samuel Butler's life through that of his hero, Ernest Pontifex. Here, the servant Ellen pawns Ernest's watch, and his parents suspect the worst . . .*

To Imagination 4:43
Wuthering Heights 4:10, 30, 34, *34-35*, 35, 36-41, *36-41*, 43, 46, 48, 50, 52
Brooke, Rupert Chawner 13:77, *78*, 82, 87
   birth 13:78
   Cathleen Nesbitt and 13:79
   death 13:78, 79, *79*, 86
   Royal Navy commission 13:79
   sonnets 13:78
      Grantchester 13:78
      Jealousy 13:78
      1914 Sonnets 13:79, 86
      Peace 13:79, 86
      Soldier, The 13:79, 86
      Tiare Tahiti 13:79
Browning, Elizabeth Barrett 8:82, 91; 12:37, 43
Browning, Robert 6:90
Bulwer-Lytton, Edward 3:13; 12:34, 52, 58
   Not so Bad as We Seem 12:58
   Strange Story, A 12:52
Bunyan, John 1:46, 57, *57*, 66, 76; 8:33, 39; 10:21
   baptism 1:58, *59*
   birth 1:58, *58*
   career 1:70-73, *70-73*
   characters 1:68-69, *68-69*
   childhood 1:59, *60*, 67
   children 1:61, *61*, 62
   death 1:63, *63*
   imprisonment 1:*60, 61*, 62, *62*, 63, 64, 67, 70, *71*, 74
   key dates 1:59
   marriages 1:60, *61, 62*
   military service 1:60, *71*
   religious beliefs, preaching 1:59, 60, *60*, 61, 62, *62*, 63, 64, 67, 70, 71, 80
   school 1:58

works in outline 1:74-75, *74-75*
   Divine Emblems 1:72
   Grace Abounding to the Chief of Sinners 1:46, 62, 70, 74, 75, *75*
   Holy War, The 1:63, 70, 74, *74-75*
   Life and Death of Mr Badman, The 1:63, 70, 74, *74*
   Pilgrim's Progress, The 1:57, 58, 62, 63, 64-69, *64-69*, 70, *70-71*, 72, *72*, 73, *73*, 74; 8:33, *33*
   Pilgrim's Progress, The, Part II 1:70, 73, 74, 75, *75*
Burgess, Anthony 10:87
   Clockwork Orange, A 10:87
Burns, Robert 11:34, *34*
Burroughs, Edgar Rice 5:52, *52*
   Tarzan 5:52
Butler, Samuel 2:77, *77, 78, 90, 93*; 5:48
   as New Zealand sheep farmer 2:79, 80, *80*
   biography of grandfather 2:*93*
   birth 2:78
   Cambridge and 2:79, *79*
   career 2:90-93
   characters 2:88-89
   childhood 2:78
   death 2:83, 87
   Eliza Savage and 2:80, 81, *81*, 83, 91, 93
   Italy and 2:78, 81, *81*, 83
   key dates 2:79
   paintings 2:78-79, *80, 81, 83, 90-91, 92*
   Pauli and 2:79-80, 81, *81*, 83
   refusal to be ordained 2:79
   relations with father 2:78, 79, 81, 82, 87
   school 2:78-79
   self-portrait 2:83
      Alps and Sanctuaries 2:92

Authoress of the Odyssey, The 2:91, *91*, 95, *95*
Erewhon 2:80, 90, *92*, 94, *94*, 5:48
Erewhon Revisited 2:93, 94, *94*
Fair Haven, The 2:80, 90, 91, *91*, 94
First Year in the Canterbury Settlement, A 2:80
Life and Habit 2:94, 95
Life and Letters of Dr Samuel Butler, The 2:93
Notebooks 2:92
Shakespeare's Sonnets, Reconsidered 2:82-83, 90
Way of All Flesh, The 2:78, 80, 81, 82, 83, 84-89, *84-89*, 93, 96
Byron, George Gordon, Lord 4:46; 11:43; 12:8, 9, 10, 11, 13, 19, *19, 20, 20*, 22, 26, 27, *44*; 13:53, *53, 72*, 73, 76
   birth 13:58
   daughter 13:59
   death 13:59, *59*
   education 13:58
   Greece and 13:58, 59, *59*
   key dates 13:73
   lameness 13:58, *59*
   love affairs 13:58, *58*, 60
   marriage 13:59
   selected poems 13:64, 67-68, *67-68*
   Shelley and 13:59, 61
   views on Wordsworth 13:*54*, 55
      Childe Harold's Pilgrimage 13:58, *68*, 76
      Corsair, The 13:59
      Don Juan 13:59, 64, 65, 67-68, *67, 68*, 76
      English Bards and Scotch Reviewers 13:58
      Giaour, The 13:59
Byron, H. J. 2:86
   The Corsican Brothers 2:86

C

Carlyle, Thomas 2:90; 3:16, 17, 18, 24; 4:58, 67, 73, 75, 81, 98; 8:*28*; 11:29; 12:52
   French Revolution, The 3:17, 18
Carroll, Lewis (Charles Lutwidge Dodgson) 10:29, *29*, 36, 38, 39, *39*
   as ordained deacon 10:33
   as Oxford don 10:30, 31, 32, *35*
   birth 10:30, *30*
   career 10:42-45, *42-45*
   characters 10:40-41, *40-41*

child-friends 10:31, 33, 35, 42, *42,* 43, 52
childhood 10:30
choice of pseudonym 10:34, 42
death 10:35
death of mother 10:31
early writings 10:33, 42
first-class degree in Mathematics 10:31
illustrations for *Alice in Wonderland* 10:*43*
key dates 10:30
photography 10:32, *32,* 33, *34-35, 48, 48-49, 49,* 50
school 10:30, *30-31,* 31
stammer 10:31, *37*
synovitis 10:35
trip to Russia 10:32
views on Great Exhibition 10:*33*
views on professional writers 10:44
works in outline 46-47, *46-47*
  Alice in Wonderland 10:30, *30-31,* 32, 33, *33,* 34, 36-41, *36-41,* 43, *43,* 44, *44,* 45, *45,* 46, 48, *49,* 52, *82*
  Euclid and his Rivals 10:42
  Hiawatha's Photographing 10:50
  How doth the little crocodile 10:45
  Hunting of the Snark, The 10:35, 39, 43, 44, 46, *46-47,* 47
  Jabberwocky 10:34, 38, *38,* 39, 43
  Morning Clouds 10:*32*
  Phantasmagoria 10:46, 47, *47*
  Pillow Problems 10:33, 46
  Sylvie and Bruno 10:44, 45, 46, *46*
  Tangled Tale, A 10:45, 46, *46*
  Useful and Instructive Poetry 10:42
  Walrus and the Carpenter, The 10:37, 41, *41,* 43
  You are old, Father William 10:45
Cervantes, Miguel de 1:64, 86, 96; 7:*19;* 11:49
  Don Quixote 1:64, 96; 7:*19;* 11:49
Chandler, Raymond 7:92
Chaucer, Geoffrey 1:96; 13:5, *5,* 7, *9,* 12, *12,* 13, 16, 18, 26
  as Clerk of the Works 13:10, *10*
  as Controller of Wool Customs 13:*8,* 9
  as Justice of the Peace 13:10
  as linguist 13:7, *7*
  as Member of Parliament 13:10
  attacks on, robbing of 13:10, *10*
  birth 13:6
  capture by French 13:6
  career 13:20-22
  characters 13:16, *16-17*
  death 13:*10,* 11, *11*
  diplomatic missions 13:7, 8, 9

education 13:6, 7, *7,* 8
illuminated manuscript 13:*22*
John of Gaunt and 13:7, *9*
key dates 13:6
rape charge against 13:9-10
works in outline 13:23, *23*
  Book of the Duchess, The 13:7, 20
  Canterbury Tales, The 13:6, 10, 11, 12-19, *12-19,* 20, 22, *22,* 23, 27
  House of Fame, The 13:9, 20
  Legend of Good Women 13:20
  Parliament of Fowls, The 13:20, 22, 23, *23*
  Troilus and Criseyde 13:9, *9,* 20, *21,* 22, 23, *23*
Chekhov, Anton 6:66, *67;* 8:56, 59, 67, *67*
  Misery 8:67
Chesney, Sir George 5:*39*
  Battle of Dorking, The 5:*39*
Chesterton, G. K. 4:46; 5:*43*
Clark, Sir Kenneth 10:81

Cockburn, Claude 6:78
Coleridge, Samuel Taylor 1:68, 95; 12:*43,* 45, 46, *50,* 51; 13:53, *53,* 72
birth 13:56
Byron's views on 13:68
children 13:57
death 13:57
education 13:56
key dates 13:73
marriage 13:56, *57*
opium addiction 13:57, 73
Robert Southey and 13:56, *56*
selected poems 13:64, 66-67, *66-67*
views on poetry 13:76
Wordsworth and 13:54, *54, 55,* 56, 57, *57*
  Biographia Literaria 13:57, 76
  Christabel 13:66, *67,* 73
  Dejection: An Ode 13:57
  Friend, The 13:57
  Kubla Khan 13:57, 66, *66-67,* 73
  Lyrical Ballads 13:54, 57, 66, 76

The trial of the knave of hearts is the climax of Alice in Wonderland. *Lewis Carroll presents a trial of arbitrary decisions and interruptions that outrages Alice's faith in British justice.*

Rime of the Ancient Mariner
12:46; 13:57, 64, 66-67, *66*, 73,
76

Collier, Jeremy 1:56, *56*
   *Short View of the Immorality and
   Profaneness of the English Stage,
   A* 1:56, *56*

Collins, Wilkie 2:34, 37; 3:9, *9*, 13,
   15, 16, *16*; 4:80; 12:53, *53, 54,
   55, 56,* 60, *61,* 63, 72, 73, 75
   American lecture tour 12:59, *59*
   biography of father 12:*54*, 55
   birth 12:54
   burial 12:59, *59*
   career 12:66-69
   characters 12:62, 64-65, *64-65*, 66,
   69
   children 12:54, 58
   death 12:59
   Dickens and 12:56, 57, *57*, 58, *58*,
   59, *66*, 67, 68, *69*, 71
   ill health 12:58-59
   job at Antrobus & Co. 12:54, 55
   key dates 12:55
   legal training 12:55, *55, 67,* 68
   school 12:54
   short stories 12:55, 56, 57, 59, 70
   views on reading public 12:67
   wives, common-law 12:54, 56,
   57, 58
     After Dark 12:70
     Antonina 12:55, 56
     Armadale 12:69, 70, 71, *71*
     Basil 12:56
     Court Duel, A 12:56
     Dream-Woman, The 12:70,
     70-71
     Fallen Leaves, The 12:58
     Frozen Deep, The 12:57, *58, 66,*
     70, 71, *71*
     Hide and Seek 12:67
     How I Write My Books 12:68
     Last Stagecoachman, The 12:55
     Memoir 12:55
     Moonstone, The 12:59, 66, 67,
     68, 69, 70, *70*
     Queen of Hearts, The 12:57, 70
     Rambles Beyond Railways 12:56
     Rogue's Life, A 12:54
     *Tales of Terror and the
     Supernatural* 12:70, 70-71
     Woman in White, The 3:9, *9*, 13;
     12:*55*, 56, *56*, 60-65, *60-65*,
     66, *66*, 67, 68, 70, 72, 75, 76

Comte, Auguste 4:100

Congreve, William 1:55, *55*, 56
     Love for Love 1:*55*
     Way of the World 1:55, *55*

Conrad, Joseph 2:75; 5:9, *11*, 32,
   39, 42, 87, 90, 91, *91*; 6:66;
   8:18; 9:48, 53, *53, 55,* 68
   arrival in England 9:56
   birth 9:54, *54*
   career 9:66-68

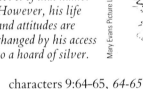

**Nostromo is the
incorruptible hero**
*of Joseph Conrad's
novel of that name.
However, his life
and attitudes are
changed by his access
to a hoard of silver.*

Mary Evans Picture Library

   characters 9:64-65, *64-65*
   children 9:58, *59*
   Civil Pension 9:58
   Congo and 9:72, 76
   death 9:59
   design of dust covers 9:*68*
   epitaph 9:59
   family 9:54
   Ford Madox Ford and 9:*67*
   gambling 9:56
   gun-running 9:54, 57
   ill health 9:55, 56, 57, 58, 59
   key dates 9:55
   magazine writing 9:67
   marriage 9:57
   naturalization as British citizen
     9:56
   naval Master's certificate 9:56, *57*
   nervous breakdown 9:58
   philosophy 9:68
   rejection of knighthood 9:59
   short stories 9:58
   smuggling 9:56, 57
   suicide attempt 9:54, *55*, 56
   supervision of apprentices 9:*66*
   trip to America 9:59
   views on fiction 9:62
   views on writing 9:66, 67, 68
   views on character 'Willems' 9:69

   works in outline 9:69-71
   youth 9:54-55
     Heart of Darkness 5:39; 9:57, 58,
     68, 69, 70, 72, 75
     Inheritors, The 9:67
     Lord Jim 9:58, 60-65, *60-65*, 69,
     72, 76
     Mirror of the Sea, The 9:57
     Nigger of the 'Narcissus', The
     9:58, 69
     Nostromo 9:58, 68, 69, 70, 76
     Outcast of the Islands, An 9:57,
     69
     Rescue, The 9:57, 58, 59, 67
     Romance 9:67
     Secret Agent, The 5:42; 9:58,
     67-68, 69, 71
     Sisters, The 9:57
     Typhoon 9:69
     Under Western Eyes 9:68, 69,
     71
     Victory 9:67
     Youth 9:58, 69

Coppard, A. E. 6:59
Coward, Noel 5:58
Cowper, William 8:7, 28
     Retirement 8:28
Crabbe, George 12:24
Cyrano de Bergerac 5:*48*, 49, 50

D

Dahl, Roald 7:82
Dampier, William 10:15; 11:25
  Voyage Round the World, A 10:15
Dante, Alighieri 5:49; 13:8, *11*, 20, *20*
  Divine Comedy 13:8, *20*
  Inferno 5:49
Darwin, Charles 2:79, 81, 83, 90, *90*, 95, 4:*98*, 100, *100*; 9:5, *5*, *6*; 10:78, *79*; 12:49
  at Cambridge 9:6
  at Edinburgh University 9:6
  birth 9:6
  childhood 9:6
  children 9:8
  death 9:10
  Down House and 9:9, *10*
  funeral 9:10
  ill health 9:8, *10*
  initiation at equator 9:*13*
  key dates 9:6
  London flat 9:8
  naturalists and 9:24, 27
  return to England 9:15
  scientific instrument 9:*15*
  theory of evolution 9:8, 13, 15, *20*, 22, *22*, 28
  theory of sexual selection 9:23, *23*
  works in outline 9:22-23
    Descent of Man, The 9:10, *22*, *23*, 27
    Expression of Emotions in Man and Animals, The 9:22
    Origin of Species, The 4:100, *100*; 9:9, 10, *11*, 15, 22, 23, 27, 28
    Voyage of the 'Beagle', The 9:12-15
Darwin, Erasmus 9:*6*; 12:13
  Zoonomia 9:*6*
Davenant, Sir William 1:52, 55, 56
  Siege of Rhodes 1:52, 56
Day Lewis, Cecil 13:91
De Quincy, Thomas 13:55, 73
  Confessions of an English Opium Eater 13:73
  Recollections of the Lake Poets 13:55
Defoe, Daniel 1:39, 96; 5:49; 9:48; 11:5, *5*, 12, 15, 24, 25, *25*, *26*, 56; 12:74
  as government propagandist 11:6, 9, *9*, 11, 18
  as secret agent 11:6, 11
  birth 11:6, *6*, 7, 11, *11*
  business ventures 11:8, *20*
  career 11:18-20, *18-20*
  characters 11:16-17, *16-17*

  childhood 11:6, *6-7*, 7
  children 11:8
  death 11:11, *11*
  handwriting 11:*20*
  imprisonment 11:10, *10*, 11, *11*
  key dates 11:7
  kidnapping by Algerian pirates 11:8
  marriage 11:8, *8*
  Monmouth's Rebellion and 11:8-9, *8*
  pillorying 11:11, *11*, 18-19
  school 11:7
  works in outline 11:21-23, *21-23*
    Captain Singleton 11:21, *21*, 24
    Colonel Jack 11:11
    Danger of the Protestant Religion Consider'd, The 11:9
    General History of the Robberies . . . of the Most Notorious Pirates, A 11:19, 24, *25*
    Hymn to the Pillory, A 11:11, *19*
    Journal of the Plague Year 11:11, *18-19*, 19, 21, 22, *22-23*
    King of Pirates, The 11:19, 24, 27
    Memoirs of a Cavalier 11:19, 20, 21, *21*
    Moll Flanders 11:11, 20, 21, 22, *22*
    Robinson Crusoe 5:49; 9:48; 11:5, 11,12-17, *12–17*, *20*, 21, 24; 12:74
    Roxana, or the Fortunate Mistress 11:19, 20, 21, 23, *23*
    Shortest Way with the Dissenters, The 11:10, 11, *18*
    Tour Through the Whole Island of Great Britain, A 11:11, 21, 22, *22-23*
    True-Born Englishman 11:18, *19*
    Worlds in the Moon 5:49
Dickens, Charles 1:94; 2:11, 18, 22, 30, 31, 34, 37, 43, 63; 3:5, *5*, *8-9*, *10*, *12*, *14*, *16*, *24-25*, 70; 4:58, 60, 63, 67, 68; 5:18, 43, 49; 9:24; 11:44, 46; 12:28, 34, 53, 56, 57, *57*, 58, *58*, 59, 62, *66*, 67, *67*
  A Tale of Two Cities and 3:20, 21, 30
  as actor 3:12, 14-15, *16*
  as social reformer 3:8, 13, 40, 41, *41*, 42, *42*, 47, 48
  birth 3:6
  burial in Westminster Abbey 3:11, *11*, 17
  career 3:24–26, *24-26*, 40-42, *40-42*
  characters 3:25–26, 38–39, *38–39*
  childhood 3:6, 7
  children 3:*8-9*, 10, *14*, 15, 16, 17
  contemporary views on 3:5, 8, 11, *13*, 15, 26, 42

  death 3:11, 16, 17, 42
  Ellen Ternan and 3:11, *11*, 15, 16, *16*
  family imprisonment for debt 3:7, 7, 8
  ill health 3:11, 16, 17, *17*, 42, *42*
  job at Warren's Blacking Factory 3:7-8, 7
  jobs as solicitors' office boy 3:8, 9
  key dates 3:7
  London and 3:50, *50*
  love of theatre 3:14, 49, 50
  Maria Beadnell and 3:9, *9*
  marriage 3:8, *9*, 10, 12, *13*
  Mary Hogarth and 3:*8*, 10-11
  Phiz and 3:41
  public reading tours 3:11, 16, 17, *17*, 26, *26*
  relationship with readers 3:26
  school 3:7, 8
  self-discipline 3:25
  self-education 3:9
  separation from Catherine 3:11, *11*, 15, 16, 17
  status as writer 3:11, 24
  use of speech patterns 3:26
  views on *Great Expectations* 3:36, 37
  views on Newgate Prison 3:*50*
  views on own art 3:40
  views on Parliament 3:9, 40
  Wilkie Collins and 3:9, *9*, 15
  works in outline 3:27-29, *27-29*, 43-45, *43-45*
    Battle of Life, The 3:27
    Bleak House 3:15, *15*, 26, 40-41, 43, 44, *44*, 50; 12:67, 97
    Child's History of England, A 3:14; 12:67
    Chimes, The 3:16, 24, 26, 27, 50
    Christmas Carol, A 3:11, 24, *24*, 27, *27*
    Cricket on the Hearth, The 3:27
    David Copperfield 2:22; 3:6, 8, *12*, *13*, 15, *24*, 26, 41, 43, *43*, 49, 50; 12:69
    Dinner at Poplar Walk, A 3:10
    Dombey and Son (Dealings with the Firm of Dombey and Son) 3:16, 24, 27, 29, *29*
    Dorsetshire Labourer, The 3:94, 96
    Frozen Deep, The 12:57, *58*, *66*, 70, 71, *71*
    George Silverman's Explanation 3:26
    Great Expectations 3:6, 7, 9, *25*, 26, 34-39, *34-39*, 43, 46, 47, *50*
    Hard Times 3:13, 26, 41-42, 43, 44, *44*
    Haunted Man, The 3:27
    Little Dorrit 3:14, 40, 42, 43, 45, *45*
    Mystery of Edwin Drood, The 2:63; 3:11, 17, 26, 43, 45, *45*, 48

Nicholas Nickleby 3:8, 26, 27, 29, *29*
Night Scene in London, A 3:47
Old Curiosity Shop, The 3:24, 27, *28-29*, *29*
Oliver Twist 3:8, 26, *26*, 27, 28, *28*, 46, 47, 49
Our Mutual Friend 3:40, 43, 45, *45*
Pickwick Papers, The 3:8, 10, *12*, 26, 27, 28, *28*, 48, 49, 50
Sketches by Boz 3:10
Tale of Two Cities, A 3:13, 17, 18–23, *18–23*, 30, 42, 43; 12:71
Trial from Pickwick 3:16
Diderot, Dennis 3:31
Disraeli, Benjamin 4:48; 11:82
Dodgson, Charles Lutwidge *see* Carroll, Lewis
Doyle, Arthur Conan, Sir 5:49; 6:54; 11:52; 12:47, 77, *77*, 98
  as Parliamentary candidate 12:82
  as sportsman 12:81, *81*
  birth 12:78
  Boer War and 12:81-82, *82*
  career 12:90-92, *90-92*
  Casement and 12:83, *83*
  characters 12:88-89, *88-89*, 92
  childhood 12:78, *78*
  children 12:80, 81, *81*, 83
  death 12:83
  key dates 12:79
  knighthood 12:82
  lecture tours 12:83
  marriages 12:80, *80*, 81, *81*, 82
  medical training 12:78, *78*, 80, *80*, 91
  school 12:78
  spiritualism and 12:82, *82*, 83, *83*
  works in outline 12:93-95, *93-95*
  World War I and 12:82-83, *83*
    Adventures of Brigadier Gerard, The 12:92
    Adventures of Sherlock Holmes, The 12:84-89, *84-89*
    Blue Carbuncle, The 12:86-87, 88, 89, *89*
    Coming of the Fairies, The 12:82
    Crime of the Congo, The 12:82
    Empty House, The 12:82, 92
    Exploits of Brigadier Gerard, The 12:81, 92, 95, *95*
    Final Problem, The 12:81, 93, *93*
    Great Boer War, The 12:82
    Great Shadow, The 12:92
    Hound of Baskervilles, The 12:92, 94, *94*
    Lost World, The 5:59; 12:92, 95, *95*
    Man with the Twisted Lip, The 12:85-86, *85*, 88, 89, *89*
    Maracot Deep, The 12:92
    Memoirs of Sherlock Holmes, The 12:93, *93*
    Micah Clarke 12:80
    Red-headed League, The 12:84
    Refugees, The 12:92
    Rodney Stone 12:94, *94*
    Scandal in Bohemia 12:84
    Sign of Four, The 12:80
    Sir Nigel 12:*92*
    Speckled Band, The 12:84-85, *85*, 88, *88*
    Study in Scarlet, A 12:80, 84, *90*, 96
    To Arms 12:82
    War in South Africa, The 12:82
    Waterloo 12:82
    White Company, The 12:80, 92, *92*, 94, *94*
Drayton, Michael 1:13; 13:48, 52
Dryden, John 1:*53*, 54, 55, 56, *56*; 10:7, 22; 11:42
Durning-Lawrence, Sir Edwin 13:31
    Bacon is Shakespeare 13:31

E

Edel, Leon 5:6
Eliot, George 2:43; 4:77, *77*, *79*; 5:6; 11:29, 44; 12:50
  birth 4:78, *78*
  career 4:90-92
  characters 4:86, 87, 88-89, *88-89*, 90, *90*, 92, *92*
  Charles Darwin and 4:*98*, 100
  childhood 4:*81*, 84, *90*
  death 4:83
  George Combe and 4:80
  George Henry Lewes and 4:78, *80*, 81, 82, *82*, 83, 90, 92, 99
  John Chapman and 4:80, 81
  key dates 4:79
  marriage to John Cross 4:83
  poetry 4:*80*, 92, 97
  pseudonym 4:78, 82-83
  religion and 4:79, *79*, 90, 96, 98, 99, 100
  research 4:82, *82*, 92
  school 4:78, *79*
  translations 4:80, 82
  travels 4:80, *81*, 83, 92
  views on art 4:90
    Adam Bede 4:78, *81*, 82, 83, 90, *90*, 91, *91*, 93, *93*
    Amos Barton 4:81
    Daniel Deronda 4:83, 92, *92*, 95, *95*
    Felix Holt, the Radical 4:91, 92, 93, 94, *94-95*
    Impressions of Theophrastus Such 4:83
    Middlemarch 4:78, 83, 90, 91, *91*, 92, 93, 94, *94*, 97
    Mill on the Floss, The 4:80, 82, 83, 84-89, *84-89*, 90, 91, 93, 96, 97, 100
    Romola 4:90, 92, 93, *93*

Holmes and Watson, *Conan Doyle's best-known creations, ponder the significance of a lost hat.*

Mansell Collection

Scenes of Clerical Life 4:*81*, 82, 90, *90*
Silas Marner 4:91, 92, 93, 95, *95*
Spanish Gypsy, The 4:92
Eliot, T. S. 5:28, *28*; 7:43; 8:57, 80, *91*; 12:66, 70
  Four Quartets, The 5:28
  Wasteland, The 5:28
Ellis, Haverlock 8:76
Emerson, Ralph Waldo 4:79, *80*; 7:18; 8:30, *32*, 35, 45
Engels, Friedrich 4:76
Etherege, Sir George 1:*53*, 54, 55
  Man of Mode 1:55
Evans, Mary Ann/Marian see Eliot, George
Evelyn, John 1:*34*, 38, 39, 43, *49*

F

Farquhar, George 1:55, 56
Fielding, Henry 1:81, *81*, 90, 91, *102, 103, 104*
  as journalist 1:82, *85*, 86, *97*
  as lawyer 1:82, *85*, 86
  as magistrate 1:87, 100, 102, 104
  attempted abduction of Sarah Andrew 1:83
  birth 1:82, *82*
  career 1:94-97, *94-97*
  characters 1:92-93, *92-93*
  childhood 1:82
  children 1:85, 87
  death 1:87, *87*
  death of Charlotte and 1:86, *86*
  dedication of *Tom Jones* 1:89-90, 95
  Dr Johnson's views on 1:87, 88
  education 1:*82-83*, 83, 84
  first play 1:*83*, 84
  formation of Bow Street Runners 1:102
  key dates 1:83
  marriages 1:85, *85*, 86-87, *94*
  views on gin-drinking 1:101-102
  works in outline 1:98-99, *98-99*
    Amelia 1:85, 87, 97, 99, *99*
    Author's Farce, The 1:84
    Grub-Street Opera, The 1:84
    Historical Register for the Year 1736, The 1:85, 94
    Jonathan Wild 1:86, 97, 98, *98*
    Joseph Andrews 1:86, 95, *95*, 96, *96-97*, 97, 98, *98*
    Journal of a Voyage to Lisbon, The 1:97, 99, *99*
    Journal from This World to the Next, A 1:96, 98, *98*
    Life and Death of Tom Thumb the Great, The 1:84, *84*, 94, *96*

Love in Several Masques 1:84
Miscellanies 1:96, 98
Modern Husband, The 1:84
Pasquin 1:85, 94
Proposal for Making an effectual Provision for the Poor, A 1:100
Shamela (An Apology for the Life of Mrs Shamela Andrews) 1:86, .95, *95*, 96
  Tom Jones 1:*84*, 85, 87, 88-93, *88-93*, *94*, 95, 97, 102, 104
  Tumble-Down Dick 1:85
  Universal Gallant, The 1:85
Fitzgerald, Francis Scott Key 7:29, *29*, 36, 47, *47*, 51, 52
  as army second lieutenant 7:31
  at Princeton 7:30, 31, *31, 42*
  birth 7:30
  career 7:42-44, *42-44*
  characters 7:40-41, *40-41*
  childhood 7:30, *30*
  death 7:33, 35
  debts 7:35
  drinking/alcoholism 7:32, 34, 35, 42, 48
  heart attacks 7:35, 44
  Hemingway and 7:*32*, 34, 35, 82, 90
  in Europe 7:33, 34, *34*
  in Hollywood 7:34, 35, *35, 44*
  key dates 7:31
  magazine stories/essays 7:32, 35, 42, *42*, 44
  marriage 7:32
  quotations 7:30, 31, 32, *32*, 33, 34, 35, 42, 43, 44, 46, 48
  Ring Lardner's description of 7:33
  school 7:30, *31*
  Sheila Graham and 7:35, *35*, 44
  tuberculosis 7:35
  works in outline 7:45-47, *45-47*
    Absolution 7:46
    Afternoon of an Author 7:44
    All the Sad Young Men 7:43, 45, 46, *46*
    Beautiful and Damned, The 7:33, 43, 45, *45*
    Crack-Up, The 7:35, 44, 45, 47
    Diamond as Big as the Ritz, The 7:44, 46
    Early Success 7:47
    Echoes of the Jazz Age 7:47
    Flappers and Philosophers 7:42, 43
    Great Gatsby, The 7:33, 34, 36-41, *36-41*, 43, 44, 45, 46, 48, 51
    Last Tycoon, The 7:35, 44, 45, 47, *47*
    Lees of Happiness 7:46
    May Day 7:44, 46
    My Lost City 7:47
    Romantic Egotist, The 7:31

Illustrated London News and Picture Library

F. Scott Fitzgerald's novels capture the spirit of the Jazz Age and bring to life its hedonistic life style and carefree young 'flappers'.

    Sensible Thing, The 7:46, *46*
    Sleeping and Waking 7:47
    Tales of the Jazz Age 7:42, 45, 46, *46*
    Tender is the Night 7:35, 44, 45, *46-47*, 47
    This Side of Paradise 7:30, 31, 32, 42, 45, *45*, 47
    Three Comrades, The (as co-writer) 7:35, *55*
Fitzgerald, Zelda Sayre 7:31, 32, *32*, 33, *33*, 34, 35, 42, 43, 45, 46, 47, *47*, 48
  Save Me the Waltz 7:35
Flaubert, Gustave 5:6, 7, *7, 9*
Fletcher, John 1:22, 55
  Cardenio (co-written with Shakespeare) 1:22
  Henry VIII (co-written with Shakespeare) 1:22
  Two Noble Kinsmen, The (co-written with Shakespeare) 1:22
Ford, Ford Madox 2:75; 5:9, *32*; 6:8; 9:58, 67, *67*
  Inheritors, The 9:67
  Romance 9:67
Forster, Edward Morgan 2:87; 3:62; 5:40; 6:9, 20; 8:91; 9:77, *77*; 11:87
  as godfather to Robert Morgan Buckingham 9:82

BBC Hulton Picture Library

The India described by E. M. Forster was in some part created by the railway, which helped the Raj penetrate the whole country.

birth 9:78
Cambridge and 9:78, 79, 83, *83*
career 9:90–92
characters 9:88–89, *88-89*
childhood 9:78
death 9:83
Egypt and 9:81, 82
essays, articles, biographies 9:83, *91, 92, 93*
Germany and 9:80
hatred of Nazism and Stalinism 9:83
honours 9:83, *83*
India and 9:81, *81,* 82, 83, 90, 92, *92,* 98, 100
Italy and 9:80, *80*
key dates 9:78
lectures 9:80
literary symbols 9:*90*
Maharajah of Dewas State Senior and 9:81, 82, *82,* 98
PEN and 9:*92*
public school 9:78
United States and 9:83
views on end of career 9:92
views on friendship 9:90
views on writing 9:91
works in outline 9:93–95, *93-95*
  Hill of Devi, The 9:*92*
  Howards End 9:78, 79, 81, 90, 91, 92, 93, 94, *94*
  Longest Journey, The 9:90, 91, 93, *93*
  Maurice 9:82, 90, 91, 92, 93, 95
  Passage to India, A 9:81, 82, 83, 84-89, *84-89,* 91, 92, 93, *96,* 100; 11:87
  Pharos and Pharillon 9:93
  Road from Colonus, The 9:91, 94
  Rock, The 9:91
  Room with a View, A 9:81, 90, 91, 93, 95, *95*
  Story of a Panic, The 9:80, 91, 94

Where Angels Fear to Tread 9:80, *80,* 90, 91, 93, *93*
Fry, Roger 8:98, *98,* 99; 9:78-79
  Vision and Design 8:99
Fuller, Thomas 1:34
  Worthies 1:34

G

Galsworthy, John 5:77, 77, *90;* 6:66; 8:90; 9:*56-57,* 68
affair with Margaret Morris 5:81, *81,* 82
as barrister 2:70, *91*
as president of PEN 5:83, *83*
as social reformer 5:81, 92, 99, *99,* 100
birth 5:78
career 5:90–93, *90-93*
D. H. Lawrence's views on 5:86
death 5:83
honours 5:82, 83
key dates 5:78
marriage 5:80
Nobel Prize 5:83, 91
nom de plume 5:90
school 5:78-79, *79*
Theatre of Ideas and 5:96, 97, 98, *98,* 99, *99, 100*
university 5:79, *80*
views on *The Forstye Saga* 5:93
World War I and 5:82, *82,* 83, 92
writing apprenticeship 5:80
  Country House, The 5:90, 92
  Dark Flower, The 5:82
  End of the Chapter 5:93
  Forsyte Saga, The 5:78, 80, 82, 84–89, *84-89,* 90, *90,* 91, 92, *92,* 93, 94
  Fraternity 5:92
  From the Four Winds 5:90
  In Chancery 5:82, 84, 85

Indian Summer of a Forsyte 5:92
Island Pharisees, The 5:90, 94, *94*
Justice 5:81, *91,* 92, 94, 95, *95, 99,* 100
Justification of the Censorship of Plays, A 5:99
Little Dream, The 5:81
Loyalties 5:94, 95, *95*
Man of Property, The 5:80, 84, 86, 87, 90, 91, 92, 94
Modern Comedy, A 5:92, 93, 94, *94-95*
On Forsyte 'Change 5:93
Patrician, The 5:82
Pigeon, The 5:82
Salvation of Swithin Forsyte, The 5:90, *91*
Silver Box, The 5:80, 92, 94, 96, 98, *99*
Silver Spoon, The 5:94
Strife 5:92, *92-93,* 94, 99
Swan Song 5:94
To Let 5:82, 84
White Monkey, The 5:94, *94-95*
Gaskell, Elizabeth 2:100; 3:13; 4:53, *53*
birth 4:54, *54-55*
characters 4:64–65, *64-65*
charity work 4:56, *57,* 59, 67, 68, 73, 74
Charles Dickens and 4:58, 67–68, *68*
Charles Eliot Norton and 4:59, *59*
Charlotte Brontë and 4:58, 59, *59,* 67
childhood 4:54, 72
children 4:56, *57,* 59, *59,* 66, *66*
death 4:59, *59,* 68
Florence Nightingale and 4:58, 59
key dates 4:54
marriage 4:56, *56*
religion 4:54, 55, 66
school 4:55
short stories 4:57, 67
sketch of Haworth 4:67
travels 4:59, *59*
views on class divisions 4:67, 68

views on *Cranford* 4:60
views on literary fame 4:66
Wives and Daughters an unfinished
   masterpiece 4:71
works in outline 4:69-71, *69-71*
writing career 4:56, 57, 62, 66-68,
   72
   Cousin Phillis 4:69, 71, *71*
   Cranford 4:*55*, 57, 58, 60-65,
    60-65, 67, *67*, 69, 72
   Dark Night's Work, A 4:70
   Ghost in the Garden Room, The
    4:70
   Grey Woman, The 4:70
   Life of Charlotte Brontë, The
    4:11, 58-59, *59*, 67, 69
   Lizzie Leigh 4:67
   Lois the Witch 4:70
   Mary Barton 4:*56*, 57, *57*, 66,
    67, 68, 69, *69*, 72, 76
   Mrs Gaskell's Tales of Mystery
    and Horror 4:69, 70, *70*
   North and South 4:58, 59, 68, 69,
    70, *70*
   Old Nurse's Story, The 4:70
   Ruth 4:67, 68, 69
   Sylvia's Lovers 4:57, 59, *68*, 69,
    70-71, *70-71*
   Wives and Daughters 4:59, 69, 71
Gautier, Theophile 2:72, 73, 75
   Mademoiselle de Maupin 2:72
Gay, John 1:84; 10:11
   Beggar's Opera, The 1:84; 10:11,
    11
Gissing, George 5:32
Godwin, William 12:6, 7, *7*, 9, 10,
   18, 19, 20; 13:60
   Enquiry Concerning Political
    Justice, An 12:7
Goethe, Johann Wolfgang von 2:7
Goldsmith, Oliver 1:*83*
Gosse, Edmund 2:74; 3:59; 5:*11*
Grant, Ulysses S. 7:9
   Memoirs 7:9
Granville-Barker, Harley 5:96, 97,
   97, 98, *98*, 99, 100
   Waste 5:99
Graves, Robert von Ranke 3:88;
   6:29, *29*, 36, *43*, 44, 52; 13:80,
   83, 91
   as 'adopted' son of Deya,
    Mallorca 6:*35*
   as Professor of Poetry at Oxford
    University 6:35
   Beryl Hodge and 6:34, *34*, 35
   birth 6:30
   career 6:42-44, *42-44*
   characters 6:40-41, *40-41*
   childhood 6:30, *30*, 31
   children 6:32, 33, 34, *34*
   death 6:35
   decline of CBE 6:35
   enlistment in British army 6:31
   heart problem 6:31

   in Cairo 6:*32*, 33
   key dates 6:31
   marriage to Nancy Nicholson
    6:31, *32*
   poetry 6:32, 33, 34, *34*, 35, 42, 43,
    44, 45
   premature obituary 6:31
   printing press 6:34, *42*
   relationship with Laura Riding
    6:33, 34, *34, 42*
   school 6:*30*, 31
   'shamming' of insanity 6:31
   siblings 6:*30*
   Siegfried Sassoon and 6:31, *33*
   study of classics 6:48
   view of himself 6:35
   works in outline 6:45-47, *45-47*
   World War I and 6:31, *31, 43*
    Antigua, Penny, Puce 6:44, 45,
     46, *46*
    Claudius the God 6:45
    Collected Poems 6:42, *44*
    Collected Short Stories 6:47, *47*
    Count Belisarius 6:44
    Dawn 6:45
    Golden Fleece, The 6:44
    Goodbye to All That 6:34, 43, 45
    Greek Myths, The 6:35, 52
    I, Claudius 6:34, 35, *35*, 36-41,
     36-41, 44, 45, 49, 50, 51, 52
    King Jesus 6:43, 45, 47, *47*
    Lawrence and the Arabs 6:43, *43*
    Long Weekend, The 6:44, 45, 46,
     46
    Myconian, The 6:47
    Nazarene Gospel Restored, The
     6:43
    Pier-Glass, The 6:45, *45*
    Proceed, Sergeant Lamb 6:44
    Reader over Your Shoulder, The
     6:44
    Reproach 6:45
    Second-Fated, The 6:35
    Sergeant Lamb of the Ninth 6:44
    Shout, The 6:44
    They Hanged My Saintly Billy
     6:44
    Toast to Ava Gardner, A 6:47
    White Goddess, The 6:35, 43, 45,
     47, *47*
    Wife to Mr Milton 6:44
Gray, Thomas 12:25; 13:74
   Elegy written in a Country
    Churchyard 12:25
Greene, Henry Graham 6:77, *77*,
   78, 83, 87; 10:58
   appendicitis 6:79
   as British intelligence agent
    6:80-81, *80*
   as playwright 6:82, *91*
   as propagandist for Ruhr
    Germans 6:79, *79*
   autobiography 6:78, 92
   birth 6:78

   career 6:90-92, *90-92*
   Catholicism and 6:79, 82, 90, *91*,
    92, 93
   characters 6:88-89, *88-89*
   childhood 6:78
   children 6:79
   film criticism 6:80, *90*
   film scripts 6:80, 82, *92, 93*
   honorary doctorate from
    Cambridge 6:*92*
   jobs 6:79
   key dates 6:79
   marriage 6:79
   move to Antibes 6:82
   Omar Torrijos and 6:83, *83*
   Oxford and 6:78, 79
   'playing' of Russian roulette 6:79
   poetry 6:78
   psychoanalysis 6:78
   public protests against oppression
    6:83
   school 6:78
   suppression of *Journey Without*
    Maps 6:80, *80*
   The Times and 6:70, 80, *80*
   travels abroad 6:79, *79*, 80, *80*, 81,
    82, *82*, 91, *91*, 96
    Brighton Rock 6:80, 90, 93, *93*
    Cheap in August 6:95, *95*
    Comedians, The 6:83, 84-89,
     84-89, 92, 93, 96
    Confidential Agent, The 6:80, 90
    Dr Fischer of Geneva 6:92
    End of the Affair, The 6:90, 93
    Fallen Idol, The 6:80
    Gun for Sale, A 6:90
    Heart of the Matter, The 6:*80*,
     81, 90, 93, 94, *94*
    Honorary Consul, The 6:92, 93
    Human Factor, The 6:81, 92
    J'Accuse – The Dark Side of Nice
     6:83
    Journey Without Maps 6:80, *80*
    Lawless Roads, The 6:80
    Living Room, The 6:91
    Loser Takes All 6:82
    Man Within, The 6:79
    May We Borrow Your Husband?
     6:92, 95, *95*
    Ministry of Fear, The 6:92
    Monsignor Quixote 6:92, 95, *95*
    Mortmain 6:95, *95*
    Our Man in Havana 6:91-92
    Power and the Glory, The 6:80,
     90, 93, *93*
    Quiet American, The 6:91, 93,
     94-95, 95
    Sort of Life, A 6:92
    Stamboul Train 6:80, 90, *90*
    Third Man, The 6:80, 81, 93,
     94, *94*
    Tick of the Clock, The 6:78
    Travels with My Aunt 6:92
    Two Gentle People 6:95, *95*

Thomas Hardy's greatest novel – *some contemporary critics called it his most obscene – is* Jude the Obscure, *the tragic tale of the stonemason, Jude Fawley.*

Mary Evans Picture Library

Greene, Robert 1:12; 13:48, 49, *49,* 50
   Groats-worth of Witte 1:12; 13:*48-49,* 49
Grenfell, Julian 13:87
   Into Battle 13:87

H

Hammett, Dashiell 7:92
Hardy, Thomas 2:76, 100; 3:51, *51, 59, 61, 63, 70, 91;* 7:43, 68; 9:68
   as architect's apprentice 3:53, *53*
   birth 3:52, *52-53,* 58-59, *58-59*
   burial arrangements 3:57
   characters 3:68-69, *68-69,* 84-85, *84-85*
   childhood 3:59
   death 3:57, *63,* 88, 96
   honours 3:*57,* 62
   ill health 3:55, 63, 87
   key dates 3:53
   marriage to Emma 3:54
   marriage to Florence 3:56
   musical talent 3:52, *52*
   poetry 3:53, 55-56, 57, *57,* 62, 63, 70, 86-91, *86-91*
   preface to *Jude the Obscure* 3:71
   preface to *Tess of the D'Urbervilles* 3:80, 83
   preface to *The Woodlanders* 3:77
   school 3:52-53
   selected poems 3:89-91
   self-education 3:53
   statement on *Far from the Madding Crowd* 3:65
   views on farm life 3:92, 94, 96
   views on life 3:58
   views on marriage 3:71
   views on sexuality 3:61, 71, *71*
   views on *The Woodlanders* 3:75
   works in outline 3:73-75, *73-75*
     After a Journey 3:87
     Afterwards 3:87
     At Tea 3:88
     At Wynyard's Gap 3:87
     Beeny Cliff 3:87, 89, 91
     Change, The 3:88
     Darkling Thrush, The 3:87, 89
     Desperate Remedies 3:53, 71
     Dream is — Which?, The 3:89, 90
     Dynasts, The 3:56, 74
     Early Life of Thomas Hardy, The 3:56-57, *58,* 59, 61, 63
     Far from the Madding Crowd 3:54, 60, 64-69, *64-69,* 71, 72, 75, 76, 77, 78, 79, *79,* 93, 94
     General Preface to the Novels and Poems 3:78
     Glimpse, The 3:87
     Going, The 3:88
     Heart Insurgent 3:72
     How I Built Myself a House 3:53
     I Found Her Out There 3:87
     In Tenebris I 3:86
     Jude the Obscure 3:55, *57,* 61, 62, 63, 71, 72, 73, 75, *75,* 77, 78, 87
     Lost Love 3:88
     Mayor of Casterbridge 3:73, *73,* 94
     Neutral Tones 3:86
     Pair of Blue Eyes, A 3:61
     Phantom Horsewoman, The 3:87
     Poems 1912-13 3:87
     Poor Man and the Lady, The 3:70
     Rain on a Grave 3:88
     Return of the Native, The 3:61, 73, 74, 93
     Ruined Maid, The 3:88, *88*
     Something Tapped 3:*88,* 89, 91
     Tess of the D'Urbervilles 3:53, 55, 57, 60, 61, 71, 72, 77, 78, 79, 80-85, *80-85,* 87, 94, 95, 96
     Trumpet Major, The 3:72, 73, 74, 78
     Two Lips 3:89, 91
     Under the Greenwood Tree 3:73, 74, 86
     Upbraiding, An 3:89, 90
     Voice, The 3:87, 89, 90
     Winter Words 3:88
     Woodlanders, The 3:73, 75, *75,* 79, *79*
Hart, Joseph C. 13:31
   The Romance of Yachting 13:31
Harte, Bret 7:8, *8, 9*
Hawthorne, Nathaniel 2:39, 44; 9:33, 34, *35,* 43
   Scarlet Letter, The 9:33
Hazlitt, William 8:*28;* 13:62
Hemingway, Ernest 6:66; 7:77, 77, 85, 87
   Africa and 7:*80,* 82, 83, 91
   as editor of *Transatlantic Review* 7:81
   as Red Cross volunteer 7:78
   as reporter 7:78, 83, *91*
   birth 7:78
   bronze medal for Normandy role 7:83
   career 7:90-92, *90-92*
   characters 7:88-89, *88-89*
   childhood 7:78, *78*
   drinking 7:83
   father's suicide and 7:78, *78,* 82, *83*
   Fitzgerald and 7:*32,* 34, 35, 82, 90
   Gertrude Stein and 7:48, 80, 81
   in Cuba 7:82, 83, *83,* 90
   in Pamplona 7:81
   James Joyce and 7:*90*
   key dates 7:79
   letters from Europe for *Toronto Star* 7:80
   marriage to Hadley Richardson 7:79-80

marriage to Martha Gellhorn 7:82
marriage to Mary Welsh 7:83
marriage to Pauline Pfeiffer 7:82
Nobel Prize 7:86, 95
Paris and 7:*79, 80*, 81, 82, 83, 90, 91
silver medal for valour 7:79
Spanish Civil War and 7:82, 84, *91, 93, 97, 98, 98*
suicide 7:83, *83*
views on Mark Twain 7:20
works in outline 7:93-95, *93-5*
wounding in action 7:78-79, *79*
  Across the River and into the Trees 7:92, *92*, 95, *95*
  Big Two-Hearted River 7:93
  Death in the Afternoon 7:91
  Farewell to Arms, A 7:79, 91, 92, 93, 94, *94*
  For Whom the Bell Tolls 7:78, 81, 82, 84-89, *84-89*, 92, 93, 98
  Garden of Eden 7:91
  Green Hills of Africa 7:91
  In Our Time 7:81, 92, 93, *93*
  Indian Camp 7:93
  Islands in the Stream 7:91
  Moveable Feast, A 7:91
  Old Man and the Sea, The 7:92, 93, 95, *95*
  Short Happy Life of Francis Macomber, The 7:82, 92
  Snows of Kilimanjaro, The 7:82, 91, *91*
  Sun Also Rises, The (Fiesta) 7:81, 93, *93*
  To Have and Have Not 7:92, 93, 94, *94*
  Torrents of Spring, The 7:81
Hobbes, Thomas 1:56
  Leviathan 1:56
Hodge Alan 6:*35*, 44, 45, 46
  Long Weekend, The 6:44, 45, 46, *46*
  Reader over Your Shoulder, The 6:44
Holden, Molly 3:*61*
Homer 6:50
  Iliad 2:82, 91, 95; 6:50
  Odyssey 2:82, 91, *91*,95, *95*
Hood, Thomas 3:92; 4:26
Howells, William Dean 7:19
Howitt, William 4:56
  Visits to Remarkable Places 4:56
Hueffer, Ford Madox *see* Ford, Ford Madox
Humboldt, Alexander von 9:*25*
  Personal Narrative 9:*25*
Hume, David 11:*43*, 44, 50, 73
  History of Great Britain 11:*43*, 50
Hunt, Leigh 13:62, *63*
Huxley, Aldous Leonard 5:52; 6:11; 8:68; 10:77, *77*, 78, 81, *82*, 83, 84, 85, 86, *90*, 96
as film scriptwriter 10:82, *82, 92*

as professor-lecturer 10:83
as teacher 10:79
at Oxford 10:79, *79*
birth 10:78
career 10:90-93, *90-93*
characters 10:88-89, *88-89*
death 10:83
death of Maria 10:83
death of mother 10:78
experiments with hallucinogenic drugs 10:82, 83, 93, *93*
eye problems/other illnesses 10:78-79, 80, 82, 83
fire in Los Angeles house 10:83
friendship with Lawrences 10:81, *91, 92*
journalism 10:80
key dates 10:78
literary honours 10:83
marriages 10:80, 83
move to Italy/South of France 10:81, *81*
Nancy Cunard and 10:*80*, 81
pacifism 10:81-82, 92
school 10:78, *78-79*
travels 10:80, 81, *81, 87*, 91
views on India/Indian mysticism 10:81, 82, *82, 91*, 92
works in outline 10:94-95, *94-95*
World War I and 10:79, *80*
Yehudi Menuhin's descriptions of 10:81, 83, *83*
  After Many a Summer 10:92, 93, 94, *94-95*, 95
  Along the Road 10:90
  Antic Hay 10:90
  Ape and Essence 10:93
  Art of Seeing, The 10:82
  Brave New World 5:52; 10:81, 83, 84-89, *84-89*, 90-91, 92, 93, 94
  Brave New World Revisited 10:83, 93
  Burning Wheel, The 10:79, *91*
  Crome Yellow 10:80, 90, 94, *94*
  Devils of Loudun, The 10:93, 95, *95*
  Doors of Perception, The 10:82, 83, 93, 94
  Ends and Means 10:92
  Eyeless in Gaza 10:81, 82, 92, 94, 95, *95*
  Gioconda Smile, The 10:82
  Grey Eminence 10:93
  Heaven and Hell 10:83, 93, *93*
  Human Condition, The 10:83
  Island 10:93, 94
  Jesting Pilate 10:81, 91
  Limbo 10:80, 90
  Little Mexican 10:90
  Mortal Coils 10:80, 90
  On the Margin 10:90
  Perennial Philosophy, The 10:92-93

  Point Counter Point 8:68-69; 10:*81*, 91, 92, 94, *94*
  Those Barren Leaves 10:90
  Time Must Have a Stop 10:92
Huysmans, J. K. 2:*61*, 72
  A Rebours 2:*61, 72*

I

Ibsen, Henrik 5:*96*, 97, 98
  Doll's House, A 5:*96*, 97

J

James, Henry 2:37, 39, 43, 44, 45, 74; 4:81, 83, 94; 5:5, *5, 6*, 12, *18*; 6:20; 7:43, 80; 8:97; 9:54, 58, *66*; 10:92; 11:58, *58*, 59, 77
Beerbohm drawing of 5:11
birth 5:6
burials 5:11
burning of letters/notebooks 5:10
career 5:18-20, *18-20*
characters 5:16-17, *16-17*
childhood 5:6
Constance Fenimore Cooper and 5:8, 9
death 5:11
first night of *Guy Domville* and 5:10
H. G. Wells and 5:32, 44
honorary degree from Harvard 5:*11*
imagery 5:15
intimate relationships 5:9-10
John Singer Sargent and 5:25
key dates 5:7
literary debut 5:6, *8*
Mark Twain and 5:25
medical treatment at Malvern 5:*9*
mother's death and 5:8
nervous breakdown 5:10
notebook sketches 5:*9*
Order of Merit 5:11
preface to *Portrait of a Lady* 5:14
serialized fiction 5:19
70th birthday 5:10
Stephen Crane and 5:28
strokes 5:11
views on American tourists 5:24
views on art 5:18
views on Civil War 5:7
views on English–American world 5:28

views on Millet 5:27
working methods 5:19-20
works in outline 5:21-23, *21-23*
  Ambassadors, The 5:10, 20, 21,
    21, 24
  American, The 5:7, 8
  Aspern Papers, The 5:19, 21, 23,
    23
  Bostonians, The 5:8, 20, 21, 23,
    23
  Europeans, The 5:19, 21, *21*
  Golden Bowl, The 5:10, 19, 20,
    21, 22, *22*
  Guy Domville 5:9, 10
  Portrait of a Lady, The 5:8, 9,
    12-17, *12-17*, 19, 20, 21, 24
  Sacred Fount, The 5:28
  Small Boy and Others, A 5:6
  Turn of the Screw, The 5:19, 21,
    23, *23*
  Washington Square 5:8, 19, 21,
    22, *22*
  Watch and Ward 5:7
  What Maisie Knew 5:21, 22, *22*
  Wings of a Dove, The 5:10, 20
Jerome, Jerome K. 12:81
Johnson, Harold 13:*31*
  *Did the Jesuits Write
  Shakespeare?* 13:*31*
Johnson, Samuel, Dr. 1:56, 87, 88;
  4:60, 63; 8:7, 19, *21*, 24
Jonson, Ben 1:10, 13, 24, 32, 55;
  3:*16*; 9:44; 13:31, 32, 51, *51*,
  52, *52*
  Alchemist, The 13:52, *52*
  Bartholomew Fair 13:*52*
  Every Man in His Humour 3:*16*;
    13:52
  Isle of Dogs, The 13:52
  Masque of Blackness, The
    13:*52*
  Sejanus 1:13
  Volpone 13:*51*, 52, *52*
Joyce, James 7:81, *90*; 8:86, *86*
  Ulysses 8:86
Juvenal 1:84

K

Keats, John 2:73; 3:87; 12:*10*, 50;
  13:53, *53, 62,* 72, 73, 76
birth 13:62
death 13:61, 62, 63, *63, 70*
education 13:62
engagement 13:63, *63*
'Great Year' 13:63, 70
key dates 13:73
selected poems 13:64, 70-71,
  70-71

Shelley and 13:62, 63, *70*
tombstone inscription 13:63
walking tour 13:62
  Belle Dame Sans Merci, La 13:63
  Endymion 13:62, 63
  Eve of St Agnes, The 13:63, *71*
  Hyperion 13:63
  Isabella; or, the Pot of Basil
    13:62, 71
  Ode on a Grecian Urn 2:73; 13:*71*
  Ode on Melancholy 13:71, *73*
  Ode to a Nightingale 13:63, 64,
    65, 70-71, *70-71, 73,* 76
  Ode to Psyche 13:71
  *On First Looking into Chapman's
  Homer* 13:62
  To Autumn 13:71
  To Solitude 13:62
Keynes, John Maynard 8:79, 96, *96,*
  99; 9:78
  *Economic Consequences of the
  Peace* 8:99
Kipling, Joseph Rudyard 1:57;
  5:*11,* 39, 59, 67; 6:54; 9:58,
  67, 68; 11:77, *77, 82,* 87, 96, *96,*
  97, 98, *98,* 99, 100; 13:*87,* 93
as curator of Lahore Museum
  11:83
as journalist 11:80, *80, 90,* 98, 100
as War Graves Commissioner
  11:*83,* 100
birth 11:78
Burne-Jones portrait of 11:*90-91*
career 11:90-92, *90-92*
characters 11:88-89, *88-89*
childhood 11:78, *78-79*
children 11:81, 82, 83, *83,* 100,
  100
Companionship of Honour 11:83

The dying poet, John Keats, spent his final weeks of life in a room beside the Spanish Steps in Rome.

court case against Beatty Balestier
  11:81-82
death 11:83, *83*
death of son John 11:83, *83,* 100,
  100
declining of Order of Merit, poet
  laureateship 11:83
education 11:79
ill health 11:80, 81, 82, 83, *90-91,*
  99
key dates 11:79
marriage 11:81
Nobel Prize for Literature 11:83
own illustrations 11:*92, 95*
views on United States 11:80
works in outline 11:93-95, *93-95*
  Absent-Minded Beggar, The
    11:*96*
  Common Form 13:93
  Baa, Baa, Black Sheep 11:79
  Barrack-Room Ballads 11:80, 91,
    93, 94, *94*
  Beyond the Pale 1:93
  Boots 11:100
  Broken-Link Handicap, The
    11:93
  Danny Deever 11:94, 99
  Departmental Ditties 11:93
  Elephant's Child, The 11:95
  From Sea to Sea 11:80
  *Gate of the Hundred Sorrows,
  The* 11:93
  If 11:91
  Jungle Books, The 11:81, 90, 92,
    93, 94, *94*

Just So Stories 11:82, 92, *92*, 93, 95, *95*
Kim 11:77, *78*, 83, 84–89, *84–89*, 90, 91, *92*
Life's Handicap 11:90
Light That Failed, The 11:79, 81, 90, 93, *93*
Mandalay 11:91, *91*, 94
Man Who Would Be King, The 5:39
Mesopotamia 13:93
Plain Tales from the Hills 11:80, 90, 93, *93*
Puck of Pook's Hill 11:90, 93, 95, *95*
Recessional 11:91
Soldiers Three 11:90, *91*, 93, 97
Something of Myself 11:79, 83, 90, 100
Stalky & Co 11:93, *94–95*, 95
They 11:82
Thrown Away 11:93
Wee Willie Winkie 11:90
Kyd, Thomas 13:*50*, 51
Spanish Tragedy, The 13:*50*, 51

L

Lamb, Charles 11:56
Langland, William 13:20, 26, 27–28
Vision of Piers Plowman 13:20, 26
Lardner, Ring 7:33
Larkin, Phillip 3:88
Lawrence, David Herbert 2:84; 4:29; 5:58, 86, 87, 90; 6:5, *5, 7, 20*; 8:57, 58, 76, 80; 10:81, *91*, 92; 12:45
as clerk 6:7
as illustrator 6:*20*
as teacher 6:7
birth 6:6
burial 6:11, *11*
career 6:18–20, *18–20*
censorship of 6:9, 13, *19*
characters 6:16–17, *16–17*
death 6:11
education 6:6, 7, *7*
Edward Garnett and 6:66
ill health 6:7, 8, 9, 11, 18
introduction to London literary life 6:8
key dates 6:7
marriage 6:8
pseudonym 6:18
Robert Graves' views on 6:43
seizure of paintings by London police 6:11, 13
travels abroad 6:8, *8–9, 9–10*, 19, *19*

views on Mexico 6:24, *24*, 25, 26, *26*, 28
views on New Mexico 6:10, *11*
views on writing 6:12, 18
works in outline 6:21–23, *21–23*
World War I and 6:9, *9*, 18
Bavarian Gentians 6:19
Boy in the Bush, The 6:10, 18, *19*
Captain's Doll, The 6:20
Daughters of the Vicar, The 6:20
Escaped Cock, The 6:20
Fox, The 6:14–15
Kangaroo 6:10, 19, *19*
Lady Chatterley's Lover 6:11, 13, 18, 19, 21, 23, *23*
Laetitia 6:19
Last Poems 6:19
Mornings in Mexico 6:26
Movements in Modern History 6:18
Mr Noon 6:18
Paul Morel 6:19
Plumed Serpent, The 6:10, 11, 19, 20, *20*, 21, 23, *23*, 24, 28
Prussian Officer, The 6:20
Rainbow, The 6:9, 13, 18, 19, 20, 21, 22, *22*
Sea and Sardinia 6:19
Ship of Death, The 6:19
Sisters, The 6:19
Sons and Lovers 6:6, 7, 8, 19, 21, *21*; 8:57, 58
Studies in Classic American Literature 6:18
Virgin and the Gipsy, The 6:12, 13, 16, *16*, 20

Trespasser, The 8:57
Wedding Ring, The 6:19
White Peacock, The 6:8, 19, 21, *21*
Woman Who Rode Away, The 6:11, 13–14, *14*, 16, *16*, 20, 25, 26
Women in Love 6:13, 18, 19, 21, 22, *22*
Le Carré, John 5:76
Lea, Hermann 3:79
Hardy's Wessex 3:78
Leacock, Stephen 5:52
Lear, Edward 9:*26*; 10:38, *38–39*; 12:50
Book of Nonsense 10:38, *38*
Owl and the Pussycat, The 10:38
Leavis, F. R. 4:92; 6:20
D. H. Lawrence, Novelist 6:20
Lewis, Matthew
Monk, The 12:*25*, 27, *27*
Lewis, Wyndham 7:81; 8:99
Lockhart, John Gibson 11:30, *34*, 35, *35*
Life of Sir Walter Scott 11:*34*
Longfellow, Henry Wadsworth 3:17; 9:43; 10:47, 50
Hiawatha 10:47, 50
Loos, Anita 10:*82*
Loudon, Mrs 9:28
Entertaining Naturalist, The 9:28
Lowell, James Russell 7:18
Lucian 5:49
Icaromenippus 5:49
True History, The 5:49

Richard Hook

The relationship between two women, *March and Banford, is disrupted by a young soldier in D. H. Lawrence's* The Fox. *At first, Banford welcomes the newcomer, but her attitudes change when she sees that he has designs on March.*

M

Macaulay, Thomas Babington 1:57;
9:97
MacDonald, George 10:34, *34*
   At the Back of the North Wind
   10:34, *34*
Mackenzie, Sir Compton 5:20, *72*,
73, 76; 6:10, 20
Mackintosh, E. A. 13:*86*, 87
   In Memoriam 13:*86*, 87
   Recruiting 13:*86*, 87
Mallarmé, Stephane 12:42
Mann, Thomas 10:93
Mansfield, Katherine 6:8, *8*; 8:53,
   53, 61, 62, 63, 72, 75, 80
  birth 8:54, *55*
  blackmail by Sobieniowski 8:59
  career 8:66–69, *66-69*
  characters 8:64–65, *64–65*
  childhood 8:54, *54*, 60
  D. H. Lawrence and 8:57, 58
  death 8:57, 59, *59*, 67, 68
  Edith Bendall and 8:55
  first meeting with Murry 8:56, 57
  ill health 8:56, 58, *58*, 59, 66, 68
  in Germany 8:56, *57*, 66
  in south of France 8:*58*, 59
  key dates 8:55
  marriage to Bowden 8:55, 57
  marriage to Murry 8:59
  miscarriage 8:56
  possible plagiarism of Chekhov
    story 8:59, 67
  pregnancy 8:55, *57*, 66
  schools 8:54, 55, *55*
  views on love 8:76
  works in outline 8:70–71, *70-71*
  World War I and 8:58
  writing style 8:60
    Aloe, The 8:67
    At the Bay 8:66
    Bliss 8:60, 62–63, *62*, 64, 65, *65*,
    70
    Child-Who-Was-Tired, The-
    8:66–67
    Daughters of the Late Colonel
    8:70, 71, *71*
    Dill Pickle, A 8:68
    Garden-Party, The 8:70
    In a German Pension 8:66, 70, *70*
    Je ne Parle pas Français 8:68, 70,
    70
    Karori 8:66
    Little Governess, The 8:63, 68
    Man Without a Temperament,
    The 8:68, 70, 71, *71*
    Miss Brill 8:66
    Pictures 8:60, 63, *63*, 64, 65, *65*,
    68, 70
    Prelude 8:58, 60, *60*, 61, *61*, 62,

    62, 64, *64*, 66, 68, 70
    Sea Child, The 8:67
    Sister of the Baroness, The 8:70,
    70
    Tiredness of Rosabel, The 8:63
Marlowe, Christopher 1:30; 13:31,
  32, 45, 48, *48*, 49, 50, *50*, 51
   Dr Faustus 13:50, *50*
   Jew of Malta, The 13:50
   Tamburlaine 13:49–50
Masefield, John 6:32
Maugham, William Somerset
  1:94; 5:53, *53, 55*, 60, *67*, 68
  as British Intelligence Agent 5:57,
    58, 70, 72, 73, 75, *75*, 76, 76
  as editor of *The Venture* 5:56
  as medical student 5:56, *56*, 62
  as member of Red Cross
    ambulance unit 5:57, *57*, 73
  at King's School 5:55, *55*
  birth 5:54, *54*
  career 5:66–68, *66-68*
  characters 5:64–65, *64-65*
  death 5:59
  death of parents and 5:54–55, *54*
  description of self 5:68
  destruction of letters 5:59
  divorce 5:58
  escape from occupied France 5:59
  Garrick Club membership 5:57
  ill health 5:55, 58
  in Heidelberg 5:55, *56*
  in Paris/Spain 5:56
  key dates 5:55
  legacy from father 5:55
  marriage 5:57
  preface to *Of Human Bondage* 5:61
  stammer 5:54, 55, *55*
  Sunday Express articles 5:59
  travels 5:58, *58*, 59, 66–67
  works in outline 5:69–71, *69-71*
    Ashenden 5:69, 70, *70*, *75*, 76
    Bishop's Apron, The 5:56
    Cakes and Ale 5:59, *67*, 68, 69,
    71, *71*
    Christmas Holiday 5:67
    Circle, The 5:58, 66
    Don Fernando 5:67
    East of Suez 5:58
    Gentleman in the Parlour, The
    5:67
    Home and Beauty 5:58
    Lady Frederick 5:56
    Liza of Lambeth 5:56, 66,
    66-67,69, *69*
    Man of Honour, A 5:56
    Moon and Sixpence, The 5:57,
    58, 66, 68, 69, *69*
    Mrs Craddock 5:66
    Narrow Corner, The 5:67
    Of Human Bondage 5:55, 60–65,
    60-65, 66, 67, *68*, 69
    On a Chinese Screen 5:67
    Our Betters 5:57, 58, 66

    Painted Veil, The 5:67, 69, 70,
    70
    Rain 5:66, 69, 70, *70*
    Razor's Edge, The 5:67, 68, 69,
    71, *71*
    Summing Up, The 5:54, 68
    Traitor, The 5:73
    Unknown, The 5:58
Maupassant, Guy de 5:8
Mayhew, Henry 2:98, 99; 3:47
   London Labour and London Poor
   2:98; 3:47
McCrae, John 13:87, *87*
   In Flanders Field 13:87, *87*
Méjans, Maurice
   Recueil des Causes Célèbres, 12:68
Melville, Herman 5:24; 9:29, *29*,
  31, 38, 39, 43, 52
  as Customs Inspector 9:*32*, 34, *44*
  birth 9:30
  career 9:42
  characters 9:40–41, *40-41*
  children 9:32, *35*
  death 9:35
  family troubles 9:30
  health 9:34
  honeymoon 9:32
  jobs 9:30
  journals 9:*42*
  key dates 9:31
  London and 9:32
  magazine writing 9:43
  marriage 9:31
  Massachusetts farm 9:33, 34, *42*
  poetry 9:43, 48
  reading 9:42
  views on fame 9:30
  views on writing 9:34
  works in outline 9:45–47, *45-47*
  youth 9:30
    Encantadas, The 9:43
    Israel Potter 9:43, 45, 47
    John Marr and Other Sailors 9:48
    Mardi 9:32, 42, 43, 45, 46, 48
    Moby-Dick 9:30, 33, 34, 35, *35,*
    36–39, 40–41, *40-41*, 43, *43*, 45,
    48, 52
    Omoo 9:31, 42, 43, 45, 48
    Pierre or The Ambiguities 9:43
    Redburn 9:32, *32*, 42, 45, 47, 48
    Typee 5:24; 9:31, *32*, 33, 42, 43,
    45, 48, 50, 52
    White-Jacket 9:32, 42, 45, 47, 48
Meredith, George 3:70
Meres, Francis 1:13; 13:42, 43
   Palladis Tamia: Wit's Treasury
   1:13
Middleton, Thomas 13:51
Mill, John Stuart 9:97
Miller, Arthur 7:*58*
Miller, Henry 6:69
Milton, John 1:67; 6:43, 54; 10:22;
  12:*10*, 15
   Paradise Lost 12:15

Mitford, Nancy 10:57
Moliere, Jean Baptiste Poquelin
    1:56, 84
    L'Avare (The Miser) 1:84
    Misanthrope, Le 1:56
Moore, G. E. 8:96
    Principia Ethica 8:96–97
Moore, George 5:56
Mortimer, Raymond 10:78
Murry, John Middleton 6:8, *8, 9,*
    10; 8:56, 57, *57,* 58, *58,* 59, 68,
    69, *69*

N

Nashe, Thomas 13:48
Nichols, Robert 13:91

O

Orwell, George 3:26; 5:52; 7:98;
    8:82; 10:87; 11:77, 87
    1984 10:87
Osbourne, Lloyd 11:58, *58, 66, 67*
    Wrecker, The (co-written with
    R. L. Stevenson) 11:66
    Wrong Box, The (co-written
    with R. L. Stevenson) 11:66
    Ebb-Tide, The (co-written with
    R. L. Stevenson) 11:66
Otway, Thomas 1:*53,* 56
    Orphan, The 1:56
    Venice Preserv'd 1:56, *56*
Ovid 6:49
    Metamorphoses, The 6:49
Owen, Wilfred 13:77, 86, 90, 92,
    93
    as teacher-tutor 13:82, *83*
    at Craiglockhart War Hospital
        13:83, 91
    birth 13:82, *82*
    death 13:82, 83, 91
    Edith Sitwell's views on 13:*83*
    education 13:82
    enlistment in Artists' Rifles 13:83
    Military Cross 13:83, 91
    Siegfried Sassoon and 13:81, 82,
        82, 83, 91, 92
        Anthem for Doomed Youth 13:83
        Apologia pro Poemate Meo 13:91
        Disabled 13:83
        Dulce et Decorum Est 13:83, *90,*
            91
        Poems 13:91

Harry Clarke/Weidenfeld Archives, London

Edgar Allen Poe's mastery of the tale of mystery and imagination is reflected in this illustration to the story of William Wilson, who is haunted by his double or doppelganger.

    Song of Songs 13:83
    Strange Meeting 13:83, 92, *92*

P

Peacock, Thomas Love 12:28
    Nightmare Abbey 12:28
Peele, George 13:48
Pepys, Samuel 1:33, *33, 34, 41, 42,*
    43, 52, 53, 55
    administrative posts 1:36, 37, *38,*
        39, *39,* 41, 45, 47, *47*
    at Cambridge 1:34, *35*
    birth 1:34
    career 1:46–49, *46-49*
    characters 1:44–45, *44-45*
    Charles II and 1:*36,* 37, *37,* 40–41,
        40, 50
    death 1:39
    death of Montagu and 1:*38,* 39
    Diary's first entry 1:40
    Election as Member of Parliament
        1:39
    key dates 1:35
    kidney stone 1:36, *36*

    library 1:35, 39, 43, 49, 50-51,
        50-51
    marriage 1:25
    retirement 1:39
    Royal Society and 1:38, 39, 48, *49*
    school 1:34
    use of shorthand 1:35, *35,* 43,
        47-48
    views on Charles I 1:*35*
        Diary 1:33, 34, *34,* 35, *35,* 36,
            36, 37, 38, *38,* 39, 40-45, *40-45,*
            46, 47, *48,* 49, 50, 51, 52, 53
        *Memoires Relating to the State of
        the Royal Navy* 1:47, *49*
Petrarch 13:8, *11,* 13, *13,* 18, 20,
    21
Philips, Katherine 1:52
    Pompey 1:52
Plutarch 1:*22,* 23
Poe, Edgar Allan 5:24, 50; 12:29,
    29, 30, 31, 34, 35, 42, 50, *51,*
    52, *52*
    as editor 12:33, 34
    at West Point 12:32
    birth 12:30
    Conan Doyle and 12:78, 90
    career 12:42-45
    characters 12:40-41, *40-41*
    death 12:35
    death of Virginia and 12:35

In his war poetry and prose memoirs, Siegfried Sassoon described his horrific experiences of trench warfare and his disillusion with thoughts of military glory.

disappearance in Baltimore 12:35
discharge from army 12:32
drinking 12:31, 34
enlistment in army 12:31, *32*
gambling 12:31
hot-air-balloon hoax story 12:48, *48*
key dates 12:31
marriage 12:33
poetry 12:42, 43, *43*
school 12:30
university 12:31
works in outline 12:46–47, *46-47*
   Adventures of One Hans Pfall 12:51
   Al Aaraaf, Tamerlane and Minor poems 12:32
   Alone 12:43
   Black Cat, The 12:45, 46, 47, *47*
   Descent into the Maelstrom, A 12:33, *44*, 45, 50
   Eleonora 12:44, *44*
   Eureka! 12:35, *42*, 45
   Facts in the Case of M. Valdemar 12:36–37, 52
   Fall of the House of Usher, The 12:34, 36, *36*, 37, *37*, 40, 41
   Gold-Bug, The 12:*32*, 43, 46, 47, *47*
   Masque of the Red Death, The 12:44, *45*, 46, 47, *47*
   Mesmeric Revelation 12:52
   MS Found in a Bottle 12:33
   Murders in the Rue Morgue, The 12:36, 38, 39, *39*, 40, 41, *41*, 78
   Narrative of Arthur Gordon Pym, The 12:38, 45, 46, *46*, 51
   Pit and the Pendulum, The 12:46, *46-47*
   Premature Burial, The 12:43
   Raven, The 12:*34*, 35, *35*, 43, *43*, 46, *46*
   Some Words with a Mummy 12:52

Tale of the Ragged Mountains, A 12:52
Tales of Mystery and Imagination 12:30
Tamerlane and other Poems 12:31
Tell-Tale Heart, The 12:45
Thousand-and-second Tale of Scheherezade, The 12:48–49
To Helen 12:31
Ulalume 12:42
Unparalleled Adventure of one Hans Pfaall, The 5:50
William Wilson 12:36, 37–38, *37*, 40, 41, *41*
Pope, Alexander 1:54, *55*, 56, 86; 10:11, 21, 23
Pound, Ezra 3:88; 5:28; 7:80, 81
   Cantos 5:28
Priestley, J. B. 5:58

R

Racine, Jean 1:56
Radcliffe, Mrs Ann 8:*20*; 12:*25*, 26, 27
   Mysteries of Udolpho, The 8:20, 23; 12:*25*, 26–27, *27*
Raleigh, Sir Walter 13:48, *48-49*
Reade, Charles 3:13
Remarque, Erich Maria
   All Quiet on the Western Front 6:43
Richard, Marthe 5:74
   I Spied for France 5:74
Richardson, Samuel 1:86, 87, 94, 95, 96, 98
   Pamela 1:86, 94, 95, *95*, 98

Rolle, Richard 13:27
Romantic Poets, The 13:53–76, *53-76*, 92
Rosenberg, Isaac 13:77, 93, *93*
   as artist 13:84, *84*, *85*
   as private in British Army 13:84
   birth 13:84
   death 13:84, 85, *85*
   Edith Sitwell's views on 13:*83*
   ill health 13:84
   school 13:84
   self-portrait 13:*84*
      August 1914 13:85
      Dead Man's Dump 13:93
      Louse Hunting 13:92
      Night and Day 13:84
      Returning, we hear the Larks 13:92, *93*
      Youth 13:85
Rossetti, Dante Gabriel 12:28
Rousseau, Jean-Jacques 3:31–32
Rowe, Nicholas 1:13
   Life of William Shakespeare, The 1:13
Ruskin, John 2:97; 5:26, *27*; 10:32; 12:56
Russel, Bertrand 6:9, *19*; 8:58; 9:78
Rutland, William 3:*62*

S

Sackville-West, Vita 8:80, 81, *83*, 91, 93, 95, *95*
Sassoon, Seigfried Loraine 6:31, *33*; 13:77, 89, 90, *90*, 93, *93*
   at Craiglockhart War Hospital 13:81, 91
   birth 13:80
   death 13:81, *81*
   education 13:80, 90
   enlistment in Sussex Yeomanry 13:80
   hunting sports 13:80, *80*
   military honours 13:80, *80*
   return to war 13:81
   Wilfred Owen and 13:81, 82, *82*, 83, 91, 92
      Aftermath 13:*92*
      Attack 13:*91*
      Blighters 13:90
      Counter-Attack 13:81, 90
      In an Underground Dressing Station 13:*90*
      In the Pink 13:90
      Memoirs of a Fox Hunting Man 13:80, 81
      Memoirs of an Infantry Officer 13:81
      Old Huntsman, The 13:81, 83, 91

Sherston's Progress 13:81
Siegfried's Journey 13:81
Soldier's Declaration, A 13:81, *81*
To the Warmongers 13:88-89
Scott, Sir Walter 1:49, 94; 4:35;
8:11; 11:29, *29, 31, 32, 34,* 36,
38, 39, 50, 52; 12:18, 19, 22,
27, 28, 78
admission to Bar 11:30
article on chivalry for
Encyclopedia Britannica 11:48
as baronet 11:34
as Clerk of Session 11:32-33
as Sheriff-Depute of Selkirkshire
11:31, 32
as soldier 11:32
bankruptcy 11:34-35
biography of Napoleon 11:35, 42
birth 11:30
career 11:42-44, *42-44*
characters 11:40-41, *40-41*
childhood 11:30, *30*
children 11:32, 35
death 11:35, *35*
declining of poet laureateship
11:33
education 11:30
George IV and 11:34, *35,* 50-51
Jane Austen's views on 11:33
key dates 11:31
lameness 11:30, *30, 32*
marriage 11:31, *33*
Mediterranean voyage 11:35
monument in Edinburgh 11:30,
30-31
Robert Burns and 11:34, *34*
works in outline 11:45-47, *45-47*
Fair Maid of Perth, The 11:45
Heart of Midlothian, The 11:44,
45, 46, *46-47*
Ivanhoe 11:33, *33,* 34, 36-41,
36-41, 44, 45, 48, *49,* 50, 51, 52
Journal 11:42, 44
Kenilworth 11:45, 47, *47*
Lady of the Lake, The 11:32,
32-33, 33, 50
Lay of the Last Minstrel, The
11:32, 43
Legend of Montrose, The 11:42
Lochinvar 11:43
Marmion 11:32, 43
Minstrelsy of the Scottish Border
11:32, 43
Old Mortality 11:44, 45, *46,* 47
Quentin Durward 11:45, 47, *47,* 50
Redgauntlet 11:44, 45, 46
Rob Roy 11:42, *44,* 45, *45*
Talisman, The 11:45, 50
Waverley 11:33, 42, *44,* 45, *45*
Shakespeare, William 1:9, *9, 11,*
13, 28, 30, *30,* 31, *31,* 32, *32,*
55, 56, 96; 7:67; 9:42; 10:85, 86,
87, 89; 11:89, 95, 96; 13:29, *29,*
47, 48, 51

authorship speculations 13:30-33,
30-33
baptism 1:10, 13
Ben Jonson and 13:51, *51,* 52
birth 1:10, *10,* 11
career 1:22-24, *22-24*
characters 1:20-21, *20-21;*
13:40-41, *40-41*
Christopher Marlowe and 13:50
comedies, selected 13:34-41,
34-41
death 1:13; 13:52
First Folio 13:31, 32, 52
inscription on gravestone 13:33
key dates 1:11
marriage 1:11
missing years 1:12
poetry 13:42-45, *42-45*
purchase of New Place 1:*12,* 13
Robert Greene and 13:49, *49*
school 1:*10-11,* 11, 22
selected tragedies 1:14-21, *14-21*
sonnets 13:31-33, *32, 33,* 42,
43-44, *43,* 46-47
will 1:13, *30;* 13:33
works in outline 1:25-27, *25-27*
Antony and Cleopatra 1:22, 27,
27
As You Like It 1:22; 13:39, *39*
Cardenio (co-written with
Fletcher) 1:22
Coriolanus 1:22
Hamlet 1:12, 14, 16-17, *16-17,*
20, *21,* 23, 24, 25, 30, 31, 32;
13:42-43, *50,* 52
Henry IV 1:23, 25, *25, 32*

Henry V 1:23, 30; 11:96
Henry VI 1:12
Henry VIII (co-written with
Fletcher) 1:22
Julius Caesar 1:22, 26, *26*
King John 1:23
King Lear 1:14, 18-19, *18-19,*
20, 21, *21,* 22, 23, 24, *24,* 25,
30, 55
Love's Labours Lost 13:44, *44*
Macbeth 1:23, 24, 25, 27, *27,* 55
Merry Wives of Windsor, The
1:*32*
Midsummer Night's Dream, A
1:52, 55; 11:95; 13:34, *34,* 40,
40, 44, *44-45*
Much Ado About Nothing 13:44
Othello 1:23, 25, 26, *26,* 30, 52
Rape of Lucrece, The 1:12;
13:32, *33,* 42, *42-43*
Richard III 1:23, 25, *25,* 30
Romeo and Juliet 1:14-15,
14-15, 20, *20,* 25, 31, 55
Sonnets 13:31-33, *32, 33,* 42, 43-44,
43, 46-47
Taming of the Shrew, The
13:36-37, *36-37,* 40, 41, *41*
Tempest, The 1:25, 55; 10:85,
86, *86;* 13:30, *45*
Titus Andronicus 1:24, *24*
Twelfth Night 1:22, 56;
13:38-39, *38-39,* 40, 41, *41*
Two Noble Kinsmen, The (co-
written with Fletcher) 1:22, 56
Venus and Adonis 1:12; 13:32,
33, 42, 43

**Many modern
readers** *find
Rebecca, the daughter
of a Jewish money-
lender, more
attractive than
Rowena, the
beautiful but
conventional heroine
of Scott's* Ivanhoe. *
Here, Rebecca defies
the passionate
attentions of the
Norman knight,
Bois-Guibert.*

Mansell Collection

Winter's Tale, The 13:49

Shaw, George Bernard 2:66, 74, 87, 93, 100; 5:10, 33, *33, 43*, 92, 97, 98, *98, 99*, 100; 8:66
  Androcles and the Lion 5:*99*
  Man and Superman 5:98
  Mrs Warren's Profession 5:99
  Plays Pleasant and Unpleasant 5:98
  Pygmalion 5:98, *100*

Shelley, Mary Godwin 5:50, 51; 12:5, *5*, 28; 13:59, 60, *60*, 61
  as Gothic writer 12:24
  birth 12:6, 9
  Byron and 12:*19*, 20
  career 12:18-21
  characters 12:16-17, *16-17, 21*
  childhood 12:6, 7
  children 12:*6*, 7, 8-9, 10, *10*
  death 12:11
  description 12:6
  elopement with Shelley 12:6, *6, 9*
  emotional breakdown 12:9-10
  introduction to *Frankenstein* 12:7, 13, 15, 18
  key dates 12:7
  literary creed 12:19
  marriage 12:8
  non-fiction 12:11
  pregnancies 12:6-7, 8, 9, 10
  Shelley's death and 12:11, 18, 19, 21, 22
  short stories 12:19, *20*, 21, 22, 23, *23*
  verse on Shelley 12:*9*
  works in outline 12:22-23, *22-23*
    Brother and Sister, The 12:22
    Euphrasia 12:20

False Rhyme, The 12:23
Frankenstein 12:5, 8, 10, 12-17, *12-17*, 19, *19*, 20, *21*, 22, 24, 28, 52
Last Man, The 12:11, 19, *19*, 20, 21, *21*, 22, 23, *23*
Lives of the Most Eminent Literary and Scientific Men 12:19
Lodore 12:19, *19*, 20
Mathilda 12:20, 22, *22*
Mortal Immortal, The 12:21, 22, 23, *23*
Rambles in Germany and Italy 12:19
Tales and Stories 12:23, *23*
Valperga 12:10, 19, *19*, 20, 22, *22*

Shelley, Percy Bysshe 4:98, *98*; 12:6, *6*, 7, *7*, 8, *8*, 9, *9*, 10, *10*, 11, 14, 18, 19, *19*, 20, 21, 22, 28, 52; 13:53, *53*, 60, 72, 76, 92
  birth 13:60
  Byron and 13:59, 61
  children 13:60, *60*, 61
  death 13:61, *61, 69*
  education 13:60, *60*
  Keats and 13:62, 63, *70*
  key dates 13:73
  marriages 13:60, 61
  selected poems 13:64, 69-70, *69-70*
  views on Wordsworth 13:*54*, 55
    Adonais 13:61, 63, *70*
    Cenci, The 13:61
    Defence of Poetry 13:76
    Hymn to Intellectual Beauty 13:61
    Julian and Maddalo 13:61
    Mask of Anarchy, The 13:61, 64, 69-70, *69*

    Necessity of Atheism 13:60, 76
    Ode to the West Wind 13:*60*, 61, *69*, 76
    Prometheus Unbound 12:14; 13:61
    Queen Mab 13:60
    To a Skylark 13:70
    When the Lamp is Shattered 13:61, *61*

Shelton, Thomas 1:35, 47, 49
  Tutor to Tachygraphy, or Short-Writing 1:35, 47

Sidney, Phillip 1:23; 11:49, *50*; 13:*32*, 48
  Arcadia 1:23

Sitwell, Osbert and Edith 13:83, *83*

Skinner, Mollie 6:10, 18
  Boy in the Bush, The 6:10, 18, *19*

Smollet, Tobias George 8:27
  Humphrey Clinker 8:27

Somerville, Alexander 3:78
  Whistler at the Plough, The 3:78

Southey, Robert 4:27; 13:56, *56*

Spenser, Edmund 9:59; 13:31, 32, 48

Stein, Gertrude 7:48, 80, 81

Steinbeck, John Ernst 1:64; 7:53, *53, 54*, 60, 62, 72, *76*
  as journalist 7:55, *56*, 57-58, 59, 63
  birth 7:54
  career 7:66-68, *66-68*
  characters 7:64-65, *64-65*
  death 7:59
  dedication of *The Grapes of Wrath* 7:63
  defence of Arthur Miller 7:*58*
  defence of *The Grapes of Wrath* ending 7:61

Robert Louis Stevenson's native city *of Edinburgh was in his thoughts however far he travelled for the sake of his delicate health. Even the forbidding Calton jail, shown here, could inspire nostalgia.*

Hemingway and 7:92
jobs 7:55, *56*, 67
key dates 7:55
marriage to Gwyndolyn Conger 7:57
marriage to Carol Henning 7:56
marriage to Elaine Scott 7:*58*, 59
Nobel Prize 7:53, 54, 59, *68*
Pulitzer Prize 7:57
school 7:55
travels abroad 7:57, 58
university 7:55
Vietnam and 7:*58-59*, 59
views on fame 7:56
views on *The Wayward Bus* 7:71
views on writing 7:67
works in outline 7:69-71, *69-71*
  Bombs Away 7:57
  Cannery Row 7:66, 67, 69, 70, *70*
  Cup of Gold 7:56
  East of Eden 7:*58*, 66, 67, 68, 69, 70, *70*
  Gift, The 7:69
  Grapes of Wrath, The 1:64; 7:56, 57, 60-65, *60-65*, 66, 67, 68, 72, 76
  Great Mountains, The 7:69
  In Dubious Battle 7:56, 66
  Leader of the People, The 7:69
  Moon is Down, The 7:57, 66
  Of Mice and Men 7:56, 57, 66, 69, 71, *71*
  Pearl, The 7:66, 67
  Promise, The 7:69
  Red Pony, The 7:69, *69*
  Sea of Cortez (with Ricketts, Ed) 7:57
  Sweet Thursday 7:70
  Tortilla Flat 7:56, *56*, 66, 69, *69*
  Travels with Charley 7:69, 71, *71*
  Wayward Bus, The 7:67, 69, 71, *71*
Stevenson, Robert Louis 3:24; 7:59; 8:20, 21; 9:48, *50*; 11:53, *53, 56-57*, 60, 62, 63, *72, 74, 76*
  birth 11:54, *54, 72*
  career 11:66-68, *66-68*
  characters 11:64–65, *64–65*
  childhood 11:54, 55, *55*
  death 11:59, *59*, 66, 68, 70
  descriptions of Edinburgh 11:72, 73, 74, 75, 76
  education 11:55
  ill health 11:54, *54*, 55, 57, 58, 59, 66, 69, 71
  key dates 11:54
  marriage 11:58
  South Seas and 11:58-59, *58, 59*, 69, 72
  travels abroad 11:57, 58, 66, *66*
  works in outline 11:69-71, *69-71*
    Amateur Emigrant, The 11:57, 66, *66*

He sent the uncouth missile hurtling through the air

  Catriona 11:69
  Child's Garden of Verses, A 11:*54*, 58, 69, *70-71, 71*
  Ebb-Tide, The (co-written with L. Osbourne) 11:66
  Edinburgh, Picturesque Notes 11:72, 76
  Kidnapped 11:58, 67, 68, 69, *69*
  Master of Ballantrae, The 11:58, 66, *67*, 68, *68*, 69
  Requiem 11:59
  Silverado Squatters, The 11:58, 66
  St Ives 11:66
  Strange Case of Dr Jekyll and Mr Hyde, The 11:58, 67, 68, 69, 71, *71*
  Travels with a Donkey in the Cevennes 11:69, 70, *70*
  Treasure Island 9:48; 11:58, 60-65, *60-65*, 66, 67, 68, 69, 76
  Weir of Hermiston 11:59, 66, 68, *68*, 69, 70, *70*
  Wrecker, The (co-written with L. Osbourne) 11:66
  Wrong Box, The (co-written with L. Osbourne) 11:66

Stevenson's adventure novel, Treasure Island, *is perhaps most notable for the character of Long John Silver. Here, the ruthless Silver dispatches an opponent with an effective, if unconventional, weapon – his crutch.*

Stoker, Bram 12:28
  Dracula 12:28
Stowe, Harriet Beecher 7:26
  Uncle Tom's Cabin 5:100; 7:26
Strachey, Lytton 8:80, *80*, 91, *91*, 96, *96*, 99, 100; 9:78, 79
  Eminent Victorians 8:99
Swift, Jonathan 1:*55, 96*; 5:48, *49*; 7:28; 9:48; 10:5, *5*, 12, 13, 14, 15, 24, 25; 11:18, 42
  as Dean of St Patrick's Cathedral, Dublin 10:10, *11*, 26, 27
  as government propagandist 10:9, *19*, 21, 23
  at Moor Park 10:7-8
  at Trinity College, Dublin 10:7, *7*
  birth 10:6, *6*
  career 10:18-21, *18-21*
  characters 10:16-17, *16-17*
  childhood abduction 10:6-7
  death 10:11, 28
  description of Ireland 10:26-27, *27*
  ill health 10:6, 8, 10
  key dates 10:6
  ordination 10:8
  portrait at 14 10:7, *7*

rumours of marriage 10:11
school 10:*6*, 7
views on science 10:9
works in outline 10:22-23, *22-23*
   Battle of the Books, The 10:22, *22*
   Bickerstaff Papers 10:19
   Cadenus and Vanessa 10:10
   Conduct of the Allies, The 10:22, 23, *23*
   Digression on Madness 10:22
   Drapier's Letters, The 10:10, 18, 27, *27*
   Gulliver's Travels 5:48, *49*; 9:48; 10:5, 6, 11, 12-17, *12-17*, 19, 21, *21*, 22
   History of Ears, A 10:20
   Journal to Stella 10:8, 9, 20, 22, 23, *23*
   Meditations on a Broomstick 10:18
   Modest Defence of the Proceedings of the Rabble in All Ages 10:20
   Modest Proposal, A 10:19, 22, 23, *23*, 26
   Tale of a Tub, A 10:8, 9, 18, 19, 20, 21, *21*, 22, *22*
   Windsor Prophesy, The 10:18
Swinburne, Algernon C. 2:*76*; 12:69
Symons, Arthur 2:74, 75, 76

T

Taylor, A. J. P. 10:68
Tennyson, Alfred Lord 2:*10*; 4:83, 100; 7:59; 8:19-20; 10:32, 34, 44, 52; 11:52
Thackeray, William Makepeace 2:5, *5*, *6*, 7; 3:54; 4:*21*, 58; 5:18; 8:27, 78; 10:12, 44; 12:28, 34, *73*, 74
   Anthony Trollope and 2:43, 44
   as artist in Paris 2:2, 8, *9*, 11
   as editor 2:7, 11, 20
   as journalist 2:9, 11, 18, *19*
   as literary celebrity 2:9
   as parliamentary candidate 2:10-11
   birth 2:6, 24
   Cambridge and 2:7, *8*, 11, *26*
   career 2:18-21, *18-19*
   characters 2:16-17, *16-17*
   childhood 2:6
   children 2:8, 9-10, 11, 18, 20
   death 2:11
   gambling 2:7
   ill health 2:10, 11, *11*, 20
   key dates 2:7
   law training 2:7
   lectures 2:10, 20
   letters 2:*9*, 19

Newspapers are seen as a malevolent force in Barchester Towers. *Trollope believed in a free press, but was suspicious of irresponsible journalism that could oust a good man like Septimus Harding from his job.*

Mansell Collection

   loss of fortune 2:8, 18
   marriage 2:7, 8
   pseudonyms 2:18
   travels 2:7, 8, 10, 18, 20, *21*
   views on America 2:*21*
   views on Napoleon 2:*26*
   visit to Waterloo 2:28, *28*
     Book of Snobs 2:18
     Denis Duval 2:11
     English Humorists of the Eighteenth Century 2:10, 20, *21*
     Four Georges, The 2:10, 20, *21*
     From Cornhill to Grand Cairo 2:18
     Great Hoggarty Diamond, The 2:18
     History of Henry Esmond Esquire, The 2:18, 20-21, 22, 23, *23*
     History of Pendennis, The 2:*10*, 21, 22, *22*
     Luck of Barry Lyndon, The 2:18, 22, *22*
     Newcomes, The 2:10, 18, 19, *19*, *20*, 21, 22, 23, *23*
     Rose and the Ring, The 2:21
     Vanity Fair 2:6, 9, 12-17, *12-17*, 16-21, *16-21*, 22, 24, 27, 28; 10:91
     Virginians, The 2:20
     Yellowplush Paper, The 2:18
Thoreau, Henry David 8:30, 31, *32*, 35
   Walden 8:*32*
Tolkien, J. R. R. 10:34
   Lord of the Rings, The 10:34
Tolstoy, Leo 2:39; 5:18; 6:67; 11:29
Townshend, Chauncey Hare 12:52
   Facts in Mesmerism 12:52
Trevelyan, G. M. 11:95
Trollope, Anthony 2:29, *29*; 7:28
   as editor of St Paul's Magazine 2:35

   as Parliamentary candidate 2:35, *43*
   birth 2:30, 48
   characters 2:40-41, *40-41*
   childhood 2:30
   children 2:33, *33*
   commission in Austrian cavalry 2:32
   death 2:35
   hunting 2:32, *33*, 35
   ill health 2:32, 35
   Ireland and 2:32-33, *43*
   key dates 2:30
   marriage 2:33
   Post Office and 2:*31*, 32, 33, *33*, 34, 35, 42, *42*, 43, 44, 47, 48, *50*, 51, 52
   postal pillar box and 48, *48*
   schools 2:30, 31
   travels 2:32, *33*, 34, *34*, 42, *42*, *50*, 51
   views on clergy 2:*37*
   views on popular press 2:38
   views on Sir Rowland Hill 2:48, 49
   views on writing 2:36, 37, 42, *42*, 44
   working schedule 2:42, *42*
   writing career 2:42-44
     Autobiography 2:34, 44, 49
     Barchester Chronicles, The 2:43, 45
     Barchester Towers 2:33, 36-41, *36-41*, 42, 43, 44, 45
     Can You Forgive Her? 2:43, 46
     Duke's Children, The 2:43, 46
     Eustace Diamonds, The 2:46, *46*
     Framley Parsonage 2:43, 44, 45
     John Caldigate 2:34
     Last Chronicle of Barset, The 2:43, 44, 45

Macdermots of Ballycloran, The
2:33, *43*
Palliser novels 2:43, *43,* 44, 45,
46, *46*
Phineas Finn 2:43, 46
Phineas Redux 2:46
Prime Minister, The 2:43, 46
Small House at Allington, The
2:43, 44, 45
Three Clerks, The 2:44, 45, 47,
47
Vicar of Bullhampton, The 2:45,
47
Warden, The 2:33, 35, 43, 44, 45
Way We Live Now, The 2:45,
46, *46*
*West Indies and the Spanish
Main, The* 2:43, 44
Trollope, Frances 2:30, *30,* 31, 32,
32, 34, 42; 7:28
*Domestic Manners of the
Americans* 2:31, 32, 42; 7:28
Factory Boy, The 2:32, *32*
Turgenev, Ivan 5:7, 7, 8, *9,* 10
Twain, Mark 1:64; 5:25, *25;* 7:5, *5,*
9, 12, 14; 8:18; 11:86
academic honours 7:10, *10-11*
as lecturer 7:8, 10, *10*
as newspaper reporter 7:7, *7,* 8, 18
as printer 7:6, *7*
as river pilot 7:6, *7, 18,* 22, 24, 25,
25
bankruptcy 7:9, *10*
birth 7:6, *6,* 25
career 7:18-20, *18-20*
characters 7:16-17, *16-17*
childhood 7:6, 25
Civil War and 7:7
death 7:11, 20
death of son 7:9
education/lack of 7:6, *11*
key dates 7:7
marriage 7:8, *9*
meaning of pen-name 7:7
publishing firm 7:9
quotations from works 7:*24-28*
tour of Mediterranean 7:8, *9,* 20,
23
Ulysses S. Grant and 7:9
views on England 7:9, *10*
views on Frances Trollope 7:28
views on publication of work 7:6
views on religion 7:*6,* 9
works in outline 7:21-23, *21-23*
*Adventures of Huckleberry Finn,
The* 1:64; 7:9, 11, 12-17, *12-17,*
18, *18,* 19, 20, 21, 24; 11:86
Adventures of Tom Sawyer, The
7:9, 11, 18, 19, 20, 21, *21*
Autobiography 7:6, *6,* 11
*Celebrated Jumping Frog of
Calaveras County and Other
Sketches, The* 7:18, 21
Connecticut Yankee in King

Arthur's Court, A 7:18, 20, 21,
23, *23*
Gilded Age, The 7:18
Innocents Abroad, The 7:8, *9,* 20,
21, 23, *23*
Jim Smiley and His Jumping Frog
7:8, *9, 18,* 21
Life on the Mississippi 7:18, 19,
21, 22, *22,* 25
*Man That Corrupted Hadleyburg,
The* 7:20, 21, 22, *22-23*
Mysterious Stranger, The 7:20
Pudd'nhead Wilson 7:11, 19, 21,
22, *22*
Roughing It 7:6-7, *7,* 9, 21
Tom Sawyer Abroad 7:21
Tom Sawyer, Detective 7:21
War Prayer, The 7:20

V

Vanbrugh, John 1:*54,* 55, 56
Verne, Jules 5:50, *50,* 51, *51,* 52, *52*
From the Earth to the Moon 5:50
Voyages Extraordinaires 5:50
Virgil 6:50
Aeneid 6:50
Voltaire (François Marie Arouet)
3:31

W

Walpole, Horace 1:102; 12:25, *25,*
26
Castle of Otranto, The 12:25, *25*
Walpole, Hugh 5:6, 10, *67;* 6:20
War Poets, The 13:77-100, *77-100*
Ward, Mrs Humphrey 8:76
Waugh, Alex 10:*54*
Waugh, Evelyn 10:53, *53, 57,* 60,
61, 62, 63, *71,* 73, 76
as member of Hyprocrites Club
10:56
as Roman Catholic 10:57, 58, 67
as teacher 10:56, 66
as war correspondent 12:57, *68*
at Oxford 10:*55,* 56, 59, *66,* 75
biography of Rossetti 10:56, 57,
66, *67*
birth 10:54
career 10:66-68, *66-68*
characters 10:64-65, *64-65*
childhood 10:54, *54*
children 10:58, *59*

death 10:59
divorce 10:57
drawing 10:*66*
in Hollywood 10:58, *58*
insomnia 10:56, 59
key dates 10:55
marriages 10:*56,* 57, 58
nervous breakdown 10:59
non-acceptance of CBE 10:59
school 10:54, *54-55,* 55, *66*
tastes 10:54
travels 10:*56-57,* 57, 59, 66
use of drugs for sleeping 10:58-59
views on Huxley's *Antic Hay*
10:90
views on writing 10:68
works in outline 10:69-71
World War I and 10:54, *55*
World War II and 10:58
Black Mischief 10:57, 66, 69
Brideshead Revisited 10:58, *58,*
67, 69, 70, *70*
Conversion 10:66
Decline and Fall 10:56, 57, 66,
67, 69, *69*
Handful of Dust, A 10:*56,* 67
Little Learning, A 10:66, 69
Loved One, The 10:58, *58,* 67,
69, 70, *70*
Men at Arms 10:58, 69, 71
Officers and Gentlemen 10:58, 69,
71
Ordeal of Gilbert Pinfold, The
10:59, 69, 71
Put Out More Flags 10:58, 69
Remote People 10:57
Rossetti: His Life and Works
10:57
Scoop 10:57, 66, 69, *69*
Scott-King's Modern Europe
10:66
Sword of Honour 10:59, 68, 69,
71, *71*
Unconditional Surrender 10:59,
69, 71
Vile Bodies 10:58, 60-65, *60-65,*
66, 67, 69, 72, 75, 76
Waugh in Abyssinia 10:57
When the Going Was Good 10:66
Webster, John 13:51
Wells, Herbert George 5:29, *29,*
30, 32-33, 38, 48, 49, 50, 51, *51,*
52, *52;* 6:4, 11; 8:18, *66,* 76, 82,
90; 9:58, 68; 10:92; 13:83
as propaganda adviser 5:34
as teacher 5:30, 31
at London premiere of *The Shape
of Things to Come* 5:*35*
Beerbohm cartoon of 5:32
birth 5:30
career 5:42-44, *42-44*
characters 4:40-41, *40-41*
childhood 5:30
children 5:32

death 5:35
education 5:30, 31
epitaph 5:39
Fabian Society and 5:33
Henry James and 5:9, 10, *11, 32,* 44
ill health 5:31, 34, 35
jobs 5:30, *31*
key dates 5:30
marriage to Isabel 5:31
nervous breakdown 5:31–32
Rebecca West and 5:33, 34, 35
self-portrait 5:*43*
Somerset Maugham and 5:58
travels to United States/Russia 5:34, *34, 35*
works in outline 5:45–47, *45-47*
  Ann Veronica 5:33, 43, 45, 47, *47*
  Anticipations 5:42
  Essay in Autobiography 5:42
  First Men in the Moon, The 5:50
  History of Mr Polly, The 5:33, 43, 45, 47, *47*
  In the Days of the Comet 5:42–43
  Invisible Man, The 5:31, 42, 45, 46, *46,* 51, *51,* 52
  Island of Dr Moreau, The 5:31, 36, 42, 45, *45*
  Kipps 5:43, 45, 46, *46*
  Love and Mr Lewisham 5:43, *43*
  Modern Utopia, A 5:42
  Men Like Gods 10:92
  Mr Britling Sees it Through 5:34
  New Machiavelli, The 5:33, 43
  Outline of History, The 5:34, 44
  Painted Veil, The 5:67, 69, 70, *70*
  Science of Life, The 5:44
  Shape of Things to Come, The 5:*35,* 44, *44*
  Short History of the World 5:44
  Time Machine, The 5:31, 36, 42, 45, *45*
  Tono-Bungay 5:43, 45, 46, *47*
  War in the Air, The 5:42
  War of the Worlds, The 5:31, 35, 36-41, *36-41,* 42, 45, 50
  Work, Wealth and Happiness of Mankind, The 5:44
  Worlds Set Free, The 5:42
West, Rebecca 5:33, *33,* 34, 35; 8:76
Wharton, Edith 5:9, 10, *10*
White, Gilbert 9:26
  Natural History of Selborne 9:26
Whiting, John 10:95
  Devils, The 10:95
Whitman, Walt 9:*43,* 86
Wilde, Oscar 2:53, *53, 55, 58-59, 68;* 9:79; 12:28
  aestheticism and 2:72, 75, 76
  as editor of *The Woman's World* 2:57, 66, *67*
  birth 2:54, *54*

Mary Evans Picture Library

Cafe Royal and 2:73
childhood 2:54
children 2:*56,* 57, 59
conversion to Roman Catholic Church 2:59, 76
death 2:59
exile in France 2:59, *59*
imprisonment 2:58, 59, *59,* 69, 75
key dates 2:55
lecture tours 2:56, *56,* 57, *66,* 67
marriage 2:*56,* 57
Oxford and 2:*54,* 55, *55*
Pall Mall Gazette and 2:57
quotes 2:53, 54, 55, 56, *56,* 57, 58, 59, 62, 63, 67, 71, 73, 74
  Doctor Thorne 2:43, 45
  Ballad of Reading Gaol, The 2:59, 69, 71, *71*
  Canterville Ghost, The 2:66, 69, *69*
  De Profundis 2:59, 66
  Duchess of Padua, The 2:56
  Fisherman and his Soul, The 2:67
  Happy Prince and Other Tales, The 2:57, 66, 69, 70, *70*
  House of Pomegranates, A 2:67
  Ideal Husband, An 2:67, *67*
  Importance of Being Earnest, The 2:57, 67, *67,* 68, 69, 71, *71*
  Lady Windermere's Fan 2:57, 66, 67, 69, 71, *71*
  Lord Arthur Savile's Crime and Other Stories 2:66, 69, *69*
  Model Millionaire, The 2:69
  Nightingale and the Rose, The 2:70
  Picture of Dorian Gray, The 2:55, 60–65, *60-65,* 66, 67, 69, 72, 73

Dorian Gray, the hero of Oscar Wilde's novel, *visits a Chinese-run opium 'den', in search of further sensual experience and ultimately of oblivion.*

  Poems 2:56
  Salome 2:*68,* 69, 70, *70,* 75
  Selfish Giant, The 2:70
  Sphinx without a Secret, The 2:69
  Woman of No Importance, A 2:67, 68
Wilson, Edmund 7:31, 47
Wollstonecraft, Mary 12:6, 9, *9,* 27; 13:60
  Thoughts on the Education of Daughters 12:9
  Vindication of the Rights of Woman, A 12:9
Woolf, Leonard 8:58, 68, 79, 81, *81,* 82, *82,* 83, *83,* 91, 92, 96, *97,* 98, 99, 100; 9:79, *80*
  Civilised Man, A 8:99
Woolf, Virginia 2:87; 3:57, 71; 4:94; 5:28; 8:22, 77, *77, 81, 82;* 9:*80*
  attempted suicide 8:80, 82
  birth 8:79, *79*
  career 8:90–92, *90-92*
  characters 8:88–89, *88-89*
  childhood 8:78, *78,* 80, *90*
  death of father 8:79
  death of mother 8:78, *78,* 79
  diary entries 8:80–81, 82, 83, 86, 90, 92
  engagement to Lytton Strachey 8:*80*
  farewell letters 8:83, *83*
  feminist writing 8:92, 99, 100

influence of Bloomsbury on 8:96, 97, *97*
key dates 8:78
marriage 8:80, 81
Murry/Mansfield and 8:57, 58, 59, 67-68, *68*, 76
nervous breakdowns 8:78, *78*, 80-81, 82, 91
reviews/essays 8:79, 80, 92
suicide 8:83, *83*, 93
suicide pact with Leonard 8:82
views on *To the Lighthouse* 8:84, 86
works in outline 8:93-95
   Anon 8:83
   Between the Acts 8:92, 93, 95, *95*
   Flush 8:82, 91
   Jacob's Room 8:91, 93, *93*
   Kew Gardens 8:92
   Monday or Tuesday 8:91
   Mrs Dalloway 8:91, 93, 94, *94*
   Night and Day 8:91
   Orlando 8:81, 91, 92, 93, 95, *95*, 100
   Room of One's Own, A 8:81, 91, *91*, 92, 99, 100
   To the Lighthouse 8:81, 82, 84-89, *84-89, 90*, 91, 93
   Voyage Out, The 8:79, 80, 91, 93, *93*

Waves, The 8:82, 90, 93, 94, *94*
Years, The 8:91
Wordsworth, Dorothy 13:54, *54*
Wordsworth, William 1:67; 8:9; 11:56; 12:50, 51; 13:53, *53,* 66, 72, *73,* 76
affair with Annette Vallon 13:54
as Poet Laureate 13:54, 55
birth 13:54
Byron's views on 13:68
children 13:54, 55, *55*
Coleridge and 13:54, *54,* 55, 56, 57, *57*
death 13:55
education 13:54
key dates 13:73
legacies 13:54, 55
marriage 13:55, *55*
selected poems 13:64-65, *64-65*
views on Shakespeare's sonnets 13:32
   Advertisement and Preface 13:76
   Daffodils 13:54, *65*
   Guide to the Lakes 13:55
   Intimations of Immortality from Recollections of Early Childhood 13:55, 64-65, *64-65*
   Lyrical Ballads 13:54, 57, 66, 76
   My Heart Leaps Up 13:65, *65*

   Prelude, The 13:55, *55, 73,* 76
   Tables Turned, The 13:76
   Tintern Abbey 13:54, *64,* 76
Wycherley, William 1:54, 55, *55,* 56
   Country Wife, The 1:55
   Plain Dealer, The 1:*55,* 56

Y

Yeats, W. B. 2:*73,* 74, 76
Yonge, Charlotte M. 9:28
   Herb of the Field, The 9:28
Younghusband, Sir George 11:96
   Soldier's Memories in Peace and War, A 11:96

Z

Zola, Emile 5:7

INDEX OF LITERATURE

Throughout his writing life, Mark Twain drew upon his experiences as a Mississippi river pilot.

Note Page numbers in italic type refer to illustrations.

A

A Rebours (Huysmans) 2:*61*, 72
Absent-Minded Beggar, The (Kipling) 11:*96*
Absolution (Fitzgerald) 7:46
Across the River and into the Trees (Hemingway) 7:92, *92*, 95, *95*
Adam Bede (G. Eliot) 4:*78*, *81*, 82, 83, 90, *90*, 91, *91*, 93, *93*
Adonais (P. B. Shelley) 13:61, 63, *70*
Adventures of Brigadier Gerard, The (Conan Doyle) 12:92
Adventures of Huckleberry Finn, The (Twain) 1:64; 7:9, 11, 12-17, *12-17*, 18, *18*, 19, 20, 21, 24; 11:86
Adventures of One Hans Pfall (Poe) 12:51
Adventures of Sherlock Holmes, The (Conan Doyle) 12:84–89, *84-89*
Adventures of Tom Sawyer, The (Twain) 7:9, 11, 18, 19, 20, 21, *21*
Advertisement and Preface (Wordsworth) 13:76

Aeneid (Virgil) 6:50
After a Journey (Hardy) 3:87
After Dark (Collins) 12:70
After Many a Summer (Huxley) 10:92, 93, 94, *94-95*, 95
Aftermath (Sassoon) 13:*92*
Afternoon of an Author (Fitzgerald) 7:44
Afterwards (Hardy) 3:87
Agnes Grey (A. Brontë) 4:10, 24, 28, 32, 44, 47, *47*
Al Aaraaf, Tamerlane and Minor Poems (Poe) 12:32
Alchemist, The (Jonson) 13:52, *52*
Alice in Wonderland (Carroll) 10:30, *30-31*, 32, 33, *33*, 34, 36-41, *36-41*, 43, *43*, 44, *44*, 45, *45*, 46, 48, *49*, 52, 82
All Quiet on the Western Front (Remarque) 6:43
All the Sad Young Men (Fitzgerald) 7:43, 45, 46, *46*
Almayer's Folly (Conrad) 9:56, 57, *57*, 69
Aloe, The (Mansfield) 8:67
Alone (Poe) 12:43
Along the Road (Huxley) 10:90
Alps and Sanctuaries (Butler) 2:92
Amateur Emigrant, The (Stevenson) 11:57, 66, *66*
Ambassadors, The (James) 5:10, 20, 21, *21*, 24
Amelia (Fielding) 1:85, 87, 97, 99, *99*
American, The (James) 5:7, 8
Amos Barton (G. Eliot) 4:*81*
Androcles and the Lion (Shaw) 5:*99*
Ann Veronica (Wells) 5:33, 43, 45, 47, *47*
Annadale (Collins) 12:69, 70, 71, *71*
Anon (Woolf) 8:83
Anthem for Doomed Youth (Owen) 13:91
Antic Hay (Huxley) 10:90
Anticipations (Wells) 5:42
Antigua, Penny, Puce (Graves) 6:44, 45, 46, *46*
Antonina (Collins) 12:55, 56
Antony and Cleopatra (Shakespeare) 1:22, 27, *27*
Ape and Essence (Huxley) 10:93
Apologia pro Poemate Meo (Owen) 13:91
Arabian Nights, The 4:43
Arcadia (Sidney) 1:23
Arrow of Gold, The (Conrad) 9:57, *68*
Art of Seeing, The (Huxley) 10:82
As You Like It (Shakespeare) 1:22; 13:39, *39*
Ashenden (Maugham) 5:69, 70, *70*, *75*, 76
Aspects of the Novel (Forster) 9:93
Aspern Papers, The (James) 5:19, 21, 23, *23*

At Tea (Hardy) 3:88
At the Back of the North Wind (MacDonald) 10:34, *34*
At the Bay (Mansfield) 8:66
At Wynyard's Gap (Hardy) 3:87
Attack (Sassoon) 13:*91*
August 1914 (Rosenberg) 13:85
Author's Farce, The (Fielding) 1:84
Authoress of the Odyssey, The (Butler) 2:91, *91*, 95, *95*
Autobiography (Trollope) 2:34, 44, 49
Autobiography (Twain) 7:6, *6*, 11
Avare, L' (The Miser) (Moliere) 1:84

B

Baa, Baa, Black Sheep (Kipling) 11:79
Bacon is Shakespeare (Durning-Lawrence) 13:31
Ballad of Reading Gaol, The (Wilde) 2:59, 69, 71, *71*
Barchester Towers (Trollope) 2:33, 36-41, *36-41*, *42*, 43, 44, 45
Barrack-Room Ballads (Kipling) 11:80, 91, 93, 94, *94*
Bartholomew Fair (Jonson) 13:*52*
Bartleby (Melville) 9:43
Basil (Collins) 12:56
Battle of Dorking, The (Chesney) 5:*39*
Battle of Life, The (Dickens) 3:27
Battle of the Books, The (Swift) 10:22, *22*
Bavarian Gentians (Lawrence) 6:19
Beautiful and Damned, The (Fitzgerald) 7:33, 43, 45, *45*
Beeny Cliff (Hardy) 3:87, 89, 91
Beggar's Opera, The (Gay) 1:84; 10:11, *11*
Belle Dame Sans Merci, La (Keats) 13:63
Between the Acts (Woolf) 8:92, 93, 95, *95*
Beyond the Pale (Kipling) 11:93
Bickerstaff Papers (Swift) 10:19
Big Two-Hearted River (Hemingway) 7:93
Billy Budd (Melville) 9:35, 44, 45, 46, 83, *92*
Biographia Literaria (Coleridge) 13:57, 76
Bishop's Apron, The (Maugham) 5:56
Black Cat, The (Poe) 12:45, 46, 47, *47*
Black Mischief (Waugh) 10:57, 66, 69
Bleak House (Dickens) 3:15, *15*, 26, 40-41, 43, 44, *44*, 50; 12:67, 97

Blighters (Sassoon) 13:90

Bliss (Mansfield) 8:60, 62–63, *62*, 64, 65, *65*, 70

Blossoming World, The (Bates) 6:59

Blue Carbuncle, The (Conan Doyle) 12:86–87, 88, 89, *89*

Book of Nonsense (Lear) 10:38, *38*

Book of Snobs, The (Thackeray) 2:18

Book of the Duchess, The (Chaucer) 13:7, 20

Boots (Kipling) 11:100

Bostonians, The (James) 5:8, 20, 21, 23, *23*

Boy in the Bush, The (Skinner/ Lawrence) 6:10, 18, *19*

Brachygraphy (Gurney) 3:8

Brave New World (Huxley) 5:52; 10:81, 83, 84–89, *84–89*, 90–91, 92, 93, 94

Brave New World Revisited (Huxley) 10:83, 93

Breath of Fresh Air, A (Bates) 6:59

Brideshead Revisited (Waugh) 10:58, *58*, 67, 69, 70, *70*

Brighton Rock (Greene) 6:80, 90, 93, *93*

Broken-Link Handicap, The (Kipling) 11:93

Brother and Sister, The (M. Shelley) 12:22

Burning Wheel, The (Huxley) 10:79, *91*

C

Cadenus and Vanessa (Swift) 10:10

Cakes and Ale (Maugham) 5:59, 67, 68, 69, 71, *71*

Can You Forgive Her? (Trollope) 2:43, 46

Cannery Row (Steinbeck) 7:66, 67, 69, 70, *70*

Canterbury Tales, The (Chaucer) 13:6, 10, 11, 12–19, *12–19*, 20, 22, *22*, 23, 27

Canterville Ghost, The (Wilde) 2:66, 69, *69*

Cantos (Pound) 5:28

Captain Singleton (Defoe) 11:21, *21*, 24

Captain's Doll, The (Lawrence) 6:20

Captive of Seville, The (Alcott) 8:32

Cardenio (Shakespeare/Fletcher) 1:22

Carolling (Robinson) 10:*50-51*

Castle of Otranto, The (Walpole) 12:25, *25*

Catriona (Stevenson) 11:69

Celebrated Jumping Frog of Calaveras County and Other Sketches, The (Twain) 7:18, 21

Celestial Omnibus, The (Forster) 9:93, 94

Cenci, The (P. B. Shelley) 13:61

Chance (Conrad) 9:59, 68, 69, 71

Change, The (Hardy) 3:88

Charlotte's Row (Bates) 6:69, *69*

Cheap in August (Greene) 6:95, *95*

Child's Garden of Verses, A (Stevenson) 11:*54*, 58, 69, 70-71, *71*

Child's History of England, A (Dickens) 3:14; 12:67

Child-Who-Was-Tired, The- (Mansfield) 8:66-67

Childe Harold's Pilgrimage (Byron) 13:58, *68*, 76

Chimes, The (Dickens) 3:16, 24, 26, 27, 50

Christabel (Coleridge) 13:66, *67*, 73

Christmas Carol, A (Dickens) 3:11, 24, *24*, 27, 27

Christmas Holiday (Maugham) 5:67

Circle, The (Maugham) 5:58, 66

Civilisation (Bell) 8:99

Clarel (Melville) 9:43

Claudius the God (Graves) 6:45

Clockwork Orange, A (Burgess) 10:87

Collected Poems (Graves) 6:42, *44*

Collected Short Stories (Graves) 6:47, *47*

Colonel Jack (Defoe) 11:11

Colonel Julian (Bates) 6:71

Comedians, The (Greene) 6:83, 84-89, *84-89*, 92, 93, 96

Coming of the Fairies, The (Conan Doyle) 12:*82*

Common Form (Kipling) 13:93

Common Objects of the Country (Wood) 9:26

Complete Poems (E. Brontë) 4:46

Conduct of the Allies, The (Swift) 10:22, 23, *23*

Confessions of an English Opium Eater (De Quincey) 9:42; 13:73

Confidence Man, The (Melville) 9:43

Confidential Agent, The (Greene) 6:80, 90

Connecticut Yankee in King Arthur's Court, A (Twain) 7:18, 20, 21, 23, *23*

Conversion (Waugh) 10:*66*

Coriolanus (Shakespeare) 1:22

Corsair, The (Byron) 13:59

Corsican Brothers, The (H. J. Byron) 2:86

Count Belisarius (Graves) 6:44

Counter-Attack (Sassoon) 13:81, 90

Country House, The (Galsworthy) 5:*90*, 92

Country Wife, The (Wycherley) 1:55

Court Duel, A (Collins) 12:56

Cousin Phillis (Gaskell) 4:69, 71, *71*

Crack-Up, The (Fitzgerald) 7:35, 44, 45, 47

Cranford (Gaskell) 4:*55*, 57, 58, 60-65, *60-65*, 67, *67*, 69, 72

Cricket on the Hearth, The (Dickens) 3:27

Crime of the Congo, The (Conan Doyle) 12:82

The village of Cranford is ruled by a group of gossipy, but mostly good-hearted, spinsters and widows.

Crome Yellow (Huxley) 10:80, 90, 94, *94*

Cruise of the Breadwinner, The (Bates) 6:*68*

Cup of Gold (Steinbeck) 7:56

D

D. H. Lawrence, Novelist (Leavis) 6:20

Daffodil Sky, The (Bates) 6:59, 68, 69, 70, *70*

Daffodils (Wordsworth) 13:54, *65*

Danger of the Protestant Religion Consider'd, The (Defoe) 11:*9*

Daniel Deronda (G. Eliot) 4:83, 92, *92*, 95, *95*

Danny Deever (Kipling) 11:94, 99

Dark Flower, The (Galsworthy) 5:82

Dark Night's Work, A (Gaskell) 4:70

Darkling Thrush, The (Hardy) 3:87, 89

Darling Buds of May, The (Bates) 6:59, 68, 69, 70, *70*

Daughters of the Late Colonel (Mansfield) 8:70, 71, *71*

Daughters of the Vicar, The (Lawrence) 6:20

Byron's hero, Don Juan, *is forced to leave Spain when his affair with Julia is discovered by her husband.*

David Copperfield (Dickens) 2:22; 3:*6*, 8, *12*, *13*, 15, *24*, 26, *41*, 43, *43*, 49, 50; 12:*69*

Dawn (Graves) 6:45

De Profundis (Wilde) 2:59, 66

Dead Man's Dump (Rosenberg) 13:93

Death in the Afternoon (Hemingway) 7:91

Decameron, The (Boccaccio) 13:*11*

Decline and Fall (Waugh) 10:56, 57, 66, 67, 69, *69*

Defence of Poetry (P. B. Shelley) 13:76

Dejection: An Ode (Coleridge) 13:57

Denis Duval (Thackeray) 2:11

Departmental Ditties (Kipling) 11:93

Descent into the Maelstrom, A (Poe) 12:33, *44*, 45, 50

Descent of Man, The (Darwin) 9:10, *22*, *23*, 27

Desperate Remedies (Hardy) 3:53, 71

Devils of Loudun, The (Huxley) 10:93, 95, *95*

Diamond as Big as the Ritz, The (Fitzgerald) 7:44, 46

Diary (Pepys) 1:33, 34, *34*, 35, *35*, 36, *36*, 37, 38, *38*, 39, 40-45, *40-45*, 46, 47, *48*, 49, 50, 51, 52, 53

Dictionary of National Biography 11:19

Did the Jesuits Write Shakespeare? (Johnson) 13:*31*

Digression on Madness (Swift) 10:22

Dill Pickle, A (Mansfield) 8:68

Disabled (Owen) 13:83

Divine Comedy (Dante) 13:8, *20*

Divine Emblems (Bunyan) 1:72

Doctor Thorne (Trollope) 2:43, 45

Doll's House, A (Ibsen) 5:*96*, 97

Dombey and Son (Dealings with the Firm of Dombey and Son) (Dickens) 3:16, 24, 27, 29, *29*

Domestic Manners of the Americans (Frances Trollope) 2:31, 32, 42; 7:28

Don Fernando (Maugham) 5:67

Don Juan (Byron) 13:59, 64, 65, 67-68, *67*, *68*, 76

Don Quixote (Cervantes) 1:64, 96; 7:*19*; 11:49

Doors of Perception, The (Huxley) 10:82, 83, 93, 94

Dorsetshire Labourer, The (Hardy) 3:94, 96

Dr Faustus (Marlowe) 13:50, *50*

Dr Fischer of Geneva (Greene) 6:92

Dracula (Stoker) 12:28

Drapier's Letters, The (Swift) 10:10, 18, 27, *27*

Dream is – Which?, The (Hardy) 3:89, 90

Dream-Woman, The (Collins) 12:70, *70-71*

Duchess of Padua, The (Wilde) 2:56

Duke's Children, The (Trollope) 2:43, 46

Dulce et Decorum Est (Owen) 13:83, *90*, 91

Dynasts, The (Hardy) 3:56, 74

E

Early Life of Thomas Hardy, The (Biography) 3:56-57, *58*, 59, 61, 63

Early Success (Fitzgerald) 7:47

East of Eden (Steinbeck) 7:*58*, 66, 67, 68, 69, 70, *70*

East of Suez (Maugham) 5:58

Ebb-Tide, The (Stevenson/Osbourne) 11:66

Echoes of the Jazz Age (Fitzgerald) 7:47

Economic Consequences of the Peace (Keynes) 8:99

Edinburgh, Picturesque Notes (Stevenson) 11:*72*, 76

1880 (Beerbohm) 2:72

Elegy written in a Country Churchyard (Gray) 12:25

Eleonora (Poe) 12:44, *44*

Elephant's Child, The (Kipling) 11:95

Elinor and Marianne (Austen) 8:8

Elizabeth and her German Garden (Von Arnim) 9:80

Eminent Victorians (Strachey) 8:99

Emma (Austen) 8:*10*, 11, *18*, *21*, 22, 23, *23*

Empty House, The (Conan Doyle) 12:82, 92

Encantadas, The (Melville) 9:43

Enchantress, The (Bates) 6:71

End of the Affair, The (Greene) 6:90, 93

End of the Chapter (Galsworthy) 5:93

Ends and Means (Huxley) 10:92

Endymion (Keats) 13:62, 63

English Bards and Scotch Reviewers (Byron) 13:58

English Humorists of the Eighteenth Century (Thackeray) 2:10, 20, *21*

Enquiry Concerning Political Justice, An (Godwin) 12:7

Entertaining Naturalist, The (Mrs Loudon) 9:28

Erewhon (Butler) 2:80, 90, *92*, 94, *94*; 5:48

Erewhon Revisited (Butler) 2:93, 94, *94*

Escaped Cock, The (Lawrence) 6:*20*

Essay in Autobiography (Wells) 5:42

Euclid and his Rivals (Carroll) 10:42
Eugenie Granet (Balzac) 5:19
Euphrasia (Poe) 12:35, *42*, 45
Eureka! (Poe) 12:35, *42*, 45
Europeans, The (James) 5:19, 21, *21*
Eustace Diamonds, The (Trollope)
    2:46, *46*
Eve of St Agnes, The (Keats) 13:63, *71*
Every Man in His Humour (Jonson)
    3:*16*; 13:52
Exploits of Brigadier Gerard, The
    (Conan Doyle) 12:81, 92, 95, *95*
Expression of Emotions in Man and
    Animals, The (Darwin) 9:22
Eyeless in Gaza (Huxley) 10:81, 82,
    92, 94, 95, *95*

F

Factory Boy, The (Frances Trollope)
    2:32, *32*
Facts in the Case of M. Valdemar (Poe)
    12:36–37, 52
Fair Haven, The (Butler) 2:80, 90,
    91, *91*, 94
Fair Maid of Perth, The (Scott) 11:45
Fair Stood the Wind for France (Bates)
    6:58, 59, 68, *68*, 69, *69*
Fall of the House of Usher, The (Poe)
    12:34, 36, *36*, 37, *37*, 40, *41*
Fallen Idol, The (Greene) 6:80
Fallen Leaves, The (Collins) 12:58
Fallow Land, The (Bates) 6:58, 66,
    67, 73
False Rhyme, The (M. Shelley) 12:23
Far from the Madding Crowd (Hardy)
    3:54, 60, 64–69, *64–69*, 71, 72,
    75, 76, 77, 78, 79, *79*, 93, 94
Farewell to Arms, A (Hemingway)
    7:79, 91, 92, 93, 94, *94*
Felix Holt, the Radical (G. Eliot) 4:91,
    92, 93, 94, *94-95*
Final Problem, The (Conan Doyle)
    12:81, 93, *93*
First Impressions (Austen) 8:8, *13*, 15
First Men in the Moon, The (Wells)
    5:50
First Year in the Canterbury
    Settlement, A (Butler) 2:80
Fisherman and his Soul, The (Wilde)
    2:67
Flappers and Philosophers (Fitzgerald)
    7:42, 43
Fleurs de Mal, Les (Baudelaire) 2:72
Flower Fables (Alcott) 8:32, 42, 45, *45*
Flush (Woolf) 8:82, 91
For Whom the Bell Tolls
    (Hemingway) 7:78, 81, 82,
    84–89, *84–89*, 92, 93, 98

Forsyte Saga, The (Galsworthy)
    5:78, 80, 82, 84–89, *84-89*, 90,
    90, 91, 92, *92*, 93, 94
Four Georges, The (Thackeray) 2:10,
    20, *21*
Four Quartets (T. S. Eliot) 5:*28*
Fox, The (Lawrence) 6:14–15
Framley Parsonage (Trollope) 2:43,
    44, 45
Frankenstein (M. Shelley) 12:5, 8, 10,
    12–17, *12-17*, 19, *19*, 20, *21*, 22,
    24, 28, 52
Fraternity (Galsworthy) 5:92
French Revolution, The (Carlyle)
    3:17, 18
Friend, The (Coleridge) 13:57
From Cornhill to Grand Cairo
    (Thackeray) 2:18
From Sea to Sea (Kipling) 11:80
From the Earth to the Moon (Verne)
    5:50
From the Four Winds (Galsworthy)
    5:90
Frozen Deep, The (Collins and
    Dickens) 12:57, *58*, *66*, 70, 71,
    71

G

Garden of Eden (Hemingway) 7:91
Garden-Party, The (Mansfield) 8:70
Gate of the Hundred Sorrows, The
    (Kipling) 11:93
Gathering Waterlilies (Emerson)
    10:*52*
General History of the Robberies . . . of
    the Most Notorious Pirates, A
    (Defoe, probably) 11:19, 24, *25*
Gentleman in the Parlour, The
    (Maugham) 5:67
George Silverman's Explanation
    (Dickens) 3:26
Ghost in the Garden Room, The
    (Gaskell) 4:70
Giaour, The (Byron) 13:59
Gift, The (Steinbeck) 7:69
Gilded Age, The (Twain) 7:18
Gioconda Smile, The (Huxley) 10:82
Glimpse, The (Hardy) 3:87
Going, The (Hardy) 3:88
Gold-Bug, The (Poe) 12:*32*, *43*, 46,
    47, *47*
Golden Fleece, The (Graves) 6:44
Good Wives see Little Women, Part II
Goodbye to All That (Graves) 6:34,
    43, 45
Grace Abounding to the Chief of
    Sinners (Bunyan) 1:46, 62, 70,
    74, 75, *75*

When Pip prepares to leave the forge
because of his Great Expectations, *Joe asks*
for no money, only that they remain 'ever the
best of friends'.

Grantchester (Brooke) 13:78
Grapes of Wrath, The (Steinbeck)
    1:64; 7:56, 57, 60–65, *60-65*, 66,
    67, 68, 72, 76
Great Boer War, The (Conan Doyle)
    12:82
Great Expectations (Dickens) 3:6, 7,
    9, *25*, 26, 34–39, *34-39*, 43, 46,
    47, *50*
Great Gatsby, The (Fitzgerald) 7:33,
    34, 36–41, *36-41*, 43, 44, 45, 46,
    48, 51
Great Hoggarty Diamond, The
    (Thackeray) 2:18
Great Mountains, The (Steinbeck)
    7:69
Great Shadow, The (Conan Doyle)
    12:*92*
Greek Myths, The (Graves) 6:35, 52
Green Hills of Africa (Hemingway)
    7:91
Grey Eminence (Huxley) 10:82
Grey Woman, The (Gaskell) 4:70
Groats-worth of Witte (R. Greene)
    1:12; 13:*48-49*, 49
Grub-Street Opera, The (Fielding)
    1:84
Guide to the Lakes (Wordsworth)
    13:55
Gulliver's Travels (Swift) 5:48, *49*;
    9:48; 10:5, 6, 11, 12–17, *12-17*,
    19, 21, *21*, 22
Gun for Sale, A (Greene) 6:90
Guy Domville (James) 5:9, 10

H

Hamlet (Shakespeare) 1:12, 14, 16-17, *16-17*, 20, *21*, 23, 24, 25, 30, 31, 32; 13:42-43, *50*, 52

Handful of Dust, A (Waugh) 10:*56*, 67

Happy Prince and Other Tales, The (Wilde) 2:57, 66, 69, 70, *70*

Hard Times (Dickens) 3:13, 26, 41-42, 43, 44, *44*

Hardy's Wessex (Lea) 3:79

Haunted Man, The (Dickens) 3:27

Heart of Darkness (Conrad) 5:39; 9:57, 58, 68, 69, 70, 72, 75

Heart of Midlothian, The (Scott) 11:44, 45, 46, *46-47*

Heart of the Matter, The (Greene) 6:*80*, 81, 90, 93, 94, *94*

Hearts Insurgent (Hardy) 3:72

Heaven and Hell (Huxley) 10:83, 93, *93*

Henry IV (Shakespeare) 1:23, 25, *25, 32*

Henry V (Shakespeare) 1:23, 30; 11:96

Henry VI (Shakespeare) 1:12

Henry VIII (Shakespeare/ Fletcher) 1:22

Hiawatha (Longfellow) 10:47, 50

Hiawatha's Photographing (Carroll) 10:50

Hide and Seek (Collins) 12:67

Hill of Devi, The (Forster) 9:*92*

Historical Register for the Year 1736, The (Fielding) 1:85, 94

History of Ears, A (Swift) 10:20

History of Great Britain (Hume) 11:*43*, 50

History of Henry Esmond Esquire, The (Thackeray) 2:18, 20-21, 22, 23, *23*

History of Mr Polly, The (Wells) 5:33, 43, 45, 47, *47*

History of Pendennis, The (Thackeray) 2:*10*, 21, 22, *22*

Holy War, The (Bunyan) 1:63, 70, 74, *74-75*

Home and Beauty (Maugham) 5:58

Honorary Consul, The (Greene) 6:92, 93

Hospital Sketches (Alcott) 8:*43*, 44, 45

Hound of the Baskervilles, The (Conan Doyle) 12:92, 94, *94*

House of Fame, The (Chaucer) 13:9, 20

House of Pomegranates, A (Wilde) 2:67

House of Women, A (Bates) 6:76

How doth the little crocodile (Carroll) 10:45

Mansell Collection

***Sir Walter Scott filled** Ivanhoe with thrilling adventure. Here the Black Knight (King Richard the Lionheart in disguise) storms the castle of the Norman villains.*

How I Built Myself a House (Hardy) 3:53

How I Write My Books (Collins) 12:68

Howards End (Forster) 9:78, *79*, 81, 90, 91, 92, 93, 94, *94*

Human Condition, The (Huxley) 10:83

Human Factor, The (Greene) 6:81, 92

Humphrey Clinker (Smollett) 8:27

Hunting of the Snark, The (Carroll) 10:35, 39, 43, 44, 46, *46-47*, 47

Hymn to Intellectual Beauty (P. B. Shelley) 13:61

Hymn to the Pillory, A (Defoe) 11:11, *19*

Hyperion (Keats) 13:63

I

I, Claudius (Graves) 6:34, 35, *35*, 36-41, *36-41*, 44, 45, 49, 50, 51, 52

I Found Her Out There (Hardy) 3:87

I Spied for France (Richard) 5:74

Icaromenippus (Lucian) 5:49

Ideal Husband, An (Wilde) 2:67, *67*

Iliad (Homer) 2:82, 91, 95; 6:50

Importance of Being Earnest, The (Wilde) 2:57, 67, *67*, 68, 69, 71, *71*

Impressions of Theophrastus Such (G. Eliot) 4:83

In a German Pension (Mansfield) 8:66, 70, *70*

In an Underground Dressing Station (Sassoon) 13:*90*

In Chancery (Galsworthy) 5:82, 84, 85

In Dubious Battle (Steinbeck) 7:56, 66

In Flanders Field (McCrae) 13:87, *87*

In Memoriam (Mackintosh) 13:*86*, 87

In Our Time (Hemingway) 7:81, 92, 93, *93*

In Tenebris I (Hardy) 3:*86*

In the Days of the Comet (Wells) 5:42-43

In the Pink (Sassoon) 13:90

Indian Camp (Hemingway) 7:93

Indian Summer of a Forsyte (Galsworthy) 5:92

Inferno (Dante) 5:49

Inheritors, The (Ford and Conrad) 9:67

Innocents Abroad, The (Twain) 7:8, *9, 20,* 21, 23, *23*

Intimations of Immortality from Recollections of Early Childhood (Wordsworth) 13:55, 64-65, *64-65*

Into Battle (Grenfell) 13:87

Invisible Man, The (Wells) 5:31, 42, 45, 46, *46*, 51, *51*, 52

Isabella; or, the Pot of Basil (Keats) 13:62, 71

Island (Huxley) 10:93, 94

Island of Dr Moreau, The (Wells) 5:31, 36, 42, 45, *45*

Island Pharisees, The (Galsworthy) 5:90, 94, *94*

Islands in the Stream (Hemingway) 7:91

Isle of Dogs, The (Jonson) 13:52

Israel Potter (Melville) 9:43, 45, 47

Ivanhoe (Scott) 11:33, *33,* 34, 36-41, *36-41,* 44, 45, 48, *49,* 50, 51, 52

J

J'Accuse – The Dark Side of Nice (Greene) 6:83

Jabberwocky (Carroll) 10:34, 38, *38, 39,* 43

Jacaranda Tree, The (Bates) 6:59, 68

Jacob's Room (Woolf) 8:91, 93

Jane Eyre (C. Brontë) 4:7, 10, 12-17, *12-17,* 20, *20,* 21, *21,* 22, 23, 25, 26, 28, 69; 12:*73*

Je ne Parle pas Français (Mansfield) 8:68, 70, *70*

Jealousy (Brooke) 13:78

Jesting Pilate (Huxley) 10:81, 91

Jew of Malta, The (Marlowe) 13:50

Jim Smiley and His Jumping Frog (Twain) 7:8, *9, 18,* 21

Jo's Boys (Alcott) 8:35, 44, 45, 47, *47*

John Caldigate (Trollope) 2:*34*

John Marr and Other Sailors (Melville) 9:48

Jonathan Wild (Fielding) 1:86, 97, 98, *98*

Joseph Andrews (Fielding) 1:86, 95, *95,* 96, *96-97,* 97, 98, *98*

Journal (Scott) 11:42, 44

Journal from This World to the Next, A (Fielding) 1:96, 98, *98*

Journal of a Voyage to Lisbon, The (Fielding) 1:97, 99, *99*

Journal of the Plague Year (Defoe) 11:11, *18-19,* 19, 21, 22, *22-23*

Journal to Stella (Swift) 10:8, 9, 20, 22, 23, *23*

Journey Without Maps (Greene) 6:80, *80*

Jude the Obscure (Hardy) 3:55, *57,* 61, 62, 63, 71, 72, 73, 75, *75,* 77, 78, 87

Julian and Maddolo (P. B. Shelley) 13:61

Julius Caesar (Shakespeare) 1:22, 26, *26*

Jungle Books, The (Kipling) 11:81, 90, 92, 93, 94, *94*

Just So Stories (Kipling) 11:82, 92, *92,* 93, 95, *95*

Justice (Galsworthy) 5:81, *91,* 92, 94, 95, *95, 99,* 100

Justification of the Censorship of Plays, A (Galsworthy) 5:99

K

Kangaroo (Lawrence) 6:10, 19, *19*

Karori (Mansfield) 8:66

Kenilworth (Scott) 11:45, 47, *47*

Kew Gardens (Woolf) 8:92

Kidnapped (Stevenson) 11:58, 67, 68, 69, *69*

Kim (Kipling) 11:77, *78,* 83, 84-89, *84-89,* 90, 91, *92*

King Jesus (Graves) 6:43, 45, 47, *47*

King John (Shakespeare) 1:23

King Lear (Shakespeare) 1:14, 18-19, *18-19,* 20, 21, *21,* 22, 23, 24, *24,* 25, 30, 55

King of Pirates, The (Defoe) 11:19, 24, 27

Kipps (Wells) 5:43, 45, 46, *46*

Kubla Khan (Coleridge) 13:57, 66, *66-67,* 73

L

Lady Chatterley's Lover (Lawrence) 6:11, 13, 18, 19, 21, 23, *23*

Lady Frederick (Maugham) 5:56

Lady of the Lake, The (Scott) 11:32, *32-33,* 33, 50

Lady Windermere's Fan (Wilde) 2:57, 66, 67, 69, 71, *71*

Lady with Lilacs, The (Hughes) 10:*49*

Laetitia (Lawrence) 6:19

Last Chronicle of Barset, The (Trollope) 2:43, 44, 45

Last Man, The (M. Shelley) 12:11, 19, *19,* 20, 21, *21,* 22, 23, *23*

Last Poems (Lawrence) 6:19

Last Stagecoachman, The (Collins) 12:55

Last Tycoon, The (Fitzgerald) 7:35, 44, 45, 47, *47*

Lawless Roads, The (Greene) 6:80

Jane Eyre was only one of the many educated, but poor, gentlewomen forced to earn their living by teaching in charity schools. Like her, they must often have felt 'degraded' and 'dismayed'.

Lawrence and the Arabs (Graves) 6:43, *43*

Lay of the Last Minstrel, The (Scott) 11:32, 43

Leader of the People, The (Steinbeck) 7:69

Lees of Happiness (Fitzgerald) 7:46

Legend of Good Women (Chaucer) 13:20

Legend of Montrose, The (Scott) 11:42

Leviathan (Hobbes) 1:56

Life and Death of Mr Badman, The (Bunyan) 1:63, 70, 74, *74*

Life and Death of Tom Thumb the Great, The (Fielding) 1:84, *84*, 94, *96*

Life and Habit (Butler) 2:94, 95

Life and Letters of Dr Samuel Butler, The (Butler) 2:*93*

Life of Charlotte Brontë, The (Gaskell) 4:11, 58–59, *59, 67*, 69

Life of Samuel Johnson, The (Boswell) 11:*34*

Life of Sir Walter Scott (Lockhart) 11:*34*

Life of William Shakespeare, The (Rowe) 1:13

Life on the Mississippi (Twain) 7:*18*, 19, 21, 22, *22*, 25

Life's Handicap (Kipling) 11:90

Light That Failed, The (Kipling) 11:79, 81, 90, 93, *93*

Limbo (Huxley) 10:80, 90

Little Dorrit (Dickens) 3:14, 40, 42, 43, 45, *45*

Little Dream, The (Galsworthy) 5:81

Little Governess, The (Mansfield) 8:63, 68

Little Learning, A (Waugh) 10:66, 69

Little Men (Alcott) 8:34, 42, 44, 45, 46, *46*

Little Mexican (Huxley) 10:90

Little Women (Alcott) 8:30, 33, *33*, 34, 36–41, *36–41*, 42, 43, 44, 45

Little Women, Part II (Good Wives) (Alcott) 8:44, 45, 46, *46*

Lives of the Most Eminent Literary and Scientific Men (M. Shelley) 12:19

Living Room, The (Greene) 6:*91*

Liza of Lambeth (Maugham) 5:56, 66, *66–67*, 69, *69*

Lizzie Leigh (Gaskell) 4:67

Lochinvar (Scott) 11:43

Lodore (M. Shelley) 12:19, *19*, 20

Lois the Witch (Gaskell) 4:70

London Labour and the London Poor (Mayhew) 2:98; 3:47

Long Weekend, The (Graves/ Hodge) 6:44, 45, 46, *46*

Longest Journey, The (Forster) 9:90, 91, 93, *93*

Lord Arthur Savile's Crime and Other Stories (Wilde) 2:66, 69, *69*

Lord Jim (Conrad) 9:58, 60–65, *60–65*, 69, 72, *76*

Lord of the Rings, The (Tolkien) 10:34

Loser Takes All (Greene) 6:82

Lost Love (Hardy) 3:88

Lost World, The (Conan Doyle) 5:49; 12:92, 95, *95*

Louse Hunting (Rosenberg) 13:92

Love and Mr Lewisham (Wells) 5:43, *43*

Love and Self-love (Alcott) 8:42

Love for Love (Congreve) 1:*55*

Love for Lydia (Bates) 6:59, 60–65, *60–65*, 68, 71, 72, 75, 76

Love in Several Masques (Fielding) 1:84

Love's Labours Lost (Shakespeare) 13:44, *44*

Loved One, The (Waugh) 10:58, *58*, 67, 69, 70, *70*

Loyalties (Galsworthy) 5:94, 95, *95*

Luck of Barry Lyndon, The (Thackeray) 2:18, 22, *22*

Lyrical Ballads (Wordsworth/ Coleridge) 13:54, 57, 66, 76

M

Macbeth (Shakespeare) 1:23, 24, 25, 27, *27*, 55

Macdermots of Ballycloran, The (Trollope) 2:33, *43*

Mademoiselle de Maupin (Gautier) 2:72

Man and Superman (Shaw) 5:98

Man of Mode (Etherege) 1:55

Man of Property, The (Galsworthy) 5:80, 84, 86, 87, 90, 91, 92, 94

Man That Corrupted Hadleyburg, The (Twain) 7:20, 21, 22, *22–23*

Man Who Would Be King, The (Kipling) 5:39

Man with the Twisted Lip, The (Conan Doyle) 12:85–86, *85*, 88, 89, *89*

Man Within, The (Greene) 6:79

Man Without a Temperament, The (Mansfield) 8:68, 70, 71, *71*

Mandalay (Kipling) 11:91, *91*, 94

Mansfield Park (Austen) 8:11, 22, *22*

Maracot Deep, The (Conan Doyle) 12:92

Marble Woman, The (Alcott) 8:33

Mardi (Melville) 9:32, 42, 43, 45, 46, 48

Marmion (Scott) 11:32, 43

Mary Barton (Gaskell) 4:*56*, 57, *57*, 66, 67, 68, 69, *69*, 72, 76

Mask of Anarchy, The (P. B. Shelley) 13:61, 64, 69–70, *69*

Masque of Blackness, The (Jonson) 13:*52*

Masque of the Red Death, The (Poe) 12:44, *45*, 46, 47, *47*

Master of Ballantrae, The (Stevenson) 11:58, 66, *67*, 68, *68*, 69

Mathilda (M. Shelley) 12:20, 22, *22*

Maurice (Forster) 9:82, 90, 91, 92, 93, 95

May Day (Fitzgerald) 7:44, 46

May We Borrow Your Husband? (Greene) 6:92, 95, *95*

Mayor of Casterbridge, The (Hardy) 3:73, *73*, 94

Meditations (Boyle) 10:18

Meditations on a Broomstick (Swift) 10:18

Memoir (Collins) 12:55

Memoires Relating to the State of the Royal Navy (Pepys) 1:47, *49*

Memoirs (Grant) 7:9

Memoirs of a Cavalier (Defoe) 11:19, 20, 21, *21*

Memoirs of a Fox-Hunting Man (Sassoon) 13:80, 81

Memoirs of an Infantry Officer (Sassoon) 13:81

Memoirs of Sherlock Holmes, The (Conan Doyle) 12:93, *93*

Men at Arms (Waugh) 10:58, 69, 71

Men Like Gods (Wells) 10:92

Merry Wives of Windsor, The (Shakespeare) 1:*32*

Mesmeric Revelation (Poe) 12:52

Mesopotamia (Kipling) 13:93

Metamorphoses, The (Ovid) 6:49

Micah Clarke (Conan Doyle) 12:80

Middlemarch (G. Eliot) 4:*78*, 83, 90, 91, *91*, 92, 93, 94, *94*, 97

Midsummer Night's Dream, A (Shakespeare) 1:52, 55; 11:95; 13:34, *34*, 40, *40*, 44, *44–45*

Mill, The (Bates) 6:58

Mill on the Floss, The (G. Eliot) 4:80, 82, 83, 84–89, *84–89*, 90, 91, 93, 96, 97, 100

Ministry of Fear, The (Greene) 6:92

Minstrelsy of the Scottish Border (Scott) 11:32, 43

Mirror of the Sea, The (Conrad) 9:57

Misanthrope, Le (Moliere) 1:56

Miscellanies (Fielding) 1:96, 98

Misery (Chekhov) 8:67

Miss Brill (Mansfield) 8:66

Moby-Dick (Melville) 9:30, 33, 34, 35, *35*, 36–39, 40–41, *40–41*, 43, *43*, 45, 48, 52

Model Millionaire, The (Wilde) 2:69

Modern Comedy, A (Galsworthy) 5:*92*, 93, 94, *94–95*

Modern Husband, The (Fielding) 1:84

Modern Utopia, A (Wells) 5:42

Modest Defence of the Proceedings of the Rabble in All Ages (Swift) 10:20

Modest Proposal, A (Swift) 10:19, 22, 23, *23*, 26

Moll Flanders (Defoe) 11:11, 20, 21, 22, *22*

Monday or Tuesday (Woolf) 8:91

Monk, The (Lewis) 12:*25*, 27, *27*

Monsignor Quixote (Greene) 6:92, 95, *95*

Moods (Alcott) 8:33, 43, 45

Moon and Sixpence, The (Maugham) 5:57, 58, 66, 68, 69, *69*

Moon is Down, The (Steinbeck) 7:*57*, 66

Moonstone, The (Collins) 12:59, 66, 67, 68, 69, 70, *70*

Morning Clouds (Carroll) 10:*32*

Mornings in Mexico (Lawrence) 6:26

Mortal Coils (Huxley) 10:80, 90

Mortal Immortal, The (M. Shelley) 12:21, 22, 23, *23*

Mortmain (Greene) 6:95, *95*

Moveable Feast, A (Hemingway) 7:91

Movements in Modern History (Lawrence) 6:18

Mr Britling Sees it Through (Wells) 5:34

Mr Noon (Lawrence) 6:18

Mrs Craddock (Maugham) 5:66

Mrs Dalloway (Woolf) 8:91, 93, 94, *94*

Mrs Eglantine (Bates) 6:71

Mrs Gaskell's Tales of Mystery and Horror (Gaskell) 4:69, 70, *70*

Mrs Warren's Profession (Shaw) 5:99

MS Found in a Bottle (Poe) 12:33

Much Ado About Nothing (Shakespeare) 13:*44*

Murders in the Rue Morgue, The (Poe) 12:36, 38, 39, *39*, 40, 41, *41*, 78

My Heart Leaps Up (Wordsworth) 13:65, *65*

My Lost City (Fitzgerald) 7:91

Myconian, The (Graves) 6:47

Mysteries of Udolpho, The (Radcliffe) 8:*20*, 23; 12:*25*, 26-27, *27*

Mysterious Stranger, The (Twain) 7:20

Mystery of Edwin Drood, The (Dickens) 2:63; 3:11, 17, 26, 43, 45, *45*, 48

N

Narrative of Arthur Gordon Pym, The (Poe) 12:38, 45, 46, *46*, 51

Narrow Corner, The (Maugham) 5:67

Natural History of Selborne (White) 9:26

Nazarene Gospel Restored, The (Graves) 6:43

BBC Hulton Picture Library

When he is drunk, *Michael Henchard sells his wife and child to a sailor. Horrified at his action, Henchard vows not to drink for 20 years, and in his new sobriety eventually becomes* Mayor of Casterbridge. *But his past catches up with him, and he is doomed.*

Necessity of Atheism (P. B. Shelley) 13:60, 76

Neutral Tones (Hardy) 3:86

New Age, The 8:56, 57, 66, *66*, 76, 76

New Machiavelli, The (Wells) 5:33, 43

Newcomes, The (Thackeray) 2:10, 18, 19, *19*, *20*, 21, 22, 23, *23*

Nicholas Nickleby (Dickens) 3:*8*, 26, 27, 29, *29*

Nigger of the 'Narcissus', The (Conrad) 9:58, 69

Night and Day (Rosenberg) 13:84

Night and Day (Woolf) 8:91

Night Scene in London, A (Dickens) 3:47

Nightingale and the Rose, The (Wilde) 2:70

Nightmare Abbey (Peacock) 12:28

1984 (Orwell) 10:87

1914 Sonnets (Brooke) 13:79, 86

No Name (Collins) 12:69, 70, 71

North and South (Gaskell) 4:58, 59, 68, 69, 70, *70*

Northanger Abbey (Austen) 8:8, *19*, 20, *20*, 22, 23, *23*, 24, *24*, 26, 27; 12:28

Nostromo (Conrad) 9:58, 68, 69, 70, 76

Not so Bad as We Seem (Bulwer-Lytton) 12:58

Notebooks (Butler) 2:92

O

Ode on a Grecian Urn (Keats) 2:73; 13:71

Ode on Melancholy (Keats) 13:71, 73

Ode to a Nightingale (Keats) 13:63, 64, 65, 70-71, *70-71*, 73, 76

Ode to Psyche (Keats) 13:71

Ode to the West Wind (P. B. Shelley) 13:*60*, 61, *69*, 76

Odyssey (Homer) 2:82, 91, *91*, 95, *95*

Of Human Bondage (Maugham) 5:55, 60-65, *60-65*, 66, 67, *68*, 69

Of Mice and Men (Steinbeck) 7:56, 57, 66, 69, 71, *71*

Officers and Gentlemen (Waugh) 10:58, 69, 71

Old Curiosity Shop, The (Dickens) 3:24, 27, *28-29*, 29

Old Huntsman, The (Sassoon) 13:81, 83, 91

Old Man and the Sea, The (Hemingway) 7:92, 93, 95, *95*

Old Mortality (Scott) 11:44, 45, *46*, 47

Old Nurse's Story, The (Gaskell) 4:70

Oliver Twist (Dickens) 3:*8*, 26, *26*, 27, 28, *28*, 46, 47, 49

Omoo (Melville) 9:31, 42, 43, 45, 48

On a Chinese Screen (Maugham) 5:67

On First Looking into Chapman's Homer (Keats) 13:62

On Forsyte 'Change (Galsworthy) 5:93

On the Margin (Huxley) 10:90

Ordeal of Gilbert Pinfold, The (Waugh) 10:59, 69, 71

Origin of Species, The (Darwin) 4:100, *100*; 9:9, 10, *11*, 15, 22, 23, 27, 28

Orlando (Woolf) 8:81, 91, 92, 93, 95, *95*, 100

Oroonoko (Behn) 1:*53*

Orphan, The (Otway) 1:56

Othello (Shakespeare) 1:23, 25, 26, *26*, 30, 52

Our Betters (Maugham) 5:57, 58, 66

Our Man in Havana (Greene) 6:91-92

INDEX OF LITERATURE

Our Mutual Friend (Dickens) 3:40, 43, 45, *45*
Outcast of the Islands, An (Conrad) 9:57, 69
Outline of History, The (Wells) 5:34, 44
Owl and the Pussycat, The (Lear) 10:38

P

Painted Veil, The (Maugham) 5:67, 69, 70, *70*
Pair of Blue Eyes, A (Hardy) 3:61
Palladis Tamia: Wit's Treasury (Meres) 1:13
Palliser novels (Trollope) 2:43, *43*, 44, 45, 46, *46*
Pamela (Richardson) 1:86, 94, 95, *95*, 98
Paradise Lost (Milton) 12:15

The interaction of Darcy's pride and Elizabeth's prejudice drives the action of Jane Austen's novel. However, both realise their mistakes, and all ends happily.

Parliament of Fowls, The (Chaucer) 13:20, 22, 23, *23*
Pasquin (Fielding) 1:85, 94
Passage to India, A (Forster) 9:81, 82, 83, 84-89, *84-89*, 91, 92, 93, *96*, 100; 11:87
Passionate Friends, The (Wells) 5:33
Patrician, The (Galsworthy) 5:92
Paul Morel (Lawrence) 6:19
Pauline's Passion and Punishment (Alcott) 8:33, *42*, 43, 45
Peace (Brooke) 13:79, 86
Pearl, The (Steinbeck) 7:66, 67
Perennial Philosophy, The (Huxley) 10:92-93
Personal Narrative (Humboldt) 9:*25*
Persuasion (Austen) 8:20, 21, 22, 23, *23*, 24, 26, 28
Peter Pan (Barrie) 11:*68*; 12:81
Phantasmagoria (Carroll) 10:46, 47, *47*
Phantom Horsewoman, The (Hardy) 3:87
Pharos and Pharillon (Forster) 9:93
Phineas Finn (Trollope) 2:43, 46
Phineas Redux (Trollope) 2:46
Pickwick Papers, The (Dickens) 3:*8*, 10, *12*, 26, 27, 28, *28*, 48, 49, 50
Picture of Dorian Gray, The (Wilde) 2:55, 60-65, *60-65*, 66, 67, 69, 72, 73
Pictures (Mansfield) 8:60, 63, *63*, 64, 65, *65*, 68, 70
Pier-Glass, The (Graves) 6:45, *45*
Pierre or The Ambiquities (Melville) 9:43
Pigeon, The (Galsworthy) 5:*82*
Pilgrim's Progress, The (Bunyan) 1:57, 58, 62, 63, 64-69, *64-69*, 70, 70-71, 72, *72*, 73, *73*, 74; 8:33, *33*
Pilgrim's Progress, The, Part II (Bunyan) 1:70, 73, 74, 75, *75*
Pillow Problems (Carroll) 10:33, 46
Pit and the Pendulum, The (Poe) 12:46, *46-47*
Plain Dealer, The (Wycherley) 1:*55*, 56
Plain Tales from the Hills (Kipling) 11:80, 90, 93, *93*
Plaine Man's Pathway to Heaven, The 1:61
Plays Pleasant and Unpleasant (Shaw) 5:98
Plots and Counterplots (Alcott) 8:45, 47, *47*
Plumed Serpent, The (Lawrence) 6:10, 11, 19, 20, *20*, 21, 23, *23*, 24, 28
Poacher, The (Bates) 6:66, 76
Poems (Brontës) 4:10, 22, 35, 44, 46
Poems (Owen) 13:91
Poems (Wilde) 2:56
Poems 1912-13 (Hardy) 3:87

Point Counter Point (Huxley) 8:68-69; 10:*81*, 91, 92, 94, *94*
Pompey (Philips) 1:52
Poor Man and the Lady, The (Hardy) 3:70
Portrait of a Lady, The (James) 5:8, 9, 12-17, *12-17*, 19, 20, 21, 24
Power and the Glory, The (Greene) 6:80, 90, 93, *93*
Poyntz Hall (Woolf) 8:83
Practice of Piety, The 1:61
Prelude (Mansfield) 8:58, 60, *60*, 61, *61*, 62, *62*, 64, *64*, 66, 68, 70
Prelude, The (Wordsworth) 13:55, *55*, *73*, 76
Premature Burial, The (Poe) 12:*43*
Preparing for Market (Currier) 9:*34-35*
Pride and Prejudice (Austen) 4:25; 8:8, 10, 11, 12-17, *12-17*, 18, 19, 21, 22; 10:82, *92*
Prime Minister, The (Trollope) 2:43, 46
Principia Ethica (Moore) 8:96-97
Proceed, Sergeant Lamb (Graves) 6:44
Professor, The (C. Brontë) 4:10, 18, *18*, 22, 26
Prometheus Unbound (P. B. Shelley) 12:14; 13:61
Promise, The (Steinbeck) 7:69
Prophetic Books (Blake) 13:72
Proposal for Making an Effectual Provision for the Poor, A (Fielding) 1:100
Prussian Officer, The (Lawrence) 6:20
Puck of Pook's Hill (Kipling) 11:90, 93, 95, *95*
Pudd'nhead Wilson (Twain) 7:11, 19, 21, 22, *22*
Purple Plain, The (Bates) 6:*58*, 59, 68, *68*
Put Out More Flags (Waugh) 10:58, 69
Pygmalion (Shaw) 5:98, *100*

Q

Queen Mab (P. B. Shelley) 13:60
Quentin Durward (Scott) 11:45, 47, *47*, 50
Quiet American, The (Greene) 6:91, 93, *94-95*, 95

R

Rain (Maugham) 5:66, 69, 70, *70*
Rain on a Grave (Hardy) 3:88
Rainbow, The (Lawrence) 6:9, 13, 18, 19, 20, 21, 22, *22*
Rambles Beyond Railways (Collins) 12:56
Rambles in Germany and Italy (M. Shelley) 12:19
Rape of Lucrece, The (Shakespeare) 1:12; 13:32, *33*, 42, *42-43*
Rape upon Rape (Fielding) 1:84, *95*
Raven, The (Poe) 12:*34*, 35, *35*, 43, *43*, 46, *46*
Razor's Edge, The (Maugham) 5:67, 68, 69, 71, *71*
Recessional (Kipling) 11:91
Recollections of the Lake Poets (De Quincey) 13:55
Recruiting (Mackintosh) 13:*86*, 87
Recueil des Causes Célèbres (Méjans) 12:68
Red Pony, The (Steinbeck) 7:69, *69*
Red-headed League, The (Conan Doyle) 12:84
Redburn (Melville) 9:32, *32*, 42, 45, 47, 48
Redgauntlet (Scott) 11:*44*, 45, 46, *46*
Refugees, The (Conan Doyle) 12:92
Remote People (Waugh) 10:57
Report on the Sanitary Conditions of the City of Edinburgh (Littlejohn) 11:76
Reproach (Graves) 6:45
Requiem (Stevenson) 11:59
Rescue, The (Conrad) 9:57, 58, 59, 67
Retirement (Cowper) 8:28
Return of the Native, The (Hardy) 3:61, 73, 74, 93
Returning, we hear the Larks (Rosenberg) 13:92, *93*
Richard III (Shakespeare) 1:23, 25, *25*, 30
Rime of the Ancient Mariner (Coleridge) 12:46; 13:57, 64, 66-67, *66*, 73, 76
Rival Prima Donnas, The (Alcott) 8:42
Road from Colonus, The (Forster) 9:91, 94
Rob Roy (Scott) 11:42, *44*, 45, *45*
Robinson Crusoe (Defoe) 5:49; 9:48; 11:5, 11, 12-17, *12-17*, 20, 21, 24; 12:74
Rock, The (Forster) 9:91
Rodney Stone (Conan Doyle) 12:94, *94*
Rogue's Life, A (Collins) 12:54

Robinson Crusoe is the only survivor of a shipwreck. Before the ship finally sinks, however, he is able to rescue enough tools and materials to enable him to survive and to face life alone on the island.

Romance (Ford and Conrad) 9:67
Romance of the Rose, The 13:20, *21*
Romance of Yachting, The (Hart) 13:31
Romantic Egotist, The (Fitzgerald) 7:31
Romeo and Juliet (Shakespeare) 1:14-15, *14-15*, 20, *20*, 25, 31, 55
Romola (G. Eliot) 4:90, 92, 93, *93*
Room of One's Own, A (Woolf) 8:81, 91, *91*, 92, 99, 100
Room with a View, A (Forster) 9:81, 90, 91, 93, 95, *95*
Rose and the Ring, The (Thackeray) 2:21
Rossetti: His Life and Works (Waugh) 10:57
Roughing It (Twain) 7:*6-7*, 7, 9, 21
Rover, The (Behn) 1:53
Roxana, or The Fortunate Mistress (Defoe) 11:19, 20, 21, 23, *23*
Ruined Maid, The (Hardy) 3:88, *88*
Ruth (Gaskell) 4:67, 68, 69

S

Sacred Fount, The (James) 5:28
Salome (Wilde) 2:*68*, 69, 70, *70*, 75
Save Me the Waltz (Zelda Fitzgerald) 7:35
Scandal in Bohemia (Conan Doyle) 12:84
Scarlet Letter, The (Hawthorne) 9:33
Scarlet Sword, The (Bates) 6:68, 69, 70, *70*
Scenes of Clerical Life (G. Eliot) 4:*81*, 82, 90, *90*
Science of Life, The (Wells) 5:44
Scoop (Waugh) 10:*57*, 66, 69, *69*
Scott-King's Modern Europe (Waugh) 10:66
Scouting for Boys (Baden-Powell) 11:52
Sea and Sardinia (Lawrence) 6:19
Sea Child, The (Mansfield) 8:67

INDEX OF LITERATURE

Sea of Cortez (Steinbeck/Ricketts) 7:57

Secret Agent, The (Conrad) 5:42; 6:44; 9:58, 67-68, 69, 71

Sejanus (Jonson) 1:13

Selfish Giant, The (Wilde) 2:70

Sense and Sensibility (Austen) 8:8, 11, 18, 19, 20, *21*, 22, *22*

Sensible Thing, The (Fitzgerald) 7:46, *46*

Sergeant Lamb of the Ninth (Graves) 6:44

Seven by Five (Bates) 6:71, *71*

Shakespeare's Sonnets, Reconsidered (Butler) 2:82-83, 90

Shamela (An Apology for the Life of Mrs Shamela Andrews) (Fielding) 1:86, 95, *95*, 96

Shape of Things to Come, The (Wells) 5:*35*, 44, *44*

Sherston's Progress (Sassoon) 13:81

Ship of Death, The (Lawrence) 6:19

Shirley (C. Brontë) 4:19, 20, *20*, 21, *21*, 22, 23, *23*

Short Happy Life of Francis Macomber, The (Hemingway) 7:82, 92

Short History of the World (Wells) 5:44

Short View of the Immorality and Profaneness of the English Stage, A (Collier) 1:56, *56*

Shortest Way with the Dissenters, The (Defoe) 11:10, 11, *18*

Shout, The (Graves) 6:44

Sick Rose, The (Blake) 13:75

Siege of Rhodes (Davenant) 1:52

Siegfried's Journey (Sassoon) 13:81

Sign of Four, The (Conan Doyle) 12:80

Silas Marner (G. Eliot) 4:91, 92, 93, 95, *95*

Silver Box, The (Galsworthy) 5:80, 92, 94, 96, 98, *99*

Silver Spoon, The (Galsworthy) 5:94

Silverado Squatters, The (Stevenson) 11:58, *66*

Sir Gawain and the Green Knight 13:20

Sir Nigel (Conan Doyle) 12:*92*

Sister of the Baroness, The (Mansfield) 8:70, *70*

Sisters, The (Conrad) 9:57

Sisters, The (Lawrence) 6:19

Sketches by 'Boz' (Dickens) 3:10, 27, 28, 50

Sleeping and Waking (Fitzgerald) 7:47

Sleepless Moon, The (Bates) 6:59

Small Boy and Others, A (James) 5:*6*

Small House at Allington, The (Trollope) 2:43, 44, 45

Snows of Kilimanjaro, The (Hemingway) 7:82, 91, *91*

Soldier, The (Brooke) 13:79, 86

This frontispiece to an edition of Treasure Island encapsulates all the adventurous elements that have inspired devotion in generations of readers.

Soldier's Declaration, A (Sassoon) 13:81, *81*

Soldier's Memories in Peace and War, A (Younghusband) 11:96

Soldiers Three (Kipling) 11:90, *91*, 93, *97*

Some Words with a Mummy (Poe) 12:52

Something of Myself (Kipling) 11:79, 83, 90, 100

Something Tapped (Hardy) 3:*88*, 89, 91

Song of Songs (Owen) 13:83

Songs of Experience (Blake) 13:75, *75*

Songs of Innocence (Blake) 13:75, 76

Sonnets (Shakespeare) 13:31-33, *32*, *33*, 42, 43-44, *43*, 46-47

Sons and Lovers (Lawrence) 6:6, 7, 8, 19, 21, *21*; 8:57, 58

Sort of Life, A (Greene) 6:92

Spanish Gypsy, The (G. Eliot) 4:92

Spanish Tragedy, The (Kyd) 13:*50*, 51

Speckled Band, The (Conan Doyle) 12:84-85, *85*, 88, *88*

Spella Ho (Bates) 6:58, 76

Sphinx without a Secret, The (Wilde) 2:69

St Ives (Stevenson) 11:66

Stalky & Co. (Kipling) 11:93, *94-95*, 95

Stamboul Train (Greene) 6:80, 90, *90*

Story of a Panic, The (Forster) 9:80, 91, 94

Strange Case of Dr Jekyll and Mr Hyde, The (Stevenson) 11:58, 67, 68, 69, 71, *71*

Strange Meeting (Owen) 13:83, 92, *92*

Strange Story, A (Bulwer-Lytton) 12:52

Stranger, The (Mansfield) 8:70, 71, *71*

Strife (Galsworthy) 5:92, *92-93*, 94, 99

Studies in Classic American Literature (Lawrence) 6:18

Study in Scarlet, A (Conan Doyle) 12:80, 84, *90*, 96

Summing Up, The (Maugham) 5:54, 68

Sun Also Rises, The (Fiesta) (Hemingway) 7:81, 93, *93*

Susan (Austen) 8:8

Swan Song (Galsworthy) 5:94

Sweet Thursday (Steinbeck) 7:70

Sword of Honour (Waugh) 10:59, 68, 69, 71, *71*

Sylvia's Lovers (Gaskell) 4:57, 59, *68, 69, 70-71, 70-71*

Sylvie and Bruno (Carroll) 10:44, 45, 46, *46*

T

Tables Turned, The (Wordsworth) 13:76

Tale of a Tub (Swift) 10:8, 9, 18, 19, 20, 21, *21*, 22, *22*

Tale of the Ragged Mountains, A (Poe) 12:52

Tale of Two Cities, A (Dickens) 3:13, 17, 18-23, *18-23*, 30, 42, 43; 12:71

Tales and Stories (M. Shelley) 12:23, *23*

Tales of Mystery and Imagination (Poe) 12:30

Tales of Terror and the Supernatural (Collins) 12:70, *70-71*

Tales of the Jazz Age (Fitzgerald) 7:42, 45, 46, *46*

Talisman, The (Scott) 11:45, 50

Talks with Elizabethans 13:31

Tamburlaine (Marlowe) 13:49-50

Tamerlane and other Poems (Poe) 12:31

Taming of the Shrew, The (Shakespeare) 13:36-37, *36-37*, 40, 41, *41*

Tangled Tale, A (Carroll) 10:45, 46, *46*

Tarzan (Burroughs) 5:52

Tell-Tale Heart, The (Poe) 12:45

Tempest, The (Shakespeare) 1:25, 55; 10:85, 86, *86*; 13:30, *45*

Tenant of Wildfell Hall, The (A. Brontë) 4:11, 32, 45, *45*, *46-47, 47*

Tender is the Night (Fitzgerald) 7:35, 44, 45, *46-47*, 47

Tess of the D'Urbervilles (Hardy) 3:53, 55, 57, 60, 61, 71, 72, 77, 78, 79, 80-85, *80-85*, 87, 94, 95, 96

TH (Holden) 3:*61*

They (Kipling) 11:82

They Hanged My Saintly Billy (Graves) 6:44

Third Man, The (Greene) 6:80, 81, 93, 94, *94*

This Side of Paradise (Fitzgerald) 7:30, 31, 32, 42, 45, *45*, 47

Those Barren Leaves (Huxley) 10:90

Thoughts on the Education of Daughters (Wollstonecraft) 12:9

Thousand-and-second Tale of Scheherezade, The (Poe) 12:48-49

Three Comrades (co-written by Fitzgerald) 7:35, *44*

Threepenny Opera, The (Brecht) 5:*100*

Through the Looking-Glass see *Alice in Wonderland*

Thrown Away (Kipling) 11:93

Tiare Tahiti (Brooke) 13:79

Tick of the Clock, The (Greene) 6:78

Time Machine, The (Wells) 5:31, 36, 42, 45, *45*

Time Must Have a Stop (Huxley) 10:92

Tintern Abbey (Wordsworth) 13:54, *64*, 76

Tiredness of Rosabel, The (Mansfield) 8:63

Titus Andronicus (Shakespeare) 1:24, *24*

To a Skylark (P. B. Shelley) 13:*70*

To Arms (Conan Doyle) 12:82

To Autumn (Keats) 13:71

To Have and Have Not (Hemingway) 7:92, 93, 94, *94*

To Helen (Poe) 12:31

To Imagination (E. Brontë) 4:43

To Let (Galsworthy) 5:82, 84

To Solitude (Keats) 13:62

To the Lighthouse (Woolf) 8:81, 82, 84-89, *84-89, 90*, 91, 93

To the Warmongers (Sassoon) 13:88-89

Toast to Ava Gardner, A (Graves) 6:47

Tom Jones (Fielding) 1:*84*, 85, 87, 88-93, *88-93, 94*, 95, 97, 102, 104

Tom Sawyer Abroad (Twain) 7:21

Tom Sawyer, Detective (Twain) 7:21

Tono-Bungay (Wells) 5:43, 45, 46, 47

Torrents of Spring, The (Hemingway) 7:81

Tortilla Flat (Steinbeck) 7:56, *56*, 66, 69, *69*

Tour Through the Whole Island of Great Britain, A (Defoe) 11:11, 21, 22, *22-23*

Travels with a Donkey in the Cevennes (Stevenson) 11:69, 70, *70*

Travels with Charley (Steinbeck) 7:69, 71, *71*

Travels with My Aunt (Greene) 6:92

Treasure Island (Stevenson) 9:48; 11:58, 60-65, *60-65*, 66, 67, 68, 69, 76

Trespasser, The (Lawrence) 8:57

Trial from Pickwick (Dickens) 3:16

Triple Echo, The (Bates) 6:59, 68, 69, 71, *71*

Troilus and Criseyde (Chaucer) 13:9, *9*, 20, *21*, 22, 23, *23*

True History, The (Lucian) 5:49

True-Born Englishman (Defoe) 11:18, *19*

Trumpet Major, The (Hardy) 3:72, 73, 74, 78

Tumble-Down Dick (Fielding) 1:85

Turn of the Screw, The (James) 5:19, 21, 23, *23*

Tutor to Tachygraphy, or Short-Writing (Shelton) 1:35, 47

Twelfth Night (Shakespeare) 1:22, 56; 13:38-39, *38-39*, 40, 41, *41*

Two Gentle People (Greene) 6:95, *95*

Two Lips (Hardy) 3:89, 91

Two Noble Kinsmen, The (Shakespeare/Fletcher) 1:22

Two Sisters, The (Bates) 6:55, 56, 66, 67

Typee (Melville) 5:24; 9:31, *32*, 33, 42, 43, 45, 48, 50, 52

Typhoon (Conrad) 9:69

U

Ulalume (Poe) 12:42

Ulysses (Joyce) 8:86

Uncle Tom's Cabin (Stowe) 5:100; 7:*26*

Unconditional Surrender (Waugh) 10:59, 69, 71

Under the Greenwood Tree (Hardy) 3:73, 74, 86

Under the Hill (Beardsley) 2:74

Under Western Eyes (Conrad) 9:68, 69, 71

Universal Gallant, The (Fielding) 1:85

Unknown, The (Maugham) 5:58

Unloved Wife, The (Alcott) 8:32

Unparalleled Adventure of one Hans Pfaall, The (Poe) 5:50

Upbraiding, An (Hardy) 3:89, 90

Useful and Instructive Poetry (Carroll) 10:42

The young Ernest Pontifex discovers the untrustworthiness of parents in The Way of All Flesh. His mother draws him to her, but only to wheedle out a confession of some misdeed.

V

Valperga (M. Shelley) 12:10, 19, *19,* 20, 22, *22*

Vanished World, The (Bates) 6:59, 72, 73, 76

Vanity Fair (Thackeray) 2:6, 9, 12–17, *12-17,* 16–21, *16-21,* 22, 24, 27, 28; 10:91

Vathek (Beckford) 12:25, 26, *26,* 27

Venice Preserv'd (Otway) 1:56, *56*

Venus and Adonis (Shakespeare) 1:12; 13:32, *33,* 42, 43

Vicar of Bullhampton, The (Trollope) 2:45, 47

Victory (Contrad) 9:67

Vile Bodies (Waugh) 10:58, 60–65, *60-65,* 66, 67, *67,* 69, 72, 75, 76

Villette (C. Brontë) 4:*10,* 11, 18, *18,* 19, 20, 21, 22, *22,* 26, 27

Vindication of the Rights of Woman, A (Wollstonecraft) 12:9

Virgin and the Gipsy, The (Lawrence) 6:12, 13, 16, *16,* 20

Virginians, The (Thackeray) 2:20

Vision and Design (Fry) 8:99

Vision of Piers Plowman (Langland) 13:20, 26

Visits to Remarkable Places (Howitt) 4:56

Voice, The (Hardy) 3:87, 89, 90

Volpone (Jonson) 13:*51,* 52, *52*

Voyage of the 'Beagle', The (Darwin) 9:12–15

Voyage Out, The (Woolf) 8:79, 80, 91, 93, *93*

Voyage Round the World, A (Dampier) 10:15

Voyagers, The (Bates) 6:56

Voyages Extraordinaires (Verne) 5:50

W

Walden (Thoreau) 8:32

Walrus and the Carpenter, The (Carroll) 10:37, 41, *41,* 43

War in South Africa, The (Conan Doyle) 12:82

War in the Air, The (Wells) 5:42

War of the Worlds, The (Wells) 5:31, 35, 36–41, *36-41,* 42, 45, 50

War Prayer, The (Twain) 7:20

Warden, The (Trollope) 2:33, 35, 43, 44, 45

Washington Square (James) 5:8, 19, 21, 22, *22*

Waste (Granville–Barker) 5:99

Wasteland, The (T. S. Eliot) 5:28

Watch and Ward (James) 5:7

Waterloo (Conan Doyle) 12:82

Waugh in Abyssinia (Waugh) 10:57

Waverley (Scott) 11:33, 42, *44,* 45, *45*

Waves, The (Woolf) 8:82, 90, 93, 94, *94*

Way of All Flesh, The 2:78, 80, 81, 82, 83, 84–89, *84-89,* 93, 96

Way of the World (Congreve) 1:55, *55*

Way We Live Now, The (Trollope) 2:45, 46, *46*

Wayward Bus, The (Steinbeck) 3:67, 69, 71, *71*

Wedding Ring, The (Lawrence) 6:19

Wee Willie Winkie (Kipling) 11:90

Weir of Hermiston (Stevenson) 11:59, 66, 68, *68,* 69, 70, *70*

West Indies and the Spanish Main, The (Trollope) 2:43, *44*

What Maisie Knew (James) 5:21, 22, *22*

When the Going Was Good (Waugh) 10:66

When the Lamp is Shattered (P. B. Shelley) 13:61, *61*

Where Angels Fear to Tread (Forster) 9:80, *80,* 90, 91, 93, *93*

Whistler at the Plough, The (Somerville) 3:78

White Company, The (Conan Doyle) 12:80, 92, *92,* 94, *94*

White Goddess, The (Graves) 6:35, 43, 45, 47, *47*

White Monkey, The (Galsworthy) 5:94, *94-95*

White Peacock, The (Lawrence) 6:8, 19, 21, *21*

White-Jacket (Melville) 9:32, 42, 45, 47, 48

Wife to Mr Milton (Graves) 6:44

William Wilson (Poe) 12:36, 37–38, *37,* 40, 41, *41*

Windsor Prophesy, The (Swift) 10:18

Wings of a Dove, The (James) 5:10, 20

Winter Words (Hardy) 3:88

Winter's Tale, The (Shakespeare) 13:49

Wives and Daughters (Gaskell) 4:59, 69, 71

Woman in White, The (Collins) 3:9, *9,* 13; 12:*55,* 56, *56,* 60–65, *60-65,* 66, *66,* 67, 68, 69, 70, 72, 75, 76

Woman of No Importance, A (Wilde)
  2:67, 68
Woman Who Rode Away, The
  (Lawrence) 6:11, 13-14, *14*, 16,
  16, 20, 25, 26
Women in Love (Lawrence) 6:13, 18,
  19, 21, 22, *22*
Woodlanders, The (Hardy) 3:73, 75,
  75, 79, *79*
Work (Alcott) 8:43
*Work, Wealth and Happiness of
  Mankind, The* (Wells) 5:44
World in Ripeness, The (Bates)
  6:59
World Set Free, The (Wells) 5:42

Worthies (Fuller) 1:34
Wrecker, The (Stevenson/
  Osbourne) 11:66
Wrong Box, The (Stevenson/
  Osbourne) 11:66

Y

Years, The (Woolf) 8:91
Yellow Book, The 2:74, 75, *75*

Yellowplush Papers, The (Thackeray)
  2:18
You are old, Father William (Carroll)
  10:45
Youth (Conrad) 9:58, 69
Youth (Rosenberg) 13:85

Z

Zoonomia (Darwin, Erasmus) 9:6

GLOSSARY

abridge To shorten or condense a book. Novels are often abridged when they are serialised in magazines or newspapers. *See also* bowdlerise.

abstract A summary of a piece of writing.

abstract poem Verse that depends for its effect on the sound rather than the sense of the words.

act The major means of dividing up a play. An act is usually sub-divided into a number of scenes.

action The main story of a literary work.

adaptation The re-forming of a piece of literature to suit another medium. For example, a novel must be adapted if the story is to be performed as a stage play or movie.

addendum (Latin) Something added to a book, such as an appendix.

Aestheticism The belief that art is an end in itself, generally summarised in the phrase, 'Art for art's sake'.

alexandrine A line of poetry made up of 12 syllables, and since the 16th century, the most usual meter in French poetry.

allegory A story, written in prose or poetry, which has two meanings: one the obvious or surface meaning, the other a deeper meaning. Christ's parables are allegories, while John Bunyan's *Pilgrim's Progress* describes human life in allegorical terms.

alliteration The use of repeated consonants for literary effect.

allusion In writing, a reference to another person, event or work of art.

anachronism A person or thing in the wrong period of time. One of the most famous anachronisms in English literature is the striking clock in Shakespeare's *Julius Caesar* — an anachronism since such clocks did not exist in classical Rome.

anagram The rearrangement of the letters of one word to form another.

analogue A story that can be paralleled in other cultures. For example, the Biblical story of Noah is echoed by the Greek myth of Deucalion, who survived a catastrophic flood sent by the gods.

ananym A word or name written backwards. Samuel Butler's novel *Erewhon* is an ananym for 'Nowhere'.

anecdote A brief story about a person or event.

annotation Commentary on the text of a book.

anonymous In literature, a work with no named author. Much folk literature is anonymous.

anthology A collection of prose or poetry by the same author or on the same theme.

anti-hero A leading character of a work of literature who does not display the qualities traditionally associated with the hero — nobility, bravery, resourcefulness. Cervantes' Don Quixote was an early anti-hero.

antonym A word having the opposite meaning to another: for example, hard and soft.

aphorism A short generalisation that is sometimes witty. Proverbs are sometimes aphoristic.

archaism Old or obsolete language, either in the use of words or sentence structure, used for effect.

argot (French) Slang, usually used by social outcasts.

aside In drama, a short speech spoken to the audience that, by convention, is not heard by the other characters in the play.

autobiography An account of a person's life written by him- or herself.

ballad A song or poem that tells a story.

bard A Celtic poet, or a modern Welsh poet. Commonly used as a half-serious description of a poet — Shakespeare is the 'Bard of Avon'.

beat poets American poets of the late 1950s, who included Jack Kerouac and Allen Ginsberg.

best–seller Can be narrowly defined as a book that is selling more than any other work, but is now used by publishers to describe any high-selling title. The Bible is a best-seller in both senses of the term.

bibliography A list of books on a particular subject.

biography An account of a person's life by someone else.

blank verse Unrhymed poetry with lines of ten syllables. Shakespeare wrote in blank verse.

blurb A sometimes exaggerated description, written by the publisher, of the contents of a book which is printed on the cover.

bowdlerise To expurgate or remove passages considered offensive or obscene; derived from Thomas Bowdler who edited *The Family Shakespeare* in the early 19th century.

burlesque Exaggerated parody of a piece of literature or music.

canon Works generally accepted to be by a particular writer.

canto A sub-division of an epic poem.

caricature A portrait in literature (or art) which distorts a person's most obvious features with the intention of laughing at him.

Cavalier poets English poets of the early 17th century, including Lovelace and Herrick.

chanson A love song of the medieval troubadour poets.

Chicago critics Literary critics of the 1950s associated with the University of Chicago.

chronicle A list of events in the order they happened, often compiled by a contemporary. The *Anglo-Saxon Chronicles* are a well-known example.

classicism The styles and themes of writers of ancient Greece and Rome. Also used of later writers and other artists who followed the classical rules of restraint, proportion and harmony.

climax The point in a work of literature at which the plot is resolved.

closet drama A play that is intended to be read instead of performed.

coin To invent a new word or phrase.

convention A device or form that is generally and implicitly accepted by the author and readers or audience. For example, the audience of a play accepts the convention that a character's thoughts may be expressed in a soliloquy; in real life, talking to oneself is regarded with suspicion.

coup de théâtre (French) An unexpected twist in the plot of a play.

couplet Two successive rhyming lines in poetry.

cycle A number of plays, poems or stories with a common theme, such as *The Canterbury Tales*.

dénouement (French) The unravelling of the plot at the end of the story.

deus ex machina (Latin) A device or character who unexpectedly resolves a difficult situation in the plot.

dialogue The conversation between the characters in a play.

dime novel An exciting work of fiction popular in the late 19th century; so called because it cost a dime.

discourse A spoken or written discussion on a learned topic.

drama A work performed on the stage by actors.

dramatic irony An occasion in a play when the audience understands the meaning of a speech or event, but the characters do not.

dramatis personae (Latin) The characters in a play.

dramatise To make a stage or television play from another literary genre, such as a novel.

duologue A conversation between two characters in a drama.

Eisteddfod (Welsh) An assembly of bards.

elegy A poem which laments a person or an event.

Elizabethan Term used to describe the second half of the 16th century in England. Shakespeare, Spenser, Bacon, and Jonson were all Elizabethan writers.

empathy The identification of the reader or audience-member with the feelings or situation of a fictional character.

Enlightenment Literary and philosophical movement of the mid-17th to the mid-18th centuries, characterised by faith in human reason. Also called the Age of Reason.

entertainment A term used by Graham Greene to describe his lighter novels.

epic A long poem which tells a story of often mythical heroes.

epigram A brief, witty comment in prose or verse.

epistle A letter, usually in verse, to a friend or patron.

epistolary novel A novel, popular in the 18th century, written in the form of letters between the characters.

eponymous A character who gives his or her name to the title of a work of literature. King Lear is the eponymous hero of Shakespeare's play.

essay A usually short piece of prose writing on a particular topic.

fable A short story with a moral. Aesop's fables are the best known.

farce A play in which character is subordinate to a complicated and humorous plot.

fiction An imaginative work in prose, such as a novel or short story.

foreword A short introduction to a book, often by someone other than the author.

free verse Poetry with irregular meter and line length.

genre (French) A type or class of literature.

ghost-writer An author who writes a book for someone who then takes the credit.

glossary A list of unfamiliar or difficult words used in a book.

Gothic novel A tale of horror popular at the turn of the 18th century.

hero/heroine The most important male/female character in a literary work.

homonym Two words which sound and are spelled the same but which have different meanings.

hyberbole Exaggeration for literary effect.

introduction A chapter at the beginning of a book which states the author's ideas or intentions in writing the book.

irony A speech in which the true meaning is opposite to the literal meaning, or an event, usually welcome, that is ill-timed.

Jacobean The early 17th century in England. Shakespeare, Drayton, and Donne were Jacobeans.

Lake Poets Wordsworth, Coleridge, and Southey.

lay A short lyrical or narrative poem. It is usually sung.

legend A story containing elements both of true history and of myth.

leitmotif (German) A recurrent theme in an author's works.

linguistics The scientific study of language.

lyric poem A short poem expressing personal feelings.

masque An allegorical drama of the 16th and 17th centuries.

melodrama A play in which complex characterisation is less important than a thrilling plot.

metaphor A literary device in which something is described in terms of something else.

GLOSSARY

Metaphysical poets English poets of the early 17th century including Donne, Marvell and Carew.

meter The pattern or rhythm of syllables in verse.

narrative verse A poem that tells a story.

novel A work of fiction written in prose containing characters and incident.

ode A lyric poem.

oxymoron A figure of speech combining apparently contradictory words.

parody A mocking imitation of an author's writings.

pathos The evocation of pity or sorrow.

play A drama usually performed on stage. *See also* closet drama.

plot The story or events of a work of literature.

poem A literary work written in verse.

prose Direct language which may be written or spoken; not verse.

refrain A line or lines repeated, especially at the end of the stanza, in a poem.

romance A story of heroic and fantastic characters and events; in general use, a story of love.

Romanticism The belief in spontaneity of thought, the power of the imagination and the importance of personal expression.

saga Medieval stories in prose about kings, heroes or warriors.

scenario The outline of the plot and characters of a play or movie.

school Writers who agree upon the style, themes or purpose of their work. The Bloomsbury group was a school.

setting The time and place in which the action of a work of fiction happens.

simile A figure of speech in which one thing is compared to another. It always uses the words 'as' or 'like' in the comparison.

soliloquy A speech in a play in which a character, alone on the stage, expresses his or her thoughts.

sonnet A rhyming poem of 14 lines.

stanza A number of lines of verse, which can be compared to a paragraph in prose.

style The way a particular writer expresses him- or herself.

symbol An object which represents something else; for example, a dove commonly symbolises peace.

synonym A word that means the same as another.

theme The central idea of a literary work.

tragedy A drama concerned with the misfortunes of people of power, who have some flaw of character which makes their downfall inevitable.

troubadour A poet of the south of France between 1100 and 1350.

turning point The moment in a work of fiction that the plot changes direction and moves towards its conclusion.

unities In drama, the belief that the action should take place during one day, in the same place, and that there should be one plot. The unities were observed by 17th-century French dramatists, but were usually ignored by English playwrights.

yarn A story.

Zeitgeist (German) The trends of thought and feeling of a historical period.